Case Studies
of beginning teachers

Theodore J. Kowalski
Ball State University

Roy A. Weaver
Ball State University

Kenneth T. Henson
Eastern Kentucky University

Longman
New York & London

Case Studies of Beginning Teachers

Longman, 10 Bank Street, White Plains, N.Y. 10606

Associated companies:
Longman Group Ltd., London
Longman Cheshire Pty., Melbourne
Longman Paul Pty., Auckland
Copp Clark Pitman, Toronto

Senior acquisitions editor: Laura McKenna
Production editor: Dee Amir Josephson
Cover design: Betty Sokol
Production supervisor: Richard Bretan

6 7 8 9 10-MA-0099

Contents

Preface

After more than a decade of intense efforts to reform public elementary and secondary education, most leaders in government, business, and the teaching profession acknowledge that meaningful and lasting improvement cannot be achieved by simply intensifying what is already in place. Rather there is growing consensus that substantive changes to the structure and operation of schools are required. One essential element of the rebuilding process is the professionalization of America's teaching force. Put simply, teachers in restructured schools need to gain greater independence and authority in their practice.

This book has three primary goals that are associated with advancing teaching from its current status as a quasi-profession. The first involves bridging theory and practice. Cases presented in this text are designed to compliment textbooks that expose students to modern theories of psychology and pedagogy. By engaging in cases, students can apply professional knowledge to problems faced by first-year teachers.

Secondly, the cases included in this text are designed to build and refine decision-making skills. Historically, teaching has been highly controlled. That is, teachers have had little decision-making power about curriculum and even about instructional approaches. As teachers gain professional status, they will be expected to make critical decisions, either independently or as part of a team. These decisions can range from instructional alternatives, to psychological interventions, to governance issues for the school. To teach decision-making skills, the cases are purposely not taken to their conclusion. This allows students to place themselves in the shoes of the beginning teacher and decide how they would deal with the challenge.

The final goal of this text is to provide students with experiences that permit them to understand and use the process of professional reflection. Skilled practitioners in all professions are able to use experiences productively. They do so by constantly relating their day-to-day encounters to a theoretical base. This process of reflection permits the practitioner to gain a fuller understanding of processes, challenges, and problems that are never fully rational or predictable.

Cases in this book cover a wide range of issues in educational psychology and teaching methodologies. They can be used in virtually all classroom and clinical courses in education. They are based on problems encountered by beginning teachers in contemporary school settings.

We express our gratitude to Dr. Mary Sudzina, the University of Dayton, and Dr. Michael Grady, St. Louis University, for their input and direction in developing cases. Both have acquired knowledge and experience from using cases with their students, and their collaboration was invaluable to this book. We are especially grateful to four other professional colleagues for their constructive criticisms, insights, and suggestions: Dr. Judith Bazler, Lehigh University; Dr. Billy Dixon, Southern Illinois University; Dr. Howard Drucker, California Polytechnic—San Luis Obispo; Dr. Richard Wisniewski, the University of Tennessee.

Introduction

Beginning teachers quickly learn that job-related circumstances help determine the success of their decisions and other actions. This is true because communities, schools, and students are not all alike. Teacher behavior is a mixture of economic, political, social, psychological, and pedagogical influences (Kowalski, 1993). Accordingly, effective teaching is not a routine process that requires trained individuals to respond in uniform ways to specific problems and needs. Rather, good teachers are highly educated professionals who use a reflective process that integrates professional knowledge, experience, and situational knowledge (i.e., circumstances surrounding a given situation).

The cases presented in this book are designed to help you learn the process of reflection. That is, they should serve as stimuli to make you think critically about the application of professional knowledge in the context of certain communities, schools, and students. Donald Schon (1990) has written extensively on the need for practitioners in all professions to use reflection in an increasingly complex world. He argues that technical skills alone will not assure success. The most effective professionals are those who constantly integrate experience and professional knowledge.

This book consists of cases that are focused on the work of first-year teachers. The issues presented deal with educational psychology and teaching methods, but each case is somewhat individual with regard to specific challenges, community, and type of school involved. Each central character is a beginning teacher.

DEFINING CASE STUDIES

A case is a description of an administrative situation, commonly involving a decision or problem (Erskine, Leenders, and Mauffette-Leenders, 1981). Frequently the terms *case study* and *case method* are used interchangeably. This is an error.

A *case study* is a general description of a situation that may have several purposes: (a) as a method of research, (b) as a method of evaluation, (c) as a method of policy studies, and (d) as a teaching method. Thus *case study* refers to the narrative description of the incident—not its intended purpose. *Case method,* on the other hand, specifically refers to the use of case studies as a teaching paradigm. In other words, the case method entails a technique whereby the major ingredients of a case study are presented to students for the purpose of studying behaviors or problem-solving techniques.

There are several characteristics of good cases which you should recognize:

1. They often include "disinformation"—extraneous data that may not be directly related to problems or solutions. In real life, teachers must identify the pertinent facts surrounding a situation when they engage in problem solving.
2. They are often complex. The problem presented is neither so simple that a resolution is readily available or so complex that students are mystified.
3. They provide a core of information to which theory, research, and experience can be related. This can be done in cognitive, affective, or moral domains of thinking.
4. They have multiple foci. Even when one theme may appear obvious, there are tangential issues that are intertwined.
5. They are provactive. That is, the issues and problems are significant to professional preparation.
6. They do not provide a solution. They allow each reader to weigh the circumstances within the context of their reality. (Weaver, Kowalski & Pfaller, 1994).

Opinions differ as to the format and length of case studies; they are written in various forms and lengths. The cases presented in this book are purposely not taken to conclusion. This allows you to either assume the role of decision maker or to evaluate the practices of the beginning teacher in the case.

THE CASE METHOD AS AN INSTRUCTIONAL PARADIGM

There are two universal aspects of the case method. One is the Socratic Method—teaching by asking questions and thus leading students into logical contradictions—and the other is the presentation of selected information that is included in the case study (e.g., facts about individuals, facts about school districts). This information is referred to as *situational knowledge.* Despite the fact that all readers are exposed to the same information, their perceptions and conclusions based on that information will vary. The reasons for this variance illuminate one of the primary values of working with cases. Each reader engages in a process called *abstraction.* When you read a case, you essentially filter situational knowledge through your personal values, beliefs, experiences, and acquired knowledge (Kowalski, 1991). As a result, your interpretations of a case may differ from that of your classmates.

In studying the ways in which teachers make decisions, Shavelson and Stern (1981) observed the following:

> . . . people selectively perceive and interpret portions of available information with respect to their goals, and construct a simplified model of reality. Using certain heuristics, attributions and other psychological mechanisms, people then make judgments and decisions and carry them out on the basis of their psychological model of reality. (p. 461)

These outputs become critical in experiencing the case method. They explain why individuals, even experienced practitioners, do not have identical reactions to situational knowledge. These outputs in the case method are referred to as *specific knowledge.* It is on the basis of specific knowledge that you formulate a response or course of action.

Frequently educators are puzzled by situations in which the same response to a given problem produces vastly different results. Take, for example, a specific approach to discipline. Why would a method work very well in one school and be totally ineffective in another? The answer rests largely with organizational and environmental variables. If the administrator ignores the conditions under which a decision must be made, the probability of error increases markedly. Put simply, decision-making processes in educational organizations are affected by existing conditions (Estler, 1988). More succinctly, they are affected by interpretations of existing conditions made by the decision maker.

USING THEORY TO MAKE DECISIONS

There are many misconceptions about theory. Some view it as a dream representing the wishes of an individual or group. Others perceive theory to be a supposition or speculation or a philosophy (Owens, 1991). In reality, theories are used to synthesize, organize, and classify facts that emerge from observations and collections of data in varying situations (e.g., research studies). They are developed by interfacing data collected on the same variables as they exist in different situations and/or environments.

When you need to make a decision as a teacher, you have several choices. Consider the following:

1. You can ignore the situation and hope that your failure to make a decision will not have serious repercussions.
2. You can make a decision solely on the basis of instinct. That is, you make no reference to professional knowledge, nor do you attempt to reflect on past experiences.

3. You try to get someone else to make the decision. For example, you pass the problem to a peer teacher or to the principal.
4. You make a decision by imitating the actions of another teacher without properly weighing the situational variables.
5. You make a decision on the basis of your professional knowledge and past experiences. (Kowalski and Reitzug, 1993).

Any of the first four alternatives may provide a short-term solution, but a continual reliance on these options will eventually create problems. The final option exhibits the choice of a professional. It entails the use of professional knowledge and experience to: (1) create alternative decisions (contingencies), (2) weigh the potential merits of these alternatives, and (3) select the most appropriate course of action given the situational variables.

EFFECTIVELY ENGAGING IN THE CASE METHOD

You need to realize that the purpose of working with these cases is not to arrive at the "one right answer." Rather the intentions are to: (1) allow you to use your knowledge and experience in analyzing problems faced by beginning teachers, (2) understand and appreciate how individuals filter information and arrive at decisions in different ways, and (3) learn the process of reflection. Romm and Mahler (1986) noted how cases help students to achieve these goals:

> . . . students realize that a case always has many problems, and the definition of one of these problems as the "main" problem is often subjective and arbitrary. They also realize that once a problem has been defined, it can have different reasons and be solved in different ways, depending on whose interests are being served or being given priority. (p. 695)

Cases provide an open invitation to generalize (Biddle and Anderson, 1986). They allow you to be creative and imaginative. You should gain an appreciation for different viewpoints, and most importantly, you should come to understand yourself as a teacher. Although the educated person is expected to rely on accumulated experiences and knowledge to formulate decisions, a person's behavior is never totally void of personal values and beliefs (Kowalski, Weaver, and Henson, 1990). Your values, beliefs, knowledge, and problem-solving skills all contribute to your own world of reality at the psychological level. Hence, you and your classmates will often react to cases differently. This reality makes the case method even more challenging and exciting.

REFERENCES

Biddle, B., & Anderson, D. (1986). Theory, methods, knowledge, and research on teaching. In M. Wittrock (Ed.), *Handbook of research on teaching* (3rd ed.), pp. 230–252. New York: Macmillan.

Erskine, J., Leenders, M., & Mauffette-Leenders, L. (1981). *Teaching with cases.* Ontario, Canada: University of Western Ontario School of Business Administration.

Estler, S. (1988). Decision making. In N. Boyan (Ed.), *Handbook of research on educational administration,* pp. 305–350. New York: Longman.

Kowalski, T. (1991). *Case studies on educational administration.* New York: Longman.

Kowalski, T. (1993). The case method and situational learning. *New Directions in Educational Reform, 1*(1), 27–30.

Kowalski, T., & Reitzug, U. (1993). *Contemporary school administration: An introduction.* New York: Longman.

Kowalski, T., Weaver, R., & Henson, K. (1990). *Case studies on teaching.* New York: Longman.

Owens, R. (1991). *Organizational Behavior in Education* (4th ed.). Englewood Cliffs, NJ: Prentice-Hall.

Romm, T., & Mahler, S. (1986). A three dimensional model for using case studies in the academic classroom. *Higher Education, 15*(6), 677–696.

Schon, D. (1990). *Educating the reflective practitioner.* San Francisco: Jossey-Bass.

Shavelson, R., & Stern, P. (1981). Research on teachers' pedagogical thoughts, judgements, decisions, and behavior. *Review of Educational Research, 51*(4), 455–498.

Weaver, R., Kowalski, T., & Pfaller, J. (1994). Case method teaching. In K. Pritchard and R. Sawyer (Eds.), *Handbook of college teaching: Theory and applications.* New York: Greenwood.

Fighting for Less Competition

PREPARING TO USE THE CASE

Background Information

Students in elementary and secondary schools not only differ in ability and motivation, they also grow at individualized rates. Between the ages of 11 and 15, for instance, boys often vary substantially in height and weight. Some children experience dramatic increases in height and weight during "growth spurts," whereas others grow in a more steady and limited manner. This lack of uniformity in body development has a myriad of implications for education.

Physical growth affects many facets of an individual's life. For example, personality development may be related to positive or negative perceptions of one's body. Positive self-image and peer acceptance are also associated with maturation. For effective teaching, teachers should understand: (1) the processes of human growth and development, and (2) the reasons why individuals grow and develop at different rates.

In general, boys and girls do not face the same problems as their bodies grow and mature. A boy who matures earlier than normal may be admired by his friends, seen as a leader, or excel in athletics simply because of his superior height and weight. By contrast, girls who mature at very early ages may find the situation discomforting or even threatening. They may be teased by others because their bodies start changing at an unusually early age.

In the past 25 years, increasing attention has been paid to educational issues related to human growth and development. The implications of this consideration are visible in a multitude of educational decisions ranging from type of curriculum to facility design. The movement to the middle school concept provides a highly visible change in education that is often linked to greater concerns about the growth and development of preadolescents and adolescents. In many school districts across the country, the transition period between elementary school and high school is occurring earlier in a student's life. Whereas junior high schools typically have contained grades 7, 8, and 9, by contrast, middle schools most frequently contain grades 6, 7, and 8; some middle schools begin at the fifth grade.

This case is about a beginning teacher who is employed as a physical education teacher in a new middle school. One unique facet of the school is its commitment to decentralized governance and shared decision making. The case revolves around a problem of planning a physical education curriculum and making decisions relative to athletic programs.

Topics for Reflection
1. Human growth and development
2. Maturation among preadolescents and adolescents
3. Middle-grades education
4. Site-based management
5. Curriculum development
6. Teachers and policy development

THE CASE

The School

Merry Meadow Middle School opened in the fall of this year. The $20 million facility replaced Merry Meadow Junior High School, a 74-year-old building that once served as the high school for the district. The decision to change the grade organization pattern for the school district came after two years of debate. Superintendent Sandra Nalli was the primary advocate for moving from a K–6; 7–9; 10–12 grade pattern to one of K–5; 6–8; 9–12. This was a position she consistently expressed since the first day of her employment in the district four years ago.

In part, Dr. Nalli proposed the move away from the traditional grades 7–9 junior high school for philosophical reasons; however, pragmatic considerations also weighed heavily in her decision to take this position. Clearly school districts across the state were changing to the middle school concept, and she was concerned that school districts that retained junior high schools eventually would find themselves out of step. Additionally, the junior high school facility in her district simply had to be replaced. The building had been renovated 31 years ago; and since that time, it had received only emergency repairs and an occasional coat of paint. The physical layout of the building was instructionally restrictive. Thus the superintendent argued that it was necessary not only to replace the facility, but it was also logical to move simultaneously to a middle school concept. Her ideas did not go unchallenged.

The real reasons for opposition to the superintendent's recommendation were difficult to pinpoint. Some citizens opposed the building of a new school solely because they did not want their taxes increased. For these individuals, it did not matter whether the district built a junior high school or a middle school; they were opposed to building any new school.

Some parents and teachers objected to placing the sixth-grade students in the same building with seventh- and eighth-grade students. They feared that the sixth-grade students would be exposed to a variety of undesirable behaviors at too early an age. Likewise, the parents of ninth graders who would be housed with older high school students were equally concerned about that arrangement.

The decision to build a new middle school was officially made after two new members who favored the superintendent's plan were elected to the school board, replacing two individuals who were overtly opposed to the superintendent's plan. However, even after construction had started, a number of the critics remained very vocal, including members of the professional staff in the school district.

When school opened in late August, the administration and faculty faced two major tasks. First, the school was directed to implement site-based management and become a prototype of decentralized governance and shared decision making for the remainder of the district. This meant that teachers would play a larger role in deciding the directions and operational procedures of the school, especially with regard to curriculum and instructional matters. Second, there had been little instructional planning prior to the opening of the school. Although Dr. Nalli knew that such planning would have been advantageous, she decided to defer instructional-planning activities until the school was actually functioning. She thought that the faculty would be more cooperative once they were working together in the new school.

Operations during the first year of the school were based largely on the curriculum that was in place in the former junior high school. Some modifications obviously had to be made to accommodate the sixth grade. However, structural elements of the school, such as the daily schedule, length of class periods, structure of departments, extracurricular activities, and so forth remained as they had been.

John Runkewicz was employed as the principal for the new school. Like Dr. Nalli, he did not work his way up through the ranks in this school system. Instead, he had established a reputation as an effective leader in site-based management as an assistant principal in a neighboring school district. When he became principal of the 620-student school, one of his first acts was to establish nine curriculum committees, composed of teachers and parents, who were to develop programming for future years. He gave them a great deal of freedom to pursue their goals, but he made it quite clear that they were expected to complete their assignments by April 1 of the current school year.

The Teacher

Jeb Carmichael graduated from the state's largest teacher education program with a double major in physical education and health. In college, he was a cross-country runner and ran the mile on the track team. He also was a good student, graduating cum laude.

Deciding to take the position at Merry Meadow Middle School was not difficult. Jeb saw it as a nearly ideal job. A new facility, a dynamic principal, and an opportunity to coach track were too enticing to even consider rejecting the offer made by the principal. He also was excited about the opportunity to be part of a planning committee that would be studying physical education and athletics.

Jeb's teaching assignment consisted of four periods of physical education and one period of health education. Teaching physical education, he was able to work with students at all grade levels in the school. He found this to be a valuable experience, because it reinforced and expanded his knowledge base about middle school students. For instance, he was able to see on a day-to-day basis how much the students varied in physical stature and maturity. And as he observed his students in class, he often reflected on his own experiences as a seventh- and eighth-grade student. He remembered that period of life vividly. He not only was diminutive in height, he looked like he was only 10 years old. Even now at age 22, he barely measures 5 feet 5 inches in height.

The Problem

One of the curriculum study committees created by Principal Runkewicz focused on physical education and athletic programs. Health education had been placed with science. The following individuals were appointed to this committee:

> Walter Jones, athletic director, coach, and industrial technology teacher
>
> Lillian Mallen, physical education teacher and coach
>
> Jeb Carmichael, physical education teacher and coach
>
> Bill Dukerko, parent
>
> Ann Silvers, parent

The first committee meeting was held just two weeks after the fall semester started. Walter Jones was elected chair of the committee, and his first official act was to declare that the group would meet twice each month. Also at the initial meeting, two broad objectives were identified. First, a physical education curriculum, spanning the three-year experience in the middle school, had to be written. It was to include instructional objectives and units to be covered in each grade. Second, decisions were to be made about athletic programs. Meeting this objective required consideration of the following: (1) the scope of the athletic program, (2) the mission of the program, and (3) philosophical statements about student participation in athletics.

After just three meetings, Jeb found himself disagreeing frequently with others on the committee. Discord among the group members became increasingly evident as more detailed discussions took place. An example of this occurred when Jeb submitted a proposal to include a broad range of physical education activities for the sixth and seventh grades. He suggested highly diversified activities in a number of sports, including soccer, softball, tennis, golf, and track. Lillian Mallen spoke against Jeb's proposal. She thought that it would be better to concentrate on a narrower range of activities. She also wanted the physical education activities focused on sports programs currently in existence at the school (e.g., volleyball, basketball). Both Walter Jones and Bill Dukerko, whose daughter plays basketball and volleyball on the eighth-grade teams, agreed with Lillian.

In stating his case, Jeb told them, "A relatively small number of students will eventually participate in competitive sports. I think the purpose of physical education is not to prepare students to become athletes, but instead should develop an interest in an active and healthful life among all students."

"Students can learn to be healthful and active playing basketball," Lillian shot back. "There aren't many students I see in these grades who care about soccer, golf, or tennis."

The second example of emerging conflict involved the scope of the athletic program. Jeb's proposal was to have only intramural teams at the sixth-grade level. He argued that his proposal would allow more students to participate and would delay the inevitable sorting process that occurred with competitive athletics. He made two other recommendations: (1) Sports such as soccer, tennis, and wrestling ought to be included in the intramural program; and (2) seventh-grade teams should operate with a "no-cut" policy. The other members on the committee, with the exception of Ann Silvers, openly disagreed with his proposals.

Walter Jones was the most vocal opponent, "All the middle schools I know have basketball, volleyball, and track in the sixth grade. Some even have football. We'll be putting our sports program at a disadvantage if we don't start competition at the same grade level. The kids have to get used to playing other schools."

The athletic director also reacted negatively to Jeb's other ideas. Expanding sports programs for sixth-grade intramurals and having a no-cut policy in seventh grade would cost money. He argued that neither the fiscal resources nor the additional coaches needed to implement these ideas were available.

In fighting for his ideas, Jeb was motivated by knowledge and beliefs about differences in children enrolled in the middle grades. He was trying to create a physical education and athletics program that would allow students who were late in development to have opportunities for participation and success in physical education and athletics. Emulating practices at the high school would only serve to defeat one of the primary objectives of a middle school—diversified programming to meet the various needs of individual students.

Jeb tried repeatedly to get the other committee members to recognize the needs of preadolescents and adolescents. He was particularly disappointed that Lillian was not more sensitive to these issues. Walter Jones became the major critic of Jeb's ideas about athletics. He argued that children were maturing more quickly today; hence, they were ready for team sports by sixth grade. He believed that most students liked competition, which he viewed as an effective means for developing character. Finally, he thought that the community would be upset if the school did not have interscholastic sports in the sixth grade.

Work on this committee had become the one negative experience in an otherwise great job for Jeb. He did not like being argumentative. Nor did he relish the role of stating a minority position all the time. Yet he was convinced that the committee would do nothing more than reaffirm the philosophy that was dominant in the old junior high school, where both Walter and Lillian had worked. And since both were opponents of the middle school concept, he was certain that they would be inflexible.

Jeb repeatedly brought information to the committee about human growth and development, but much of it had little impact on anyone except Mrs. Silver. Although she rarely supported Jeb overtly, it appeared that she agreed with him more often than did the other three. At least she seemed to be open minded.

As the end of the first semester drew near, Jeb thought about asking the principal to remove him from the committee. He had several major concerns. He did not want to be associated with creating a curriculum and athletic program that would be detrimental to the school and its students. Second, he did not want to become an enemy of Walter and Lillian, two individuals with whom he would have a great deal of contact for many years to come. Finally, he wondered if staying on the committee could make any difference. It seemed that the more he used facts and information to bolster his recommendations, the more his opponents became fixed in their positions.

The Challenge

Imagine that you are Jeb. First, are you comfortable that your viewpoint is professionally correct? Second, what would you do about remaining on the committee?

ISSUES FOR FURTHER REFLECTION

1. Is Walter Jones correct in his statement that children are maturing and developing more quickly today? What evidence do you have to support your answer? Is there any evidence that race or ethnicity has any effect on rate of maturation?

2. Why do you think Jeb is so against restricting the physical education curriculum to a limited number of popular sports activities?

3. What is your position about placing sixth-grade students in a middle school? What is your position about putting fifth-grade students in a middle school?

4. Have most middle schools merely emulated the athletic programs of junior high schools? If they have, is this a concern to you?

5. Do you accept Walter Jones's contention that students like competition? Why or why not?

6. Do you believe that competitive athletics builds character? Defend your response.

7. What should be the primary objectives of a physical education program in a middle school for grades 6–8?

8. Do you think Jeb's positions in this case are the product of his personal experiences? Why or why not?

9. What options does Jeb have if he stays on the committee?

10. Why would it have been better from a programmatic standpoint to have planned the curriculum before the new facility was designed?

11. Should parents have been allowed to serve on curriculum committees at Merry Meadow Middle School? What are the positive and negative ramifications of having them on the committees?

12. Since site-based management is being instituted, do you think the principal should be obligated to accept the outcome of the committee as determined by the majority? Why or why not?

13. If Jeb resigned from the committee, would you consider him to be unprofessional? Why or why not?

14. Develop a list of facts and information about human growth and development for boys and girls in the sixth, seventh, and eighth grades. Use this information to argue for or against Jeb's positions about the physical education curriculum and the athletics program in the sixth grade.

15. Why do you believe that so many people in our society see competition as important?

SUGGESTED READINGS

Campbell, S. (1991). Are middle school students normal? Early adolescents and their needs. *Schools in the Middle, 1*(12), 19–22.

Dembo, M. (1994). *Applying educational psychology in the classroom* (5th ed.). New York: Longman (see chapter 10).

George, P. (1990). From junior high school to middle school: Principals' perspectives. *NASSP Bulletin, 73*(521), 67–74.

George, P., Stevenson, C., Thomason, J., & Beane, J. (1992). *The middle school—and beyond.* Arlington, VA: Association for Supervision and Curriculum Development (see chapters 3, 4).

Good, T., & Brophy, J. (1990). *Educational psychology: A realistic approach* (4th ed.). New York: Longman (see chapter 2).

Graham, G. (1990). Physical education in U.S. schools, K–12. *Journal of Physical Education, Recreation and Dance, 61*(2), 35, 37, 39.

Griffin, S. (1988). Student activities in the middle school: What do they contribute? *NASSP Bulletin, 72*(507), 87–92.

Henson, K. (1993). *Methods and strategies for teaching in secondary and middle schools* (2nd ed.). New York: Longman (see pp. 395–399).

Hovland, D. (1990). Middle level activities program: Helping achieve academic success. *NASSP Bulletin, 74*(530), 15–18.

Kirkpatrick, B. (1987). Ultra physical education in middle schools. *Journal of Physical Education, Recreation and Dance, 58*(6), 46–49.

Lawton, E. (1987). True middle level education: Keeping student characteristics in mind. *NASSP Bulletin, 71*(502), 115–120.

Lounsbury, J. (1981). Less is more in middle school scheduling. *Principal, 60*(3), 15–17.

Manning, M. (1988). Erikson's psychosocial theories help explain early adolescence. *NASSP Bulletin, 72*(509), 95–100.

Quattrone, D. (1990). Carnegie's middle school ideals: Phases of program development. *Journal of Curriculum and Supervision, 6*(1), 52–61.

Simmons, R. (1987). Social transition and adolescent development. *New Directions for Child Development, (37),* 33–62.

Stafford, E. (1985). *Programs and practices to meet the needs of the middle school child.* (ERIC Reproduction Document Service No. ED 261 051)

Thomas, J., & Thomas, K. (1988). Development of gender differences in physical activity. *Quest, 40*(3), 219–229.

Thornburg, H. (1981). Developmental characteristics of middle schoolers and middle school organization. *Contemporary Education, 52*(3), 134–138.

Toepfer, C. (1987). Curriculum issues for middle-level schools. *National Forum: Phi Kappa Phi Journal, 67*(3), 17–18.

CASE 2

Sorting the Children

PREPARING TO USE THE CASE

Background Information

Historically, intelligence tests have played a major role in education, and both the group and individual varieties continue to be used widely. Their product, an intelligence quotient (IQ), has long been a common measure of mental ability in our society. But despite their prevalence, intelligence tests remain one of the most controversial topics in education and psychology.

Many people continue to believe that intelligence tests accurately determine a person's innate ability. According to them, an IQ is an inborn, and, thus immutable, characteristic. Those who hold these views are more likely to see young children as predestined for certain educational programs that will direct them toward selected occupations in adulthood. For them, schools serve a purpose of sorting students according to their levels of academic competence. "Tracking," a controversial process of placing students in courses based on academic ability and/or achievement, exemplifies how beliefs about people have dramatic implications for the structure and operation of schools.

In reality, an individual's intelligence is not fixed. Accordingly, intelligence tests, at best, measure intellectual functioning at a particular period in life. Further, as psychologists do not all agree as to the essence of intelligence, the literature contains varying definitions. The vast majority of experts, however, recognize that the nature of intelligence is not properly represented by a single quotient such as an IQ.

However, despite misperceptions and misuse, intelligence tests can be an essential tool for educators. They can identify students with learning disabilities, reveal information about students with serious mental deficiencies, or indicate that a student's poor performance in class is due to a verbal deficiency. Or they may be considered as one of several factors helping educators to make student placement decisions.

Those who rely on IQ scores to make critical decisions often underestimate the potential for errors in measurement. For example, a student's score may have been affected by an illness at the time of test administration. Another student may have done poorly because he or she suffers from test anxiety. Even the physical environment in which the test is administered (e.g., poor lighting, excessive noise levels) can have a significant influence on outcomes. When one considers the types of decisions that are made about people as a result of IQ scores, the potential for errors is not a trivial matter.

In recent decades, intelligence testing also has been scrutinized with regard to fairness. Are such tests, for example, free of cultural biases? Since one major element of these tests involves language skills, is a child raised in a home where Spanish is spoken exclusively at a disadvantage? With increasing frequency, educators are raising these types of questions because recurring outcomes of research studies reveal that certain minority groups have been placed in disproportionate numbers in remedial or special education classes. These data raise suspicions of cultural bias.

In this case, a beginning teacher becomes curious about referral rates, testing practices, and placement of students in special-education classes in her school. With regard to these issues, together with the assistant principal, she seeks data as to the treatment of minority students. After receiving the information, she becomes convinced that: (1) African-American students are not treated in the same way as white students, and (2) teachers may be using the referral/testing/placement process as a means of removing undesirable students from their classes.

Topics for Reflection
1. The uses of intelligence tests
2. Cultural biases in making decisions about students
3. Measuring mental ability
4. Educational program placement
5. Teacher decision making
6. Multicultural education

THE CASE

Janice Davis grew up in a middle-class, African-American family. Her father is a civil rights attorney working for the federal government; her mother is a nurse at a children's hospital where she has been employed for the past 19 years. Janice is the youngest of three children. Her oldest brother, Darrell, followed in his father's footsteps and is a lawyer. Her other brother, Samuel, is a sales representative for a manufacturing company.

When Janice graduated from a large midwestern university, she accepted a teaching position in an industrial-based community in the same state. She was assigned to teach at Randolph Elementary School on the east side of the city—a school that is housed in an unattractive rectangular building constructed circa 1954. Her decision to accept this particular position had little to do with either professional or personal goals. The teaching position at Randolph was simply the job geographically closest to her fiancé who is a third-year medical student.

Randolph Elementary School has an enrollment of 535. Many of the students come from families living below the poverty level. The school has a minority student population of approximately 35%, and almost all of the minority students are African Americans. Yet the faculty in the school is predominantly white. Besides Janice, there are three other African-American employees in the school. One is the assistant principal; one is a Chapter I reading teacher; and one is a secretary in the principal's office. In recent years, minority-student parents have had growing concerns that their children were not being treated equitably. In particular, complaints that minority students were subjected to unusually severe disciplinary action were becoming more frequent. In part, growing unrest among these parents prompted the principal to select an African American, Ned Ferren, to be his assistant principal a year ago. At the time of his selection, Ned was a teacher in another elementary school in the district.

Janice's assignment at Randolph is in the first grade. She finds working with six- and seven-year-old children to be very rewarding. Additionally, her student-teaching assignment was at this grade level, and this fact added to her self-confidence. That experience, however, took place in a very different type of community and school. In the fall semester of her senior year, she was assigned to student teach at Weldon Heights Elementary School, a recently constructed facility located in an affluent suburb of the state's largest city. There she worked with students who were largely from middle-class, professional families. Her students at Weldon Heights were spared many of the social and economic problems that she now sees every day at Randolph.

Janice's adjustment to Randolph was not easy. She herself had been raised in a community more like Weldon Heights. Through September and October, she repeatedly asked herself if she could ever get used to helping her current students deal with all their problems. Many of the boys and girls came to school poorly fed and dressed, and far too many were socially immature. It was clear that they had not been exposed to the cultural and social activities common in middle-class families (e.g., traveling, going to the zoo).

One day in early December, Janice met with the other two first- grade teachers at Randolph to discuss the purchase of supplemental materials for reading. It was during this discussion that the topic of intelligence testing first emerged. One of the teachers, Mrs. Brenton, mentioned that she had "gotten rid of" another student who was being moved to a special-education class. What particularly captured Janice's attention was the word *another*. Although she had become acquainted with referral policies, Janice had not asked that any of her students be tested. Although there were two students in her class who were having diffi-culty, she planned to wait until early in the second semester before deciding whether they should be examined by the school psychologist.

Because she had taken a cautious approach toward referrals, and given her lack of experience, Janice's curiosity was raised by her colleague's comments. She asked Mrs. Brenton how many students had been transferred from her class during the current school year.

"This was the fourth one. Maybe I just got a bad bunch of students this year."

"Oh, I don't know," said Miss Bradshaw, the other first-grade teacher. "I have had three removed from my class already."

Janice knew that referrals were not uncommon in the first grade. The role of teachers in recommending students for individual testing, especially in the first grade, was discussed in education and psychology courses she took at the university. But at Weldon Heights Elementary, referrals at any grade level were rather rare. During her entire semester of student teaching, not a single first-grade student was recommended for individual testing. Now she just discovered that the teachers in the other two first grades had already had seven students placed in special-education classes. She wondered how many in total had been tested.

In subsequent conversations with the other two first-grade teachers, Janice tried to learn more about her colleagues' attitudes and practices as to referrals and testing. She was surprised by some of their comments, especially those that related to the use of IQ scores. They acted as if this single measure was sacred. Clearly, they both believed that if a student's IQ was below a certain score, such as 75 to 78, he or she did not belong in a regular classroom. Janice asked the two teachers if they ever thought about the possibility that the test scores could be in error. She also asked them if they were concerned that some students might improperly be placed in special education.

Mrs. Brenton replied, "I suppose mistakes are made. But, that's not my responsibility. The school psychologist and staff from special education really make the placement decisions when they hold a conference with the parents. I only look for signs that a student needs to be tested. After that, it is pretty much out of my hands."

Miss Bradshaw expressed her agreement, "That's absolutely correct. Some of these parents think we make the decisions to place children in special classes, but as you know, that isn't true."

The issue of referring children for testing remained on Janice's mind. In part, she was concerned about her own responsibilities. She was starting to question whether she should be referring some of her students. Was she serving their best interests by waiting until she knew them better?

Over the course of the first semester, Janice developed a friendship with the assistant principal, Ned Ferren. One day while they were having lunch in the faculty room, she asked him about the issue of testing and placements at Randolph Elementary School.

"I know a little about it. Mr. Wilson (the principal) is the one who goes to the case conferences. He feels he should be personally involved in these matters. He attends all of them, and I have never been asked to attend."

"I just can't stop thinking about the number of students who have been placed in special education from the other two first grades this year," Janice told him.

Since no self-contained special-education classes were housed at Randolph, students who were deemed as needing such programs automatically had to change schools. The only special-education programs housed at Randolph were speech and hearing therapy and a learning-disability (LD) program. Both functioned on a resource room basis; in other words, students left their regular classrooms for brief periods for special instruction or therapy.

Janice commented further, "Seven children in one semester seems like an unusually high number of students to be placed in special education from just two first-grade rooms. Then again, maybe I'm the one who isn't noticing problems. Maybe I should be referring more students for testing. What do you know about the children who have been referred?"

Ned responded with his own question, "What do you mean?"

"Were they largely behavioral problems? Were they students who couldn't cope with school work? Were they primarily minority children?"

Ned was caught off guard by the last of her questions. Suddenly Janice had switched from expressing doubt about her ability to identify students requiring individual testing to the sensitive issue of cultural bias in the treatment of students. Immediately a yellow flag went up in his mind. Given the perceptions of many minority parents, he knew he had to be careful in discussing the matter Janice had raised. It was one thing to discuss whether intelligence tests were being used for the wrong reasons; it was another to suggest that race was an issue in referrals, testing, and placements.

"I don't know, but I don't have any reason to suspect that special-education placements are a racial issue. Is that what you're suggesting—that minority students are placed in special-education more frequently than others?" the assistant principal asked as he rose from the table.

Janice just shrugged her shoulders indicating that she wasn't sure. She looked at her watch; it was time to get back to her room.

Ned was bothered by Janice's questions, and the following day he asked his secretary to bring him the report for the fall semester on special-education placements. What he found proved to be even more disturbing. There had been 19 students referred for testing during the fall semester. Of these, 14 were minority children. Of the five white children who were tested, only one was placed in a special-education program in another school; two others were placed in the LD program at Randolph. Of the 14 minority children who were tested, 11 were placed in special-education programs in other schools; two others were placed in the LD program at Randolph.

After reading these data, Ned's first thought was to keep the information to himself. He recognized that the numbers alone were insufficient evidence of cultural bias. He also wondered if he and Janice could deal with this issue objectively. Were they being overly sensitive? If they were white, would they look at the data in the same way? These were troublesome questions, because Ned knew that the last thing he was expected to do was to increase tensions among minority parents.

Nearly two weeks passed, and Ned could not forget about the data he uncovered when he examined the report. After a great deal of agonizing, he decided to tell

Janice what he had discovered. He asked her to meet him in his office after school. Ned expected Janice to be surprised that the data were so skewed. If she was, he could not detect it.

"Ned, I had a feeling about what you would find if you looked into this matter. And you know why? I found out that all seven of the children who left the other two first-grade rooms were African Americans," Janice told him. "And I concluded that the first-grade experience was reflective of what was occurring in the entire school."

"But how do we know that the placements weren't justified? You know that many of these kids live in deplorable conditions. They're lucky if they have one parent. I think we have to be careful about jumping to conclusions."

Janice responded, "It is also true that most white children at this school live in less than desirable conditions. So I'm not sure that poverty provides a suitable explanation."

After discussing the issue for about 15 minutes, Janice had to leave because her students were returning from music class. The two decided to continue their discussion at a later time.

After leaving Janice, Ned examined in greater detail the student folders of all 19 Randolph students tested by the school psychologist that year. Based on what he read, he judged that IQ scores weighed heavily in virtually all placement decisions. Of the 11 minority children placed in special-education classes in other schools, 10 had IQ scores that ranged from 63 to 74. Each was placed in a class for mildly, mentally handicapped children.

What was even more revealing for Ned was the fact that in seven of the case conferences for minority children, a parent or guardian failed to appear. The folders contained evidence of proper notification, so the absences clearly could not be blamed on the school officials. Nevertheless, the fact remained that the placements in special education for these students were made without parental consultation or objections. Ned also discovered that one of the three white students having placement conferences was not represented by a parent or guardian. The issue of representation at the conferences was made more meaningful for him by virtue of the fact that every person who was in attendance was white. The teachers were white; the principal was white; the school psychologist was white; and the representative of the special-education division was white.

Ned called Janice and asked if she could meet with him after school. He told her he wanted to discuss the issue of referrals and placements.

Meticulously, Ned outlined for Janice information from their previous discussion as well as additional facts he had discovered. He wrote them on a small chalkboard that was on one of his office walls:

1. Even though minorities constitute only 35% of the school's enrollment, they constituted 74% of those referred for testing during the fall semester.
2. Of the minority children tested, 79% were eventually placed in special-education classes outside of Randolph. Yet, only 20% of the white students tested received the same placement.

3. Of the 13 minority students who eventually had case conferences, 54% was not represented by a parent or guardian during the conference. This was true in only one of the three case conferences involving white students.

4. In each case conference held at the school during the fall semester, every representative of the school district was white.

Mentally, Janice sat there telling herself that she would have preferred that her suspicions were incorrect. But the facts presented by her assistant principal were just too convincing.

"Ned, what do we do now?" Janice asked.

"I don't really know. I wish I knew more about this whole issue of IQ testing and special-education placements. We both would look like fools if we raised these concerns and then got blasted out of the water by psychologists and the special-education personnel."

After a brief pause, Ned continued, "Janice, you may be in a better position to get these concerns out in the open. After all, someone might start asking questions about why I was looking at the files. Since I don't get involved in referrals and placements, my motives would become an issue."

"But Ned, you have every right as an administrator to look into this problem. The evidence here is just overwhelming. If we don't stand up for these children, who will? You know enough about IQ tests to realize that they are very culturally biased. Overall, minority children simply do not do as well on them as white children. As educators, as African Americans, we have a responsibility to speak out on this issue."

Janice could see that Ned was troubled by her suggestion. She knew that he had his career and family to consider. It was natural for him to be apprehensive—especially considering that he was hired at Randolph to help reduce tensions among minority-student parents.

Ned finally spoke, "If someone else raises this issue publicly, I'll be in a better position to get involved. You could, for example, just say that you're concerned about testing and special-education placements and ask if data on the matter are available. That way, the question will be out in the open without revealing that we already have examined the data. What do you think?"

The Challenge

Keeping in mind all the circumstances surrounding this case, what do you think Janice should do?

ISSUES FOR FURTHER REFLECTION

1. Do you believe that intelligence tests are still controversial? Why or why not?
2. What are the differences between group intelligence tests and individual tests?
3. What does an IQ really represent?

4. Is Janice correct in her assertion that intelligence tests are culturally biased?

5. Do you think Janice has been ethical in dealing with this issue? Should she have discussed her concerns with the other two first-grade teachers? With the school psychologist? With the principal?

6. From time to time, arguments have been made that certain racial or ethnic groups have higher (or lower) average intelligence. Is there any validity to such arguments?

7. What positive use is there for intelligence tests in elementary schools?

8. Since errors of measurement are possible, what precautions ought to be taken when using IQ scores?

9. To what extent do you think IQ is based on heredity? On environmental circumstances?

10. Some educational psychologists have warned that minorities may be vulnerable to being labeled *retarded* because their intelligence test outcomes are being interpreted from a culture-based perspective. What does this mean?

11. Do you think that most teachers have sufficient knowledge about the intellectual development of young children? What evidence do you have to support your response?

12. Make a list of environmental factors that could affect the intellectual development of preschool children.

13. What does the term *psychometrics* mean?

14. One of the most widely used individual intelligence tests is the Wechsler Intelligence Scale for Children (WISC). It has two subtests: (a) verbal scale, and (b) performance scale. Do you know what each attempts to measure? Why would significant differences in a child's scores on the two scales be of interest to educators?

15. If Janice does what Ned suggests, how do you think Mrs. Brenton and Miss Bradshaw will react?

SUGGESTED READINGS

Beckum, L. (1983). Testing and the minority child. *New Directions for Testing and Measurement, 19*, 39–47.

Chinn, P., & Hughes, S. (1987). Representation of minority students in special classes. *Remedial and Special Education, 8*(4), 41–46.

Dembo, M. (1994). *Applying educational psychology in the classroom* (5th ed.). New York: Longman (see chapter 8).

Elliott, R. (1988). Tests, abilities, race, and conflict. *Intelligence, 12*(4), 333–350.

Farrell, W., Olson, J., Malloy, W., & Boykin, W. (1983). Discrimination in educational placement and referral. *Integrated Education, 21*(6), 120–123.

Fields, J., & Kumar, V. (1982). How teachers use the group IQ test scores. *Journal of School Psychology, 20*(1), 32–38.

Good, T., & Brophy, J. (1990). *Educational psychology: A realistic approach* (4th ed.). New York: Longman (see chapter 23).

Gregory, S., & Lee, S. (1986). Psychoeducational assessment of racial and ethnic minority groups: Professional implications. *Journal of Counseling & Development, 64*(10), 635–637.

McCombs, R., & Gay, J. (1988). Effects of race, class, and IQ information on judgments of parochial grade school teachers. *Journal of Social Psychology, 128*(5), 647–652.

Miller-Jones, D. (1989). Culture and testing. *American Psychologist, 44*(2), 360–366.

Neisworth, J., & Bagnato, S. (1992). The case against intelligence testing in early intervention. *Topics in Early Childhood Special Education, 12*(1), 1–20.

Partenio, I., & Taylor, R. (1985). The relationship of teacher ratings and IQ: A question of bias? *School Psychology Review, 14*(1), 79–83.

Reilly, T. (1991). Cultural bias: The albatross of assessing behavior-disordered children and youth. *Preventing School Failure, 36*(1), 50–53.

Reschly, D. (1991). The effects of placement litigation on psychological and educational classification. *Diagnostique, 17*(1), 6–20.

Sharma, S. (1986). Assessment strategies for minority groups. *Journal of Black Studies, 17*(1), 111–124.

Svanum, S., & Bringle, R. (1982). Race, social class, and predictive bias: An evaluation using WISC, WRAT, and teacher ratings. *Intelligence, 6*(3), 275–286.

Williams-Dixon, R. (1991). Disproportionate mental retardation placement of minority students. *Reading Improvement, 28*(3), 133–137.

CASE 3

A Matter of Style

PREPARING TO USE THE CASE

Background Information

Respecting and encouraging creativity is an important responsibility for teachers as they make decisions about instruction. While much of the organization of instruction focuses on order, practice, and tasks related to achievement, emphasis should be placed on nurturing independence, flexibility, and originality. Experience is an essential condition for creativity. The most creative persons need time to acquire the knowledge and skills related to the creative act.

To enhance creativity, teachers are expected to use appropriate instructional strategies. A variety of approaches are available, including brainstorming, creative thinking, divergent thinking, and problem solving. The use of puzzles, games, simulations, open discussions, creative writing, and multimedia are appropriate for encouraging creativity.

While it was once believed that high intelligence was an antecedent to creativity, research has not supported this thought. Giftedness and creativity are not synonymous. Giftedness refers to intellectual ability, while creativity is most often associated with special talent, in such areas as the fine arts, leadership, mathematics, sciences, and literature.

In organizing opportunities for creative activity, it is important for teachers to understand that each child is capable, in some way, of engaging in such activity. Dreaming and imagining are normal aspects of children's lives and are ready-made sources for structuring creative activities. Legends, fables, analogies, and metaphors provide other rich resources. The organization of creative activities in the classroom will be limited only by the creative imagination of teachers.

In this case a first-year home economics teacher becomes upset by the continual absences of one of her students. Upon investigation, she learns that the student is an outstanding pianist, who much prefers practicing to attending the home economics class. It is also disturbing to her that a music teacher provides written notes to endorse the student's absences. In the end, the teacher must decide whether to punish the student in order to change her behavior, to develop more individualized activities for the student, or to use a combination of punishment and individualized instruction.

Topics for Reflection
1. Achievement
2. Cognitive development
3. Cognitive goals
4. Human growth and development
5. Individual differences
6. Intelligence testing and IQ
7. Parental influence/involvement
8. Peer relations
9. Self-concept, confidence, and esteem

THE CASE

Katie Nelson, a student at Mason County High School, spent the summer studying at the Interlocken Music Camp. During the final competition she won the Beethoven Medal, signifying the top performance in the piano division. Her ten years of study with harpsichord and piano instructor Hardin Watson had paid off.

As a result of her performance Katie was eligible for the Medallion Competition in Chicago in January—a prelude to a possible concert at Carnegie Hall. As she planned her practice sessions, she hoped to schedule two hours at school each day—one hour during study hall and another hour during a scheduled music class. She knew she would need to rehearse four hours each weekday to master Aram Khachaturian's ''Toccata'' and Ernest Bloch's ''Sea Poems.''

Within Mason County, Katie became an instant celebrity. A front page headline in the *Mason Bulletin* the morning after her performance read: ''Katie Nelson May Play Carnegie.'' Two local radio stations aired her Interlocken performance, and she was interviewed on a television program. There was a parade in her hometown of Anchorville, where nearly all of the 1,400 residents lined Main Street to cheer Katie upon her return.

When she started school, she was hounded for autographs by students. Many of the teachers took time in class to have Katie share the highlights of summer camp, her winning performance, and how she might get to Carnegie Hall. It took her three days to get into the school routine.

Because of the attention given to her the first week of school, Katie had not been able to get in four hours of practice each day. She had hoped to practice two hours each morning during the second and third periods. She had English first period, a study hall second, music third, then lunch, followed by home economics, mathematics, history, and science.

Berlin Malenski, her third-period music teacher, accommodated to her schedule by allowing her to practice on Monday, Wednesday, and Friday. But he insisted she participate in music class two days a week. Under ordinary circumstances, Katie would have been able to use her study hall time to practice. However, because she had to spend time practicing each night, Katie needed study hall to prepare for her afternoon classes. Although she was talented as a musician, school work never came easy for Katie. Through careful organization, hard work, and an outgoing personality, she plodded through school as an average student.

Gradually, Katie began to skip her home economics class. She missed one class during the second week of school. She did not tell anyone where she was going, but went to one of the three soundproof practice rooms in the music wing of the school. Before the bell rang at the end of the period, Mr. Malenski, as he made a habit of doing, peered through the window to each of the practice rooms. When he saw Katie practicing, he knocked on the door and entered, saying: "Katie, what are you doing here?"

"Practicing," she responded.

"I know that," Mr. Malenski said, chuckling. "Did someone write a pass for you?"

"No." Katie said.

"You know you can get in trouble for missing a class without a written excuse," Mr. Malenski said.

"Why don't you write one for me?" Katie asked.

Mr. Malenski hesitated, then said: "Look, I don't approve of your missing one of your classes to practice. What class is it?"

"Just home ec," Katie said. "You know—cooking, food, family stuff."

"Who is your teacher?" Mr. Malenski asked.

"Ms. Wells. She's new this year."

Rhonda Wells had come to Mason County High School with superior recommendations. She was a member of Kappa Delta Pi, graduated magna cum laude, had served as both president and vice-president of the Student Education Association, and had been recognized as an "Outstanding Future Teacher" by the state Association of Colleges of Teacher Education. She sees her strengths as an in-depth understanding of the home economics field as well as planning, organization, and discipline. She believes that most problems in the classroom arise from the lack of careful lesson planning and implementation. She stands firm on rules.

During the first day of classes, Ms. Wells had clearly stated orally and in course outlines what she expected of students. She discussed attendance, noting that she would deduct points for each absence. She described the level of quality expected in homework, projects, and tests, indicating how each would be evaluated.

Ms. Wells is eager to share her love of home economics with her students. "There's so much information that can be applied on a daily basis to help improve the quality of students' lives," Ms. Wells believed. She entered the year hoping her enthusiasm for the subject would quickly become contagious.

With some reluctance Mr. Malenski wrote a note, indicating he endorsed Katie's absence because of "preparation for a critically important musical event."

Berlin Malenski is considered "a soft touch" by students who have musical talent and hope to pursue a musical career beyond high school. He identifies with these students, for he once aspired to work as a professional musician. His talent fell short. After several auditions, he realized he would never attain his dream.

Mr. Malenski is an ardent advocate for a strong music curriculum. He believes that the music curriculum is as important as physics, chemistry, English, or any other subject. Since coming to Mason County, he has added "History of Music" and "Music Theory" courses to the curriculum. He has volunteered for and served on district-wide curriculum committees "to protect the integrity of the fine arts."

To Mr. Malenski, music is his life. He has not married because he believes that the time needed to build a quality music program precludes building other relationships. In a sense, he is married to his job. Most weeknights and weekends he works with music groups at school and in the community. Routinely, he devotes 10 to 14 hours each day to his work. For this effort he has received state and national recognition.

That night Mr. Malenski received a phone call from Merriem Nelson, Katie's mother. Mrs. Nelson expressed her appreciation of Mr. Malenski for having written the pass, and she added that when Katie came home from school, she seemed relieved and more relaxed. She noted the extreme pressure Katie felt—from the demands of her piano instructor Hardin Watson, the difficulty of her schoolwork, and the intensity of her own dedication.

Mr. Malenski said he understood.

"I hope you really do," Mrs. Nelson said. "Please continue to provide support. You're the only teacher Katie can rely on." Mr. Malenski felt good. It was nice getting a compliment from a parent.

On Wednesday of the following week, Mr. Malenski made his routine check of the practice rooms and again discovered Katie rehearsing. As before, he entered and asked, "Katie, did Ms. Wells approve your coming here to practice?"

"No." Katie said.

"Then why are you here?" Mr. Malenski asked.

Looking tired and near tears, Katie pleaded with Mr. Malenski. "I just don't have enough time. I feel too much pressure. You've got to help me!"

"Why don't we go talk to Ms. Wells? I'm sure she will understand," Mr. Malenski said.

"Please! No!" Katie shouted. "She'll punish me!"

Understanding her distress, Mr. Malenski wrote Katie a pass to excuse her from Ms. Wells's class that day. He had mixed feelings about his actions, but he promised Katie he would not talk with Ms. Wells.

Twice the next week Mr. Malenski wrote excuses for Katie, who had by then missed four home economics classes. Each time, Mr. Malenski received a phone call from Mrs. Nelson expressing appreciation for his support.

"I'm a patient person," Rhonda Wells thought to herself as she placed an X in her grade book to record Katie's fourth absence. As a new teacher at Mason County High School, she had assumed that the notes from Mr. Malenski were legitimate. Now she felt that regardless of the reasons Mr. Malenski might offer for Katie's absence, her continual absences were not acceptable.

She realized the status Katie held. Without doubt Katie was the most notable figure in the county. Ms. Wells also knew that Mr. Malenski was highly respected in the school and the community. Under his leadership the Mason High School Orchestra and the Mason Civic Band had received state and regional recognition.

"My home economics class is important too," Ms. Wells thought aloud. "I'm going to do something about this situation."

She decided to see if Katie might be in a practice room after school. Accordingly, after the last class of the day, Ms. Wells walked to the music area. As she approached, she saw both Katie and Mr. Malenski standing in the hallway and talking.

As she neared them, she said, "Could we talk for a few minutes?"

Startled by her sudden approach and embarrassed, Katie responded nervously as she glanced at her watch, "Not right now. I have to be home in five minutes."

"Katie's right. She needs to go home now. But I'll be happy to stay and talk with you," Mr. Malenski said.

As Katie walked away, Mr. Malenski escorted Ms. Wells to his office. Once they were seated, he started: "I know why you're here. And I don't blame you for being upset."

"How would you feel if you had a student who was absent as often as Katie?" Ms. Wells challenged.

"I don't believe I would be very happy," Mr. Malenski responded. "But you do understand how important music is to Katie, don't you?"

"Of course I do," Ms. Wells replied. "But what I teach is as important to me as music is to Katie. And I let my students know on the first day of classes how important I believe home economics is by explaining my attendance policy."

"I've given some thought to Katie's attendance problem. And I've talked with her mother," Mr. Malenski said. "Rather than focusing so much on your attendance policy, punishing Katie, and making her even more disinterested and unhappy with your class, could you think of a way to design an activity that recognized her creative talent and interest in music?"

"I'm not certain that I can. I'm so upset with Katie," Ms. Wells responded.

"Please think about it," Mr. Malenski pleaded.

She concluded the conversation, saying: "I'll give your suggestion some thought."

She spent that night thinking of alternatives. She tried to put herself in Katie's place. Would rigidly enforcing the rules get her back to class? Would punishment make her more interested in the subject?

As she considered Mr. Malenski's suggestion for trying to design an instructional activity related to Katie's talent and interests, she brainstormed possibilities. Perhaps I could get Katie more interested in the course by letting her complete an independent study on food preparation and presentation related to musical events—festivals, chamber music, orchestras, rock concerts. "This seems bizarre to me," she thought, "but maybe it's worth trying."

The Challenge

What should Ms. Wells do?

ISSUES FOR FURTHER REFLECTION

1. Given what you know about Katie's talent and interests, which of the following approaches do you believe would be most effective in dealing with her continual absences? Enforce the rules and provide an appropriate punishment? Design a special activity related to her interests? Enforce the rules, but also design a special activity?

2. Would another approach, one not mentioned in question 1, be more effective? Explain.

3. If Ms. Wells decided to enforce her attendance policy, what punishment would you propose as appropriate? How do you believe Katie would react to the punishment you propose?

4. Do you believe Mr. Malenski's idea of relating a special activity in home economics to Katie's interest in music would be successful? Defend your answer.

5. If Ms. Wells went ahead with plans to individualize an activity for Katie, do you believe it would build an expectation on Katie's part for more independent-study opportunities? If such an expectation were to develop, would you judge it as a problem? Defend your answer.

6. How might you get Mr. Malenski to be more involved in supporting Katie's attendance in your class?

7. In what ways might you enlist the support of Katie's mother?

8. What additional information would you need in order to make a decision?

SUGGESTED READINGS

Bjorkland, D. (1992). Development differences in the acquisition and maintenance of an organizational strategy. *Journal of Experimental Child Psychology, 54*(3), 434–448.

Blase, J. (1987). The politics of teaching: The teacher-parent relationship and the dynamics of diplomacy. *Journal of Teacher Education, 38*(2), 53–60.

Borkowski, J. (1992). Metacognitive theory: A framework for teaching literacy, writing, and math skills. *Journal of Learning Disabilities, 25*(4), 253–257.

Cohen, E. (1989). Can classrooms learn? *Sociology of Education, 62*(2), 75–94.

Cornell, N. (1986). Encouraging responsibility: A discipline plan that works. *Learning, 15*(2), 46–49.

Dembo, M. (1994). *Applying educational psychology in the classroom* (5th ed.). New York: Longman (see chapters 2, 3, 4, 7, 8).

Good, T., & Brophy, J. (1990). *Educational psychology: A realistic approach* (4th ed.). New York: Longman (see chapters 3, 4, 8, 15, 24).

Gorham, J., & Zakahi, W. (1990). A comparison of teacher and student perceptions of immediacy and learning: Monitoring process and product. *Communication Education, 39*(4), 354–368.

Henson, K. (1993). *Methods and strategies for teaching in secondary and middle schools* (2nd ed.). New York: Longman (see chapters 3, 5, 12, 13).

Hillard, A. (1992). Behavorial style, culture, and teaching and learning. *Journal of Negro Education,* *61*(3), 370–377.

Kimpston, R. (1992). Ways of knowing and the curriculum. *Educational Forum,* *56*(2), 153–172.

Leinhardt, G. (1992). What research on learning tells us about teaching. *Educational Leadership,* *49*(7), 20–25.

Loekavitch, J. (1986). Motivating the unmotivated student. *Techniques,* *2*(4), 317–321.

Ohlsson, S. (1992). The cognitive complexity of learning and doing arithmetic. *Journal for Research in Mathematics Education,* *23*(5), 441–467.

Pasch, M., Sparks-Langer, G., Gardner, T., Starko, A., & Moody, C. (1991). *Teaching as decision making: Instructional practices for the successful teacher.* New York: Longman (see chapters 8, 9).

Tennyson, R. (1992). An educational learning theory for instructional design. *Educational Technology,* *32*(1), 36–41.

Vosniadov, S. (1991). Are we ready for a psychology of learning and culture? *Learning and Instruction,* *61*(3), 370–377.

Wong, B. (1992). On cognitive process-based instruction: An introduction. *Journal of Learning Disabilities,* *25*(3), 150–152, 172.

A Better Way to Remember

PREPARING TO USE THE CASE

Background Information

How information is learned and remembered is of vital importance to teachers. Most learning theorists agree on a three-stage information-processing model, involving: (1) sensory register, (2) short-term memory and rehearsal, and (3) long-term memory and storage. From this view, information processed neurologically from the eyes and ears is transferred to short-term memory. Information considered valuable becomes a part of short-term memory and can be kept on reserve through a process of rehearsal or continual use. Information "held in reserve" as a part of long-term memory is said to have been built into a network based either on associations among pieces of information to be stored (a schema) or on a fixed system of information flow (semantics).

The ease with which we can remember information depends in part on:

1. How the information is organized
2. How the information is presented
3. How meaningful it is
4. How recent it is
5. How significant it appears

Understanding how information may be received and stored is vital for effective instructional planning. Making certain that the information presented is done so in meaningful and organized ways can enhance instruction. Looking for ways to transfer learning from one instructional context to another is equally important.

In this case a first-year teacher develops a creative, instructional approach for helping students better remember the structure and lyrics of poetry. Using a rehearsal technique, the teacher promotes more interest and meaning in the subject by organizing the lesson around contemporary music enjoyed by the students. The teacher planned this lesson as a part of an instructional sequence covering poetry concepts. As the success of the lesson spreads through the school, another teacher asks to borrow it.

Topics for Reflection
1. Cognitive development
2. Cognitive goals
3. Critical thinking
4. Instructional strategies
5. Motivation
6. Problem solving
7. Ethical concerns
8. Learning theory
9. Conflict resolution

THE CASE

Paul Santini, a veteran teacher of 16 years, had grown tired of school opening procedures. He found the initial faculty meeting "a waste of time." He took a book, paper, and pen to the meeting and took a seat in the back of the room.

The year before he had begun sharing feelings of being burned out. "I'm tired of fighting lethargic, disinterested youth," he had thought. In recent years he spent much less time revising lessons, depending largely on materials he had used previously. On occasion he tried to cajole other teachers into giving him lesson plans and accompanying materials and tests. At the same time, he began to experience more serious discipline problems.

Privately, other teachers noticed a dramatic change in Paul Santini's personality. He was more abrasive, quick to react to conflict, disorganized, uncompromising, opinionated, and sarcastic. He seldom had a kind word for anyone.

Despite his attitude Paul was still highly respected for his knowledge. He had attempted to revive his enthusiasm for teaching by attending summer seminars sponsored by the National Endowment for the Humanities. These experiences had refueled his interest in literature but had little effect on his desire to teach. In many ways spending the preceding summer at Cornell, his alma mater, had renewed a long-time dream of teaching English at a university, where he believed he would have more mature, scholarly students.

In contrast to Paul Santini, Arlene Winston, also a veteran of more than a decade of teaching, eagerly awaited the beginning of another school year. Each summer she reviewed activities used the preceding year and sought ways to improve them. Once a week she met with three other English teachers from area schools to explore trends in teaching English. Also, they discussed a novel each had read the preceding week. Arlene Winston found these informal professional development sessions inspiring. During the summer, she also enjoyed tutoring students in grammar and composition. She worked with six students twice a week in her home for three hours, charging $6 per hour per student. She felt that tutoring students who were experiencing failure helped sharpen her teaching skills.

The remainder of her summer, including an entire week preceding the opening of school, she devoted to her husband and two teenage daughters. The week before school the family vacationed at a new location each year. On weekends the family took day trips to sites of historical and cultural interest. Transporting the girls to softball and soccer practice, 4-H, and the library occupied much of her remaining time.

During the academic year, Arlene enrolled in a college course each term. "I don't need the credits. I just find learning invigorating," she had explained to her husband. Over the years, since completing the master's degree in English education, she had taken courses in anthropology, philosophy, sociology, Chinese, and art. She believed that these experiences enriched her teaching.

Carlos Burton, entering his first year of teaching, was the most enthusiastic of the three English teachers. Since childhood he had dreamed of having his own classroom and students. With his father and grandmother as teachers, he felt he was carrying forward a family tradition. He fondly remembered the hours his grandmother had "played school" with him. She had converted a small area in the basement of her house into a classroom and furnished it with refinished oak desks, a chalkboard, and a teacher's oak desk and chair. She stored boxes there filled with discarded materials: paper, wooden blocks, worn textbooks, used workbooks, packages of crayons, containers of paints, pens, pencils, and brushes. An American flag and nineteenth-century player piano were prized objects.

Carlos's father was a chemistry teacher and a baseball and cross-country coach. As a child, his father took him to all the games and meets. He helped to chalk-line the baseball diamond, drag the field, and put down the bases. He served as an honorary bat boy. He set markers on the cross-country course. He had enjoyed the busy schedule, and he had valued the opportunity to meet so many people.

Carlos carried on his interest in athletics when he attended Lincoln State, a black college. He had excelled in track and field and baseball. He had been an active member of the speech and theater clubs. Routinely, he made the Dean's List. In the college yearbook he had been labeled "Most Likely to Succeed."

Carlos Burton's strengths are his speaking and dramatic talent, knowledge of traditional ethnic literature, belief in his ability to inspire young people, and dedication to long hours of preparation. He believes that "you get out of life what you put into it" and is convinced that his peers should work as hard as he does.

The three English teachers walked from the department faculty meeting and headed toward their classrooms.

"Really, Carlos, I want to know. Why did you choose to come to teach in the Walnut Hills schools?" Paul Santini asked.

"The schools have a superb academic reputation. I'm within a two-hour drive of my parents. And the 'perks' are outstanding," Carlos Burton replied.

"I couldn't believe the incentive package the business and industry council put together," Arlene Winston added. "A month's free rent at Shadow Lane Apartments. Discounts at selected restaurants. Help with moving expenses."

"And a starting salary of $23,000 doesn't hurt, does it?" Paul interrupted.

"No, it doesn't," Carlos said crisply.

"And breaking tradition as the first black English teacher at Centennial probably gives you pride," Paul continued.

"I can't believe you," Arlene interjected with surprise.

"Hey, no offense," Paul shot back sharply.

"That had not entered my mind," Carlos responded.

"Well, it's good to have you here," Paul said, as he turned to enter his classroom. "We'll be seeing a lot of one another."

"Goodbye," Carlos responded.

"See you tomorrow, Paul," Arlene said.

As they walked toward adjoining rooms, Arlene told Carlos, "Paul is relatively harmless. He means well, but he isn't very sensitive. He's not noted for his tact."

"That's okay," Carlos responded. "He doesn't bother me."

"I saw from the schedule that each of us has at least one section of literature," Arlene remarked, making an effort to steer the conversation away from the tension she felt.

"Yes, I have two literature classes—first and third periods," Carlos said.

"Mine are both in the afternoon," Arlene replied. "And Paul has a section first period, too, I think."

"I believe he said he did," Carlos responded.

"See you tomorrow, Carlos," Arlene said, holding out her hand to shake his.

"Welcome to Centennial. Let me know how I can help."

"Thank you, Arlene," Carlos said.

The two teachers entered their classrooms and worked on getting their rooms and materials organized for the first day of classes. About an hour later Carlos left. As he walked down the hall, he was met by Paul, who had also decided to depart.

"All set for tomorrow?" Paul asked.

"Pretty much," Carlos replied. "I'm going to give each period my best shot. I have some unique lessons planned for the week."

"I'd like to see what you're planning. We both have a section of American literature during first period," Paul noted. "Maybe we can get together and share some ideas."

"Sounds good to me," Carlos replied.

As they left the building, each teacher went his separate way.

As Carlos neared his car, he spotted Arlene Winston motioning to him.

"Carlos, I need to talk to you," she shouted, as she walked hurriedly toward him.

As she neared, she lowered her voice and said, "I overheard your conversation with Paul. I want to warn you. Paul Santini has a history of conning teachers into sharing lesson plans. He gets what he wants, but he never gives anything in return."

"Thanks, but I don't want to pass judgment. I've only been here a few days. I'll have to form my own opinions about people," Carlos said.

"Well, I wanted to share this information with you. You'll find out what I mean," she said.

"I know you have my best interests at heart," Carlos remarked. "But I hope you understand why I can't pass judgment on people before I really know them."

"Sure, Carlos, I understand," Arlene replied.

The next day Carlos's first-period class was a smashing success. He had planned a lesson to get the students interested in poetry by building on their love of music. He began the class by telling the students he wanted to introduce them to two contemporary poets. At first there were groans. But when a song by Simon and Garfunkel began playing on the record player, the students became attentive. When the song "Richard Cory" was finished, Carlos turned off the record player and awaited the students' reactions.

"That's not poetry," a student suggested immediately. "That's folk music. My mom and dad listen to that stuff all the time."

"Mine, too," another student offered. "That was Simon and Garfunkel."

"Before we decide that what you heard was not poetry, I want you to read the following handout," said Carlos, as he distributed a copy of Edwin Arlington Robinson's poem "Richard Cory."

As students were reading the poem, one said, "Looks like the lyrics to the song." Several other students agreed aloud.

After the students had all read the handout, Carlos said, "I want to play the song again. As I do, pay careful attention to the handout."

At the conclusion of the song, he asked, "What did you notice between the lyrics in the song and the words in the handout?"

Several hands went up. He looked at his seating chart and said, "Julie, did you see any differences?"

"Some of the words were different. But not many. The lyrics and the words are nearly identical," Julie responded.

Carlos continued the discussion, explaining that "Richard Cory" was a poem written by the renowned American poet Edwin Arlington Robinson.

Comparisons were made between the poem and the song in terms of word choice, sentence structure, tone, rhythm, and meaning. Enticing the students to study poetry through music had worked. The class period had gone quickly. As they left the room, the students were buzzing. They were excited about the class and looked forward to returning the next day.

Later in the afternoon Paul Santini stopped Carlos in the hallway and said, "Congratulations!"

"For what?" Carlos Burton asked.

"Students from your two American literature classes this morning are already tapping you as 'Teacher of the Year,' he said, chuckling. "They told me about your use of music to introduce them to poetry."

"What are the chances today of my getting the plaque?" Carlos joked. "I don't want to risk my popularity for too long."

"Seriously though, getting them listening to a song and then springing the poem on them was an act of genius," Paul Santini continued. "What are the chances I could try out your lesson in my first-period class tomorrow?"

"The entire lesson?" Carlos asked.

"Yes. You could give me the materials after school and coach me on what to do. That shouldn't take more than ten minutes. I'll share some of my stuff with you later on. What do you say?" Paul asked.

"I put a lot of work into the lesson. Besides, I don't think the lesson would be very meaningful for your students," Carlos said.

"What do you mean by that?" Paul challenged.

"Look, this lesson is a part of a sequence of lessons, where I introduce different poetry concepts over time. Each lesson builds on the other. You can't just take the lesson and drop it on the students," Carlos retorted.

"I don't think it matters. That's like saying that if a major war breaks out tomorrow afternoon the social studies teachers shouldn't discuss it with their students because it doesn't fit into some predetermined sequence of lessons," Paul said.

"That's not the point," Carlos said.

"Just give it some thought. Let me know tomorrow."

The Challenge

You are Carlos. Is it appropriate to share the lesson?

ISSUES FOR FURTHER REFLECTION

1. Was the lesson Carlos developed worth borrowing? Defend your answer.
2. Based on the instructional approach to the poetry lesson, how likely are the students to retain the information presented? What factors will affect the length of time they will remember?
3. What elements of information-processing theory are contained in the lesson? What elements are not?
4. If you were designing the next lesson, how would you build on the one presented in this case? Be specific about what you would do.
5. Would you give your lesson plan and materials to Paul Santini? Explain your answer.
6. If Paul did use the lesson with his students, do you believe he would be as successful? Defend your answer.
7. Toward the end of their conversation, Paul says: "I don't think it matters [referring to the relationship of the lesson to others planned in a sequence]. That's like saying that if a major war breaks out tomorrow afternoon, the social studies teachers shouldn't discuss it with their students because it doesn't fit into some predetermined sequence of lessons." Do you agree with Paul's statement? Explain.
8. What ethical issues are raised?
9. What concerns emerge in regard to professional practice?

SUGGESTED READINGS

Bjorkland, D. (1992). Development differences in the acquisition and maintenance of an organizational strategy. *Journal of Experimental Child Psychology, 54*(3), 434–448.

Borkowski, J. (1992). Metacognitive theory: A framework for teaching literacy, writing, and math skills. *Journal of Learning Disabilities, 25*(4), 253–257.

Cohen, E. (1989). Can classrooms learn? *Sociology of Education, 62*(2), 75–94.

Dembo, M. (1994). *Applying educational psychology in the classroom* (5th ed.). New York: Longman (see chapters 2, 3, 4, 7, 8).

Feezel, J. (1986). Elements of teacher communication competence. *Communication Education, 35*(3), 254–268.

Good, T., & Brophy, J. (1990). *Educational psychology: A realistic approach* (4th ed.). New York: Longman (see chapters 3, 4, 8, 15, 24).

Gorham, J., & Zakahi, W. (1990). A comparison of teacher and student perceptions of immediacy and learning: Monitoring process and product. *Communication Education, 39*(4), 354–368.

Hawthorne, R. K. (1986). The professional teacher's dilemma: Balancing autonomy and obligation. *Educational Leadership, 44*(2), 34–35.

Henson, K. (1993). *Methods and strategies for teaching in secondary and middle schools* (2nd ed.). New York: Longman (see chapters 3, 5, 12, 13).

Hillard, A. (1992). Behavorial style, culture, and teaching and learning. *Journal of Negro Education, 61*(3), 370–377.

Katzner, L. I. (1986). Teaching from an ethical sensibility. *American Secondary Education, 15*(2), 6–8.

Kimpston, R. (1992). Ways of knowing and the curriculum. *Educational Forum, 56*(2), 153–172.

Leinhardt, G. (1992). What research on learning tells us about teaching. *Educational Leadership, 49*(7), 20–25.

Ohlsson, S. (1992). The cognitive complexity of learning and doing arithmetic. *Journal for Research in Mathematics Education, 23*(5), 441–467.

Pasch, M., Sparks-Langer, G., Gardner, T., Starko, A., & Moody, C. (1991). *Teaching as decision making: Instructional practices for the successful teacher.* New York: Longman (see chapters 8, 9).

Saltis, J. (1986). Teaching professional ethics. *Journal of Teacher Education, 37*(3), 2–4.

Tennyson, R. (1992). An educational learning theory for instructional design. *Educational Technology, 32*(1), 36–41.

Tennyson, W., & Strom, S. (1986). Beyond professional standards: Developing responsibleness. *Journal of Counseling and Development, 64*(5), 298–302.

Vosniadov, S. (1991). Are we ready for a psychology of learning and culture? *Learning and Instruction, 61*(3), 370–377.

Wong, B. (1992). On cognitive process–based instruction: An introduction. *Journal of Learning Disabilities, 25*(3), 150–152, 172.

Yeazell, M. (1986). The neglected competency, moral sensibility. *Contemporary Education, 57*(4), 173–175.

Using Metacognition to Improve Achievement, Attendance, and Retention

PREPARING TO USE THE CASE

Background Information

This case is about using cognitive and metacognitive strategies to improve an entire student body's performance on standardized achievement tests and to improve student attendance and retention. But the case is also about teachers working under stress. Increased emphasis on accountability is causing contemporary teachers to feel that there is not enough time to do all they should be doing.

Reaching the level of expectations that the public places on schools today requires more than just trying harder; today's teachers must use different approaches. Maximum success also requires more than increased teacher effort; parents and students must want better achievement and must be willing to work harder to make it happen.

Much evidence suggests that significantly increasing the performance of an entire school requires a unified effort that goes beyond individual teacher efforts in their isolated classrooms. An overall strategy is needed—a plan. This case shows a faculty's struggles to devise a plan that will increase students' overall academic performance.

As you read this case, think about yourself as a member of a team that is dedicated to maximum student performance. Particularly think about the cognitive and metacognitive strategies you can help your students use to increase their learning. Finally, think about ways you can alter your teaching methods to meet the cognitive needs of a large variety of individual students.

Topics for Reflection
1. Cognitive strategies vs. metacognitive strategies
2. The effect of objectives on learning
3. Individual learning differences
4. The effect of accommodating styles preferred by students or expanding the number of styles they can use
5. The desirability and effects of identifying major concepts in each lesson

THE CASE

Until recently, Martinville could be described as a sleepy little town surrounded by a prosperous farm community. There is a relatively high per capita income, and the residents place a high value on education. Quality schools are considered a must for the youth of Martinville. Unfortunately, the town's recent growth surge has happened so quickly that schools are in critically short supply. Even though the annual revenue generated in Martinville's city limits has doubled from $1 million to slightly over $2 million in only two years, the rapid growth rate has precluded time for planning, and the schools have not seen the benefit from the unanticipated growth.

The School District

Martinville Middle School is located in a town of 20,000 people, up from 12,000 about four years ago before the rash of factory outlets began moving in. The middle school building was erected in the late 1940s. At that time, the existing high school building was given up for the junior high students and teachers to occupy, and a new building was built to house the overrun population of high school students caused by school consolidation. In 1981, the junior high was converted to a middle school.

The School and School Leadership

During the past few years, Martinville Middle School's enrollment has grown from 1,500 to 2,800 students. The increase in enrollment is spread evenly over the school's four grades (5–8). Mobile homes serve as temporary classrooms for the newer faculty members. The additional growth has allowed for a broader curriculum with multiple sections of most subjects. Most teachers are permitted to choose between teaching five sections of the same subject or teaching a total of five sections of two subjects; either choice provides a planning period.

Through the years, Martinville teachers have had relatively high salaries. A recently developed career ladder has assured that the school will remain competitive and attract quality teachers.

Martinville's principal, Dr. Jane Chapman, has led the school for the past five years. During this time she has been a strong advocate for her school. This support has been reciprocated by a faculty that appreciates her leadership.

The combination of a rapid increase in enrollment and a corresponding rapid increase in revenue made for unusual circumstances. Paradoxically, the school board has had the money to buy the best, and the members have insisted on having top standardized-test scores; yet the teachers were being challenged to plan for such an influx of students that there was no time to systematically improve the entire structure of the school district or, for that matter, even for individual schools to restructure.

The school board decided that the best way to obtain the rapid improvement that they demanded was to provide an incentives program. Quickly the central office established a performance baseline for each school in the district. This consisted of a combination of three major performance areas: attendance, retention, and achievement. Each school's average daily attendance over the past three years became that school's benchmark for attendance. The number of students that dropped out over the past three years divided by the school's total enrollment became the school's benchmark for retention, and each school's average achievement test scores over the past three years became the school's benchmark for achievement.

In each of three areas, a specific dollar amount of reward was established for each point of improvement above the school's average performance over the past three years. Thus each school's local decision-making council was left to determine how it could best raise the performance level of its students. The local school councils were permitted to use up to 90% of their bonus money as salary supplements. Since teachers constituted 50 percent of the membership on the various school councils, this reward system quickly got the attention and commitment of each school's council.

The Incident

Each year Dr. Chapman calls a three-day in-service workshop to get the school year off to a good start. Actually, about a day and a half are used for faculty development. Consultants are usually brought in for a half day, and the following day the faculty divides into groups and discusses how best to apply the skills and knowledge acquired from the consultants.

This year, Dr. Chapman dedicated only a single day to organizing the beginning of the school year. The remaining two days would be used to determine the best way to raise the achievement test scores of Martinville Middle School as far above its benchmark as possible. Upon completion of this task, the faculty representative would take the faculty's recommendations to the council. The faculty for each grade would work together and develop its own recommended plan.

After working for a day and a half, the entire faculty was assembled into the school library to hear the plan from each grade level.

Mr. Bill Thompson spoke for grade 5.

"The fifth-grade faculty decided to break every lesson down into the following designated parts: objectives, concepts, teacher activities, student activities, and test items. All math teachers (grades 5–8) will work together to develop a curriculum that will have for each day's lesson at least one cognitive objective and one affective objective, a psychomotor objective (whenever feasible), two to four major concepts, at least one teacher activity to present the concepts, at least one student activity *involving all students* to help them learn the content, and at least one test item for each objective in the day's lesson. The other faculty members will join the teachers in their disciplines to do the same."

After some questions and answers, Mr. Thompson sat down. Dr. Chapman thanked him and called on Judy White, the chair of grade 6.

"Our group held a general discussion on the current performance at our school. We concluded that the faculty could improve performance most by focusing on those students who pull the performance down—the low achievers. They are also the same students who have the poorest attendance record and the highest drop-out rate.

"These students perform poorly because they don't care and because they don't know how to do better. We decided that they would do better if we shared the rewards with them; but we don't figure the state will let us give the students cash, so for each student who increases his or her benchmark level of performance in each category (attendance and achievement), we will give that student a predetermined amount of budget money to be used to take the class on special field trips. The class could also decide to purchase special equipment and materials.

"As to their not knowing how to improve, we decided that the school should designate two days each month to teach all students how to pay closer attention in class, how to pick out the most important concepts, how to take notes, and how to study their texts. And, that's about all we had time to come up with."

Doris Williams spoke for grade 7.

"Well, as all of you know, seventh graders are at the most awkward stage in their lives. Each one tries to be like the others but can't even be like himself for longer than a few minutes.

"It's probably because we work with this diverse age-group that our group decided that the best approach would be to give a learning styles inventory to the entire school so that we can tell each student his or her preferred learning style.

"Bobby Starns said—and we all agreed with him—that we teachers would have to have some faculty development to broaden our teaching styles, because it wouldn't help for students to know their preferred styles if we weren't able to use a variety of styles."

Gene Robinette spoke for the eighth-grade teachers.

"Well, first we decided that whatever approach the school uses, it should enable students to learn about their current thinking strategies. We decided the best way to do this would be to set up some exercises. Each exercise would be a different type of learning task. Letting each student choose his or her own approach, we would have the student analyze the strategies used. The results would be a self-developed thinking-strategies portfolio for each student.

"When complete, the student would know which thinking strategies he or she used during lectures, group discussion, simulations, role playing, case studies, and independent study. Then the student would be encouraged to experiment with other strategies. For example, a student who always took complete notes during a lecture might try outlining a lecture and then might try just listening for the two or three major concepts in a lecture."

The Challenge

With this last group report given, Dr. Chapman decided to let the faculty rate and rank these recommendations in order so they could give a preferred recommendation to the school council. Suppose you were Martha Simms, how would you rank these four recommendations?

ISSUES FOR FURTHER REFLECTION

1. Which grade level recommended more cognitive strategies?
2. Which are the most powerful in raising achievement: cognitive strategies or metacognitive strategies?
3. What evidence can you offer to support the use of incentives as suggested by the sixth-grade faculty?
4. The fifth-grade faculty stressed the need to use at least one cognitive and one affective objective. Is this reasonable?
5. The eighth-grade faculty suggested having each student analyze his or her own current preferred learning strategies. Are eighth graders capable of doing this?
6. Should teachers always strive to accommodate students' style preferences? Why or why not?
7. Can students alter their learning styles?
8. Are certain reading strategies (e.g., underscoring or highlighting the major concepts) more appropriate with some texts than others? If so, explain.
9. Is the fifth-grade faculty's decision to focus all efforts on the low performers equitable? Justifiable?
10. Which of these plans are characterized more by active strategies than passive strategies?
11. Which of the strategies use inquiry?
12. One group focused on helping students improve their note-taking skills. What can the teacher do to help?

SUGGESTED READINGS

Bonds, C. W., Bonds, L. G., & Peach, W. (1992). Metacognition: Developing independence in learning. *The Clearing House, 66*(1), 56–59.

Beyer, B. K. (1991). *Teaching thinking skills: A handbook for elementary school teachers.* Boston: Allyn & Bacon.

Boschee, F. (1992). Small-group learning in the information age. *The Clearing House, 65* (2), 89–92.

Curry, L. (1990). A critique of research on teaching styles. *Educational Leadership, 48*(2), 50–52, 54–56.

Dembo, M. (1994). Applying educational psychology in the classroom (5th ed.). New York: Longman (see chapter 4).

Derry, S. K. (1990). Learning strategies for acquiring useful knowledge. In B. L. Jones & L. Idol (Eds.). *Dimensions of thinking and cognitive instruction.* Hillsdale, NJ: Erlbaum.

Farber, B. A. (1991). *Crisis in education: Stress and burnout in the American teacher.* San Francisco: Jossey-Bass.

Gold, Y., & Roth, R. A. (1993). *Teachers managing stress and preventing burnout.* Washington, DC: Falmer.

Good, T., & Brophy, J. (1990). *Educational psychology: A realistic approach* (4th ed.). New York: Longman (see chapter 13).

Henson, K. T. (1993). *Methods and strategies for teaching in secondary and middle schools* (2nd ed.). New York: Longman (see chapter 7 & appendix E).

Hyde, A. A., & Bizar, M. (1989). *Thinking in context: Teaching cognitive processes across the elementary curriculum.* White Plains, NY: Longman.

Maclure, S., & Davies, P. (Eds.). (1991). *Learning to think: Thinking to learn.* Oxford: Pergamon Press.

Marshall, C. (1991). Teachers' learning styles: How they affect student learning. *The Clearing House, 64*(4), 225–227.

McWorter, K. T. (1992). *Study and thinking skills in college* (2nd ed.). New York: HarperCollins.

Schunk, D. H. (1991). *Learning theories: An educational perspective.* New York: Macmillan.

Snider, V. (1990). What we know about learning styles from research in special education. *Educational Leadership, 48*(2), 53.

Whittrock, M. C. (1991). Generative teaching of comprehension. *Elementary School Review, 92,* 169–184.

Young, D. B. (1993). Developing thinking skills: What teachers can do. *National Association of Laboratory Schools Journal, 17*(3), 32–52.

CASE 6

Drug Abuse Is a Major Problem

PREPARING TO USE THE CASE

Background Information

In recent years, the media have been filled with bad news about the schools and bad news about the behavior of youths. Throughout the 1960s and 1970s, the increased abuse of drugs contributed to an escalating frequency of youth crimes. The growth in drug abuse continued at an unchecked pace through 1982. The good news is that since 1982 the abuse of marijuana and "hard" drugs has declined. As Wynne and Ryan (1993) explain:

> Another trend we should keep in mind is youth drug use. To identify such trends, since 1975 the University of Michigan Center for Social Research has conducted annual, anonymous surveys of a national sample of each year's graduating high school class. The respondents were asked whether and how frequently, they used specified illegal substances. The surveys disclose that the peak point of such usage was in 1981 and 1982. At that time, 65% of the respondents said they had used marijuana at least once in their lives, and 45% also had used another illegal drug (e.g., LSD, cocaine, amphetamines). Smaller numbers of respondents used such drugs monthly or daily.
>
> Since 1980–1981, youth drug use trends have fortunately moved in a more favorable direction. The center's report for the class of 1990 revealed that marijuana use had gone down to 47%, and the use of other drugs was at 29%. Still, most authorities would agree that contemporary levels of youth drug use are far higher than they were in about 1970.

We still have far to go before we reattain the levels prevailing before
the youth drug epidemic. (p. 11)

Although drug abuse has declined, the fact remains that drugs are still a
dominative reality. As long as they continue to proliferate in our society, they
will continue to be a major problem in the schools. Based on a 1989 survey,
Hawley (1990) estimates that the average classroom has five or six drug-impaired
students, and says that "Considering that one in three students reports having
been drunk over the past two weeks, and you are not even within screaming
distance from a drug-free school." (p. 310)

Although drug abuse in schools has been a serious problem for almost a half
century, our teacher-education programs have done little or nothing to prepare
future teachers to cope with this problem. Finally, with the setting of the "Goals
of 2000" the president and the governors (National Education Goals Panel, 1991)
have at least acknowledged the problem by proclaiming the following goal for
all American schools:

By the year 2000, every school in America should be free of drugs and
violence and will offer a disciplined environment conducive to learning.

Of the top six goals set by this commission, the American public rated the
above goal last (Elam, Rose, & Gallup, 1991), and 79 percent of the public said
they thought the achievement of this goal by the year 2000 is unlikely or very
unlikely. Unfortunately, a review of the literature failed to reveal an abundance
of clear-cut methods for identifying and coping with drug abusers; therefore, as
you read this case, think about avenues you may pursue to increase your personal
knowledge about the teacher's role in curtailing drug abuse in the schools.

Topics for Reflection
1. The extent of drug abuse in the school
2. The relationship between drug abuse in society and drug abuse in
   the schools
3. The effects of drug abuse on behavior
4. Ways of recognizing drug abuse
5. The public's opinion about the seriousness of drug abuse in the
   schools

THE CASE

Granada is a small, rural community in the southwestern United States. A recently
developed laser-driven irrigation system has revitalized a community that was
once destined to become a ghost town. Yet this economic boost was not enough
to totally offset the damage caused by the oil slump of the early 1980s. Most of
Granada's population are ranchers, including the owners of the town's two small

gas stations and the combination hardware and general merchandise store. Granada's post office is operated by a staff of one, and even he has a small second business that combines a laundromat with a videocassette rental operation. For a 50-mile radius, the topography is sparsely spotted with oil wells that slowly pump as though to announce the stubborn resistance of a dying community.

A constant flow of illegal immigrant farm workers from Mexico into this community has been a perpetual problem, paralleled by a worse problem—a constant flow of illegal drugs. South of the border, marijuana has become a main crop in the last decade. Its popularity has intensified the long-established drug-traffic problem in towns such as Granada, which pepper the southwestern border of the United States.

The local newspaper has been carrying articles about people making mass runs for the border. Dozens of people, mostly in their teens and twenties, are assembling at major border crossings and storming the gates, running at top speed. Their sheer numbers are overwhelming for the border patrol. Those who are caught are jailed, but some usually escape.

To escape the poor economy, others are swimming across the border, mostly at night. The rivers, composed almost entirely of raw sewage, do not deter the desperate hundreds. Adding to the danger, some would-be immigrants are killed by cave-ins of the soft river banks during flash floods, and others are drowned by the raging currents. With this level of desperation, one can imagine the temptation that drugs offer as a means of escaping poverty. Once across, the immigrants seldom leave their old habits behind. For many, these include the continuing use and sales of illicit drugs.

The School District

Because of its vast open spaces, the state has been divided into about a dozen major education service centers. This accounts for Granada Elementary's only obvious link to the outside world. Prior to reorganization, this one-school district was isolated from the rest of the state. To describe the region as remote would be grossly inadequate to many Americans who cannot imagine the vastness of the rural Southwest. Unfortunately, the remoteness of this community is equalled by its poverty. The few dollars that come into the community do not seem to find their way into the schools.

The School and School Leadership

Granada Elementary is still housed in a 1930s wooden frame building that was built specifically for the school. After a longer period than anyone will admit to remembering, the principal, Mr. Starnes Austin, is finally retiring. A much younger administrator, Mrs. Juanita Quarrels, a graduate of Granada, has accepted the vacant principalship. Like Mr. Austin, she holds a bachelor's degree in elementary education and a master's degree in educational administration, both from the local state teachers' college. Since receiving her master's degree two years ago, she has not pursued further study.

The Granada student body is small and conservative. Like their parents, many of these students view education as a means for acquiring better jobs; thus schooling is viewed as a vehicle for socioeconomic mobility. Actually, their concern for social growth is dwarfed by their more compelling desire to earn money. Although during the planting and harvest seasons a few of the parents keep their children home to work in the fields, a commonly heard expression is "Go get your education; the crops will be here when you get back." Most of the students apply their family's work ethic to their schoolwork. From their small classes have come many honor-roll high school and college students. Several Granada students have gone on to become petroleum engineers. Others have entered a variety of other professions.

The Teacher

Jeff Stewart completed his bachelor's degree in elementary education last May with a major in English and a minor in speech. He was a little nervous over his first teaching position, but his nervousness was overshadowed by his enthusiasm. Four years had seemed like eternity to someone who is as active and involved as Jeff. Having finally reached the end of the tunnel, he was eager to get his rewards. Jeff was impressed with what he saw during his interview at Granada. Mrs. Quarrels who, incidentally, because of her Southern accent refers to herself as "Miseries" Quarrels, is hospitable and knowledgeable. She knows how to accentuate the assets of her school. Her pride in the work ethic and the success of the Granada students is reflected in the many academic plaques and trophies that decorate her office.

Yet, during Jeff's interview, Mrs. Quarrels was careful not to "oversell" the school. She pointed out the advantages and the disadvantages of working in a small, rural school such as Granada. "This is a school where parents appreciate and support their children's teachers." Granada teachers have a lot of latitude. Nobody tells them what they should be teaching or how they should discipline or grade their students. But Granada teachers work hard. Even during their lunch periods all teachers are required to sit with and manage the behavior of their homeroom classes.

Jeff appreciated this honesty. Work had never bothered him. The fact that he was given five separate teaching assignments spread over three grade levels (a situation that commonly befalls new teachers in small schools) did not discourage him. And although his students ranged from a section of gifted students to a section of low achievers, Jeff was determined to put his teaching on a personal basis and help all individual students reach their potential. Granada was fortunate to have a new teacher with his level of energy and commitment.

Jeff's middle-class background is typical of many teachers. His father is an accountant for a local chain of fast-food restaurants in his hometown, and his mother is a nurse at the local hospital. Jeff, his two brothers, and one sister have always been close. Their parents are devout Baptists who believe in attending church regularly, contributing to the community, and, in short, clean living. Sometimes Jeff wonders whether this high level of support has prepared him for, or sheltered him from, understanding and helping others.

Jeff remembers from his own school experience that some students seemed to stay on track academically and socially while others were habitually depressed, and still others were always getting into trouble, academically or otherwise. He felt lucky to have had a good youth, and he wanted to express this appreciation by helping students who are less fortunate.

As the end of the first six-week period approached, Jeff's career had definitely gotten off to a good start. His nervous jitters had been replaced by a very busy schedule coupled with a deep concern for "his" students. Jeff's daily conversations focused only on his class activities and upon the youths who were in his classes. More than anything else, Jeff wanted to stimulate students to achieve their maximum potential. Jeff's students felt the results of his high level of dedication in their heavy homework assignments, although a few were not making any noticeable progress.

Jeff's concern for individual achievement levels was intensified after reading an issue of *Harper's* magazine; there he saw a list of the top discipline problems of the 1940s compared to a list of the top discipline problems of the 1980s. (See Table 1.)

One of the students who had captured Jeff's attention was a small, quiet sixth-grader named Julio Martinez. Julio was one of eleven children in a family of migrant farm workers who had moved into town during the past summer. They move five or six times a year to gather produce. Their annual route extends from Florida where they pick citrus fruits to Maine where they harvest apples, beets, and syrup.

The school records contain mostly negative comments about Julio. One note says that he has been careless with his textbooks and has repeatedly misplaced them. Another notation by a former teacher says, "He often comes to school

TABLE 1   The top disciplinary problems in 1940 and 1982

1940	1982
1. Talking	1. Rape
2. Chewing gum	2. Robbery
3. Making noise	3. Assault
4. Running in the halls	4. Burglary
5. Getting out of turn in line	5. Arson
6. Wearing improper clothing	6. Bombings
7. Not putting paper in wastebasket	7. Murder
	8. Suicide
	9. Absenteeism
	10. Vandalism
	11. Extortion
	12. Drug abuse
	13. Alcohol abuse
	14. Gang warfare
	15. Pregnancy
	16. Abortion
	17. Venereal disease

without bathing, and the other boys have introduced him to the showers in the gym.'' A note from a former counselor says that he is shy and that sometimes he has problems with his peers.

So far, neither of Julio's parents has visited the school. They have missed Parents Orientation Day and Open House. No response was received from the questionnaires mailed to absent parents, following these important events. When asked why they were absent, Julio's only response was a shoulder shrug and a mumbled, ''I dunno.'' At school, Julio's achievement could most accurately be described as nonexistent. As the first six-week period wound down, Julio had failed all five weekly tests and, in fact, had not come close to passing any of them. He was behind on eight homework assignments. Julio's problems were not limited to poor academics. In fact, this may have been one of his smallest problems. At Granada, Julio was a social misfit. Each day when he left the building for recess or physical education, his mild-mannered classroom behavior disappeared and he became noticeably aggressive. It was clear that he went out of his way to start fights, often with students who were almost twice his size. It was almost as though he wanted to be beaten.

The Incident

When working his assigned turn at ''hall duty'' (monitoring student behavior), Jeff overheard a conversation between two students who were discussing Julio. The conversation clearly indicated that Julio was using drugs. Jeff thought, ''Sure, this explains his Jekyll–Hyde behavior. But what if they were wrong? Should I confront Julio? What an injustice to falsely accuse a student of drug abuse!''

Jeff checked Julio's cumulative folder again and found out that the school counselor had recently learned that when Julio was seven, his parents had divorced, and subsequently Julio had been given up for adoption. But after only a year in his new home, Julio was awarded back to the state as a result of misconduct charges of severe neglect and alleged child abuse against his adoptive parents. His current family consists of an uncle, an aunt, and their children.

Julio's social record shows a life-long inability to get along with his peers. He has been in one fight after another, each resulting from his inability to control his temper.

Jeff considered going to the school counselor about Julio's possible drug problem, but he was not sure. The only evidence he had was Julio's bizarre contrast in behavior and a conversation between two students that he overheard. He wondered whether he should just openly offer his help. Jeff also considered asking other teachers whether they had noticed Julio's erratic behavior and whether his performance in their classes was low. Should he ask these two students why they were so convinced that Julio was on drugs? He wondered too, what if his suspicion was correct? What could he do? What should he do?

The Challenge

Suppose you were Jeff Stewart. What would you do?

ISSUES FOR FURTHER REFLECTION

1. What additional information does Jeff need?

2. To what other sources could Jeff go for information?

3. Is it ethical to discuss a student with other teachers? With other students?

4. What might happen if Jeff were to confront Julio?

5. What information do you have that is not relevant to making this decision?

6. What are some other possible causes of erratic behavior?

7. Would it be ethical to ask the two students how they know that Julio is using drugs? What possible consequence might this have?

8. Identify some immediate actions and some long-term actions that Jeff might take to help a drug abuser.

9. Examine Table 1. What implications does this information have for future teachers?

10. How can a teacher spot a student who is on drugs?

11. What community agencies can be used to help reduce drug abuse in the schools?

12. What is the potential that consultants could help arrest this problem, and where might a teacher find good consultants?

13. Where could you learn about sources of effective videotapes on prevention of drug abuse? What other types of videotapes could help?

14. What effects do personal and social backgrounds have on the ability of teachers to cope with drug-related problems?

15. Is any type of teacher-imposed punishment appropriate for student drug abusers?

16. What responsibilities, if any, do teachers have for guarding the safety of students who abuse drugs?

17. What does Jeff need to know about Julio's home life?

18. Could Julio's size affect his behavior? How?

19. What does Jeff need to know about Julio's peer relationships?

20. What can Jeff do to help Julio relax when he notices that Julio is especially tense?

21. What can Jeff do to help Julio feel good about himself, so that he will not feel a need for drugs?

22. How might Jeff determine whether Julio's problem results from his social relationships or from hereditary factors?

23. What connection, if any, do you think there is between Julio's long-term academic performance and his "temper" problem?

SUGGESTED READINGS

Dembo, M. (1994). *Applying educational psychology in the classroom* (5th ed.). New York: Longman (see chapter 4).

Elam, S. M., Rose, L. C., & Gallup, A. M. (1991). The 23rd annual Gallup poll of the public's attitude toward the school. *Phi Delta Kappan, 73*(1), 41–56.

Etscheidt, S. (1991). Reducing aggressive behavior and improving self-control: A cognitive behavioral program for behaviorally disordered adolescents. *Behavioral Disorders, 16*(2), 107–115.

Goldstein, A. P., Reagles, K. W., & Amann, L. S. (1990). *Refusal skills, preventing drug use in adolescents,* Champaign, IL: Research Press.

Good, T., & Brophy, J. (1990). *Educational psychology: A realistic approach* (4th ed.). New York: Longman (see chapter 5).

Hawley, R. A. (1990). The bumpy road to drug free schools. *Phi Delta Kappan, 72*(4), 310–314.

Henson, K. T. (1993). *Methods and strategies for teaching in secondary and middle schools* (2nd ed.). New York: Longman (see chapter 13).

National Education Goals Panel (1991). *Goals report.* Washington, DC: United States Government Printing Office.

Powell, R. R., & Garcia, J. (1991). Classrooms under the influence: Adolescents and alcoholic parents. *The Clearing House, 64*(4), 277.

Wynne, E. A., & Ryan, K. (1993). *Reclaiming our schools.* New York: Merrill.

Helping a Troubled Student

PREPARING TO USE THE CASE

Background Information

Work with middle school students is often characterized as challenging simply because the students at this level are progressing toward adolescence. To be effective, teachers must have an understanding of the physical, social, psychological, and emotional implications of this stage of life. Such information helps to explain the difficulties many students have with their personal lives—and with their work in school.

Most of us readily recognize the physical differences in preadolescents and adolescents. We can see how these differences manifest themselves in body characteristics. Detecting and understanding differences in psychosocial development, however, tend to be more difficult. While one student may develop a positive self-image with little difficulty, others may find this developmental task to be extremely painful. Insecurity, confusion, and anxiety can emerge to affect a student's behavior.

As students make the transition from childhood to adolescence, they experience alterations in their world of reality. Two examples serve to exhibit this. First as students become older, their range of experiences typically broadens. That is, they are likely to be exposed to people of different races, socioeconomic backgrounds, beliefs, and values. Second, movement into adolescence usually is accompanied by increasing levels of independence. The students want to become young men and women.

This case focuses on an eighth-grade boy from an upper-middle-class family who develops a close friendship with another boy whose socioeconomic background is quite different. When this friend's family is forced to leave the community, the boy exhibits an abrupt change in appearance and behavior. The transformation concerns school officials, and it truly alarms the boy's parents. A first-year mathematics teacher tries to reach out to help the boy refocus on his schoolwork. But her advice spawns an angry reaction from the boy's parents.

One of the lessons teachers learn very quickly is that people hold differing values and beliefs about the purposes of schooling and life. Some parents, for instance, may expect teachers to play a major role in providing guidance for their children—including direction in controversial areas such as sex education. Other parents demand that teachers restrict their activities to academic programs. These parents resent interventions into family life. Because of such differing expectations, teachers often face difficult decisions about when and how to assist troubled students. This is especially true if neither the school nor the school district offers professional employees much direction in dealing with such matters.

Topics for Reflection
1. Psychosocial development among early adolescents
2. Peer relationships among early adolescents
3. Teacher interventions in personal problems
4. The effects of social and psychological difficulties on academic performance
5. Parental/teacher conflict

THE CASE

Todd Allen and Billy Drumm first met four years ago when they were both named to a Little League all-star baseball team for their city. At first, the two did not like each other. Prior to being named to the all-star team, they had played against each other on several occasions, but they had never engaged in conversation. The coach of the all-star team assumed that they didn't get along well because they were the two superstars of the team. Each had been the player in the spotlight on his respective team. And as the all-star team practiced for the state tournament, it was evident that competition between the two was intense. Todd played shortstop and Billy was an outfielder. Both were excellent hitters.

Their talent in baseball was one of the few things the two boys had in common. Whereas Todd lived in the wealthy part of White River, Billy lived in the poorest neighborhood. Todd was an only child; Billy was the youngest of six children. Todd's father is a dentist; Billy's father had died when he was two years old. Todd's mother owns her own real estate company; Billy's mother is a waitress in a tavern. But despite the glaring differences in their socioeconomic backgrounds, and despite their initial dislike for each other, the two eventually became close friends. The success of the White River all-star team was largely responsible for the bonding that occurred. They learned quickly that if their team was to win, they both had to do well.

When Todd and Billy entered the sixth grade at White River Middle School, they had the opportunity to spend more time together. Since they attended elementary schools in different parts of the city, their prior contact was restricted to baseball. At the middle school, they had much more time to get to know each other, and they became close friends. By the end of the seventh grade, many teachers and students referred to them as "lightning" and "thunder." They were virtually inseparable.

One of the remarkable things about their friendship was the sharp contrast in their personal appearance. Todd was always neatly dressed—a model Boy Scout. Billy had long shaggy hair and dressed more like a recruit for a motorcycle gang. The boys also differed markedly in their achievement levels at school. Todd was an "A" student, Billy had little or no interest in schoolwork. Billy dreamed of becoming a professional baseball player, and he often told Todd about some of the major leaguers who never even finished high school. Todd, by contrast, knew that his parents wanted him to become a physician.

During the summer between the seventh and eighth grade, the two were playing on the same baseball team and spending a good bit of time with each other. It was during this summer that Todd's parents realized how close the two boys had become. They were not pleased with the friendship. They saw Billy as a troubled young man who was likely to lead Todd astray. Early that summer, Todd brought Billy to the house on several occasions to swim in the family pool, but Billy sensed that Todd's parents did not want him around. He felt uncomfortable around Dr. and Mrs. Allen, who were always very formal and domineering. It seemed they were always barking orders at Todd.

Todd resented his parents' rejection of his friend. Every time his parents disapproved of his behavior, they would ask him, "Did you learn that from your friend, Billy? Did he teach you these poor manners?" By mid-July, Todd's parents reached a decision that they would not allow the two boys to spend time together. Todd was told that if he disobeyed their wishes, he would be grounded for the remainder of the summer. Dr. and Mrs. Allen encouraged their son to resume his friendships with some of the children in their neighborhood.

Shortly after the two boys started eighth grade in late August, Billy Drumm's house burned to the ground. It wasn't much of a house, and a short in an electrical wire touched off a blaze that totally destroyed the residence in less than an hour. Mrs. Drumm had no insurance on the house, and the tragedy forced her to relocate her family so that they could live with her sister in another state.

Todd was devastated by Billy's departure from White River. He said little about the matter to his parents, teachers, or friends. Inwardly, however, he was angry that this had to happen. He started isolating himself. He would come home from school and sit in his room watching television for hours at a time. When he was alone in his room, he thought about Billy's house burning and how the whole situation would have been different if Billy had a father and his family had some money. He thought it was unfair that he had to lose his best friend. Gradually, his anger about the incident shifted from what had happened to Billy to what had happened to him. It was he, he concluded, who got hurt most by Billy's house being destroyed.

In the two months following Billy's departure from White River, Todd started to show signs of rebelling against authority. His stopped wearing conventional clothing and let his hair grow. You could no longer tell by looking at him that he came from an affluent family.

Todd's behavior around other people, especially adults, also underwent visible changes. He began to challenge simple statements, and on occasion even became argumentative with his teachers and parents. He became less interested in his schoolwork, and told Mr. Martin, the eighth-grade basketball coach, that he probably would not go out for the team. Increasingly, everyone who knew Todd thought that he was trying to imitate his lost friend, Billy. His parents reacted to Todd's behavioral changes by repeatedly telling him that he should have listened to them—he should have stayed away from Billy. They hoped that he would return to normal once he realized that Billy was not coming back to White River.

Todd's transformation became a focused concern for Rose Ann O'Malley, his mathematics teacher. She was troubled by his declining performance in her class. Todd's records showed that he had been an excellent student, but in her class, he was barely doing average work. On several occasions, she tried to talk to him about his schoolwork. Todd responded by telling her he was doing his best. He never admitted that he was not studying or doing homework.

One afternoon, Rose Ann was leaving school when she saw Todd sitting alone on a bench near the parking lot. He seemed to be in a trance.

"Todd, what are you thinking about?" she asked him.

"Absolutely nothing, Miss O'Malley. Absolutely nothing," he answered.

Rose Ann sat on the other end of the bench and said, "Then I guess you don't mind if we talk for a while."

"About what?" Todd inquired.

"About you. About your schoolwork. About what is troubling you."

Todd shook his head as if to say no. Then he said, "Why does everyone care about me all of sudden? My parents, the principal, and now you. What am I doing that is so terrible?"

"Nobody said you are doing terrible things. I'm concerned about you because you are a young man with tremendous potential. You can be anything you want to be. You're smart. You're a gifted athlete. You come from a fine family. I don't want you to waste all that potential."

Todd did not respond. After a moment of silence, Rose Ann continued,

"You can do much better in my class. I looked at your records. You have never made anything but 'A's in mathematics—and now, you're struggling to get a 'C'. Why, Todd? Tell me so I can help you."

It seemed that two or three minutes passed before Todd responded to his teacher.

"Did you know Billy Drumm?" he asked. Rose Ann said that she did not. Todd then told her about the fire and Billy having to move to another state.

"Billy's a good guy. My parents and teachers didn't like him because he was different. Because he came from a poor family and because he wasn't a very good student, a lot of people thought he wasn't a good guy. It seems everybody knows what they want from me. My dad and mom want me to be a doctor. Teachers keep telling me how much potential I have. What about what I want? Doesn't that matter? I used to feel sorry for Billy because he didn't have much. Now,

I realize how lucky he was. He didn't have people telling him what they expected all the time. Billy could be what he wanted to be.''

"And what do you want, Todd?"

"I'm just not sure. I know I don't want everybody deciding things for me. Since Billy moved away, I've been kind of confused. Why does someone like Billy have to have such a rotten life? Why doesn't he have a father? Why does he have to move away because his family can't afford to stay here?"

"Those are good questions, and I understand why they bother you. But you have got to start thinking about yourself. You need to concentrate on your schoolwork."

Todd looked at his teacher and said, "Well, my parents seem more concerned about how I dress and who I pal around with. They didn't like Billy, and now they want to pick all of my friends for me."

"Todd, I want you to concentrate on your schoolwork. How you dress and act is something you need to sort out for yourself. As you can plainly see at our school, not everyone chooses to dress the same way. Try to separate these two issues. Your decisions about how you want to look are one thing; your schoolwork is quite another." Having said that, Rose Ann stood up and added, "You think about that and don't hesitate to come and see me if you feel you want to talk some more."

That evening Todd had another confrontation with his parents at the dinner table. His father ordered him to get a haircut and to quit wearing an old pair of tattered jeans.

"You look like some bum going to school that way," his mother commented. "You have a closet full of nice clothes, and all you wear are those awful jeans and those old tee shirts."

"How I look and act is my business," Todd shot back.

"Well, that is where you are mistaken, young man," his father responded. "What makes you think that you know everything? Your mother and I care very deeply about your future. We know that you have to do well in school to do well in life. We're not going to let you just become a nobody."

"There are lots of people who do well in life without going to college. How do you know what I have to do? What makes you think you two have all the answers?"

Before either parent could respond, Todd continued, "I had a talk with one of my teachers this afternoon—Miss O'Malley, my math teacher. She told me that I had to sort these things out for myself. She said I have to make decisions for myself—to live up to my expectations. What makes her wrong and you right?"

Dr. Allen's face became flushed as he got up from the dinner table. Without saying another word he went into the den and got out the telephone book. He looked up the number of Rose Ann O'Malley and dialed it. He had never met the teacher, but he had heard her name mentioned once or twice.

"Hello, Miss O'Malley. This is Dr. Allen, Todd's father. I wish to speak with you about my son. Did you have a conversation with him this afternoon?"

Rose Ann said that she had, and before she could explain why, she was subjected to a five-minute lecture about how she should not be interfering in the way the Allens handled their son. Clearly, the father was angry. He expressed his feeling that the teacher had given his son bad advice. In so doing, Dr. Allen felt that Rose Ann had exacerbated the tension between him and his son.

"On what basis do you feel qualified to tell our son how he should dress or act? Are you a psychologist? Are you a parent? Don't you realize that young people like Todd are vulnerable?"

Rose Ann tried to give her version of the conversation. She explained that she was trying to help Todd refocus on his studies. She also explained how many adolescents go through periods where they search for their identities. She suggested that his behavioral changes might be just a temporary thing, and that calling attention to these matters only served to distract him from his schoolwork.

"Dr. Allen, I was only trying to help. If what I did offended you, I'm sorry. I was just trying to turn Todd around," Rose Ann explained. But Dr. Allen did not accept the apology. He reiterated his feelings that she had no business telling Todd to make his own decisions about personal appearance. Before he concluded the telephone conversation, he told her that he was referring his complaint to the principal, Mr. Watson.

"Miss O'Malley, my wife and I are both well educated. We appreciate the fact that you want to help Todd do better in school. But when it comes to how he looks and dresses, that really is none of your concern. I don't mean to be discourteous, but try to understand our view on this matter," the father said as he ended the conversation.

Neil Watson, the principal of White River Middle School, has known Dr. Allen for nearly 15 years. He is a patient of the dentist, and they both belong to the local Rotary Club. When he received the complaint about Miss O'Malley, he told Dr. Allen that she was a very good teacher who was probably just trying to help Todd. But he also assured the father that he would look into the matter immediately and report back to him.

Later that morning, Rose Ann received a note from Mr. Watson requesting that she meet with him after school that day to discuss Todd Allen.

The Challenge

Evaluate Rose Ann's behavior in this case. Do you think her actions were appropriate?

ISSUES FOR FURTHER REFLECTION

1. What do you think caused the behavioral changes in Todd?
2. Do you think there was anything abnormal about Todd's relationship with Billy?
3. Do you think that Billy was a bad influence on Todd? What evidence do you have for your conclusion?
4. Do all adolescents go through a period of questioning themselves—of seeking their identity?
5. Should schools be concerned with the psychosocial development of students? Or is it the responsibility of schools to concentrate on academic matters?

6. Do you think Todd is feeling sorry for himself? Why or why not?

7. If you were Rose Ann, would you have approached Todd the way she did? If not, what would you have done differently?

8. What is your assessment of Rose Ann's advice to Todd?

9. Do you think that Todd's parents are correct in trying to guide his future?

10. In what ways might identity confusion affect a student's academic performance?

11. Can you recall your experiences in the eighth grade? Did you have feelings of uncertainty about yourself?

12. Was it wise for Todd's parents to forbid him from seeing Billy during the summer?

13. Do you think the fact that Todd was an only child had any bearing on this case?

14. To what extent do you believe that Todd was seeking independence from his parents?

SUGGESTED READINGS

Berndt, T. (1982). The features and effects of friendship in early adolescence. *Child Development, 53*(6), 1447–1460.

Bigelow, B. (1982). On the interdependency between stage and sequence in the development of children's friendship expectations. *Journal of Psychology, 110*(1), 121–132.

Broughton, J. (1981). The divided self in adolescence. *Human Development, 24*(1), 13–32.

Cote, J., & Levine, C. (1989). The empirical test of Erikson's theory of ego identity formation. *Youth and Society, 20*(4), 388–415.

Dembo, M. (1994). *Applying educational psychology in the classroom* (5th ed.). New York: Longman (see chapter 10).

Felson, R., & Zielinski, M. (1989). Children's self-esteem and parental support. *Journal of Marriage and the Family, 51*(3), 727–735.

Good, T., & Brophy, J. (1990). *Educational psychology: A realistic approach* (4th ed.). New York: Longman (see chapter 5).

Harter, S., & Monsour, A. (1992). Developmental analysis of conflict caused by opposing attributes in the adolescent self-portrait. *Developmental Psychology, 28*(2), 251–260.

Johnson, W., & Kottman, T. (1992). Developmental needs of middle school students: Implications for counselors. *Elementary School Guidance and Counseling, 27*(1), 3–14.

Lempers, J., & Clark-Lempers, D. (1992). Young, middle, and late adolescents' comparisons of the functional importance of five significant relationships. *Journal of Youth and Adolescence, 21*(1), 53–96.

Markstrom-Adams, C. (1989). Androgyny and its relation to adolescent psychosocial well-being: A review of the literature. *Sex Roles: A Journal of Research, 21*(5-6), 325–340.

Matthews, D. (1989). Anxiety: A component of self-esteem. *Elementary School Guidance and Counseling, 24*(2), 153–159.

Moore, S., & Boldero, J. (1991). Psychosocial development and friendship functions in adolescence. *Sex Roles: A Journal of Research, 25*(9-10), 521–536.

Muus, R. (1982). Social cognition: Robert Selman's theory of role taking. *Adolescence, 17*(67), 499–525.

O'Brien, S. (1989). For parents particularly: How can I help my preadolescent? *Childhood Education, 66*(1), 35–36.

O'Brien, S., & Bierman, K. (1988). Conceptions of perceived influence on peer groups: Interviews with preadolescents and adolescents. *Child Development, 59*(5), 1360–1365.

Phelps, P. (1992). Understanding early adolescents through dialogue journals. *Teaching Education, 4*(2), 147–150.

Philibert, P. (1982). Adolescence: Season of transition. *Momentum, 13*(2), 7–9, 39–41.

Siddique, C., & D'Arcy, C. (1984). Adolescence, stress, and psychological well-being. *Journal of Youth and Adolescence, 13*(6), 459–473.

Tierno, M. (1983). Responding to self-concept disturbance among early adolescents: A psychosocial view for educators. *Adolescence, 18*(71), 577–584.

Whalen, S., & Csikszentmihalyi, M. (1989). A comparison of self-image of talented teenagers with a normal adolescent population. *Journal of Youth and Adolescence, 18*(2), 131–146.

CASE 8

Improving Sarah's Self-Concept

PREPARING TO USE THE CASE

Background Information

A variety of experiences can affect a student's self-image and self-esteem. Affection, approval, and discipline in the family and at school exemplify experiences that often have a profound effect on social, psychological, and emotional development. When students see themselves as unworthy or academically incapable, personal growth is often thwarted. Such a condition usually leads to an undesirable cycle of events in which these students attempt to avoid situations that test their social and academic skills. Not surprisingly, many of these students eventually develop negative attitudes about school.

Not infrequently, teachers observe that children who have low academic achievement also possess low self-esteem. Selecting the best approach to working with this type of a student is a major challenge. There usually is a fine line between properly motivating the student to do better and creating false hopes. For instance, a teacher's praise can be misconstrued by a student. When this occurs, there is a danger that the student will improperly judge personal achievements and potentialities. By contrast, teachers need to be concerned about students who never have an opportunity for success. For these individuals, most experiences at school serve to reinforce low self-esteem. It is in this respect that a teacher must make critical decisions about instructional interventions that involve setting tasks and issuing praise.

A person's self-assessment is not the product of any one experience. Rather, it evolves from myriad encounters in childhood. Parents, for example, may repeatedly set unrealistic tasks for their child that inevitably result in failure; and even at a preschool age, the child eventually develops a sense of hopelessness.

A person who sees success as impossible has little reason to put forth effort. It is like a young boy who is forced to be a participant in a race he knows he cannot win. Even before the start of the race, he is mentally rationalizing his performance.

A number of psychologists have suggested that student motivation is positively effected by linking personal effort and success. To accomplish this objective, the teacher must identify tasks that the student can realistically achieve—and as already noted, this is more complex than it may seem. Teachers must attempt to create opportunities for individual success in the context of a classroom of 25 to 35 students. Students rarely can be isolated from the group; and thus tasks devised for a given student do not go unnoticed by others in the class. Some students, for example, may question the teacher's fairness if he or she continually gives a particular student easy assignments.

This case focuses on a fourth-grade teacher who seeks to help a girl who he believes is not achieving at an appropriate level. Seemingly uninterested in schoolwork, the student exhibits a rare burst of enthusiasm when she is afforded the opportunity to serve as a peer tutor for the lowest achieving student in the class. The teacher struggles to give meaning to this serendipitous event. He ponders whether the experience should be repeated; and not feeling totally confident with his own deliberations, he turns to two more experienced peers for advice. Unfortunately, this approach also fails to provide a conclusive approach to dealing with the problem.

Topics for Reflection
1. Student self-esteem
2. Relationship between self-esteem and achievement
3. Identifying areas of student success
4. Building a student's level of confidence
5. Praise and rewards

THE CASE

Donald Potter grew up in a tough neighborhood in Baltimore. His father and mother were divorced when he was only three years old. Marcia Potter, his mother, worked as a clerk in a department store, and Donald and his sister, who was one year younger, spent many of their preschool days with Grandma Hawkins, Marcia Potter's mother.

Donald attended public schools and was an above-average student. In high school, he became a star on the track team. His greatest athletic achievement came in his senior year when he finished second in the low hurdles in the state finals.

Accomplishments in the classroom and athletics earned Donald a scholarship to a small state university in the South. There he majored in elementary education and maintained an active schedule in student government, his social fraternity, and athletics. He also was an excellent student, and in his senior year, he was named the outstanding graduate in the school of education.

By the time Donald graduated from college, Grandmother Hawkins had died and his sister had married. His mother was now living alone in Baltimore, and because he wanted to be near her, Donald applied for positions in that area. After a successful interview, he was employed by a county school system and assigned to teach fourth grade at Adams Elementary School.

Adams is a relatively new facility, having been built just 13 years ago. The school serves a middle-class neighborhood in suburban Baltimore; however, about 20% of the students are bused to the school from other neighborhoods as part of a desegregation plan. Approximately 25% of the teachers at the school are African Americans, but most of them have been employed at the school for less than five years. The principal, Edward Jacobsen, has been in his current post for 14 years.

For the most part, Donald was thrilled with his position at Adams Elementary School. The two other fourth-grade teachers, Deeanne Wise and Betsy Irons, were highly experienced and offered him assistance in many ways. They shared materials, provided insights about lesson planning, and even offered ''political'' advice about organizational life at Adams. Early in the school year, the three had decided to meet at least once every two weeks for one hour after school to discuss programming in the fourth grade. The meetings had led to a number of creative ideas that involved collaboration among the three teachers and their students.

Being an African-American teacher, Donald felt a special responsibility to the minority children who were bused to the school. In his class of 27 students, six were in this category. He often reflected what it would have been like for him to be bused to a suburban school when he was in the fourth grade. On the one hand, he thought it would be great because he would have had a nicer school building and more materials. But on the other hand, he wasn't sure that he would have felt very comfortable going to school in a strange community. These thoughts of his own childhood and educational experiences shaped his behavior toward the six inner-city students in his class. He tried to give each a little extra care and assistance.

Although Donald maintains an interest in each of his 27 students, Sarah Killebrew has become special for him. She is a shy student who is a bit smaller than the other girls in class. Her academic achievement has been below average even though her ability test scores suggest that she should be an above-average student. She rarely exhibits excitement about academic assignments—or anything else that occurs at school. Sarah is not, however, a behavior problem.

By early November, Donald had made a concerted effort to find out everything he could about Sarah. He examined her file; he talked to the school counselor and previous teachers; and he had a conference with her mother. Sarah had two siblings—one two years older and one three years younger. Her mother had never married, and currently she was unemployed. The family lived in a public housing project in a neighborhood much like the one in which Donald was reared. Sarah had taken group ability tests in first and third grade, and her scores indicated that she was in the ''high average'' range.

During the conference with Sarah's mother, Donald learned that Sarah had a particularly close relationship with her younger brother, Reggie. The mother indicated that Sarah was very protective of him and often was happiest when the two were together. In fact, Sarah seemed to be another person. Her shyness was less obvious and she seemed more extroverted. Reggie also attended Adams; and each day Sarah helped him get ready for school and sat with him on the bus.

Donald was troubled by two things related to Sarah: (1) She was a low achiever despite the fact that some evidence showed that she was capable of much better work, and (2) she was a "loner," who had virtually no social relationships with the other students. Despite these problems, Sarah seemed to have a great deal of common sense, and on occasion she had been creative in attempting to do school assignments.

One day when the other children were outside for recess, Donald kept Sarah in class so he could talk to her privately.

"Sarah, do you like school?" he asked her.

"It's okay," she answered.

"You know, Sarah, I think you could be a really good student if you wanted to be. That's why I wanted to talk with you. I want to know if there are some things that I could do to help you do better."

Sarah did not respond. She looked down at the floor, and it was obvious that she was not comfortable having her teacher talk to her while the other students were at recess.

"Sarah, is there some place you would rather be than in school?" he asked her.

"Yes."

"Where?"

"At home."

"Well if you were home all day, how would you learn anything?" he asked.

"I don't know," Sarah answered.

"Don't you think that school is important? Don't you think that you need to learn to do certain things?"

Again Sarah answered, "I don't know."

"Sarah, do you think you are a good student?"

She answered, "No."

"Do you think you can be a good student if you try harder?"

Again she answered, "No."

Donald's perception that Sarah had little self-confidence was strengthened by their brief conversation. He concluded that he had to help her eradicate a defeatist attitude that was a barrier to academic achievement. He chose a two-part strategy: (1) Sarah would be given relatively easy tasks that she was certain to complete, and (2) she would be praised before the class for having been successful. The first effort to move in this direction came the following day while the class was working with mathematics. Donald assigned each student a problem to complete on the front chalkboard. Sarah was given the first and least complex problem. She finished it correctly, and Donald immediately said, "What a fine job, Sarah. That was outstanding." But fourth-grade students are often quite blunt—and perceptive. One of the boys in class reacted immediately, "Mr. Potter, that's an easy problem. We all could do it." Donald saw that the comment had counterbalanced his effort to build Sarah's confidence.

Even though Sarah's achievement level was low, she was not the poorest student in the class. That dubious distinction belonged to Andy Jurovich. Like Sarah he was rather shy and wasn't really popular with the other students. But he was not one of the children bused to Adams; he lived just three blocks from the school. Andy had been retained in the first grade, and now almost always gets the lowest grades on tests and homework projects. He has an especially difficult time with spelling. There are moments when Donald wonders how Andy ever learned to spell his own name.

One day in February, the students were getting ready to go outside for recess. Donald was unhappy with Andy because he had not completed a study exercise assigned the previous day as homework. He decided to make Andy stay in the room during recess and work on the exercise so that he would be better prepared for the spelling test that afternoon. Having to skip recess was a penalty that had become rather common for Andy. Sarah was also staying inside because she was suffering from a cold. That day it was Donald's turn to supervise the playground; and as he was departing with the students he said to Sarah, "Why don't you help Andy with his homework? Maybe he can learn something from you." Donald did not think that would really happen since both students were prone to isolating themselves.

When the class returned 20 minutes later, Donald was pleasantly surprised that Andy had completed his homework. This was a rare accomplishment.

He called Sarah aside, "Did you help him do this?"

"Yes," she responded. And after a brief pause, she added, "If you want me to help Andy again, I will."

This was the first time Donald had ever seen Sarah volunteer to do anything. She even seemed to have a slight smile on her face when she talked to him. Donald made of point of telling the class how Sarah had helped Andy during recess. Again, he detected a slight smile on Sarah's face.

That afternoon, the students took their weekly spelling test. To Donald's surprise, Sarah spelled all 20 words correctly. She had never done that before. Andy spelled 11 out of the 20 words correctly—a little above average for him.

For several evenings after the experience with Andy and Sarah, Donald tried to give meaning to what had happened. What was it that caused Sarah to show an interest in helping Andy? Would it be possible to capitalize on this incident; and if so, how? Should he have the two students work together again? He decided to raise these questions with the other fourth-grade teachers when they met the next day for one of their periodic planning meetings.

Deeanne Wise and Betsy Irons listened as Donald told them about Sarah's experience with Andy. He described how she appeared to take pride in being able to help Andy, and he shared the fact that she volunteered to do it again. In summarizing the experience between Sarah and Andy, Donald told the other two teachers that it was his opinion that Sarah's self-confidence increased when she was placed in a situation where she could help someone else.

"You should know that Sarah spends a lot of time taking care of a younger brother. Maybe she is motivated by a relationship where she thinks she is helping someone else," he told his colleagues. "What do you think about creating situations where Sarah can continue working with Andy? Would that be good?"

The other two teachers were acquainted with Sarah's background, because Donald had talked about her on previous occasions. Betsy Irons was first to respond to Donald, "I don't think so. You said Sarah is not a very good student herself. Teaming her with this boy might negatively affect her own aspirations. And she will be spending her time helping Andy instead of learning things herself. What you ought to do is team her with one of your best students."

Deeanne Wise took a different position, "It could be that Sarah will learn by helping Andy. That is, she will have to study in order to help him and maybe her own achievement will improve. Teaming her with a bright student would cast her in the role of the person being helped—and given what Donald has told us, I'm not sure that she will react positively."

"I was also thinking about ways to create opportunities for Sarah to be assigned responsibilities that would make her feel important," Donald said. "Even before this incident with Andy, I was trying to create opportunities for success so that I could praise her. I found out that other students are quick to react if they think someone is getting special treatment. So I have been looking for different ways to boost her confidence and feelings of self-worth. For example, each month a student in my class is selected to design the bulletin board in the back of our room. This assignment has been tied to points that students earn for their schoolwork. A student like Sarah probably will never get a chance to do the bulletin board, because she never earns enough points. Do you think that I ought to change this practice and allow all students to have a chance to do the bulletin board? Do you think that giving Sarah tasks such as this will have a positive effect on her self-image and her attitude toward school?"

Deeanne and Betsy both agreed that giving Sarah added responsibilities could produce some improvements in her self-image—especially if she were given tasks that she could perform. However, they had trouble with issuing rewards that were not earned.

"What type of message do we send to students when we let them receive recognition without earning it?" Betsy commented. "In my room, we set specific rules about rewards and punishment, and students know that I am not going to change them. If you let Sarah design the bulletin board, how will you explain this to your students? How will you explain it to the student who should have received the honor for that month?"

"Besides, Donald. Do you really know enough about this student to determine that giving her more responsibility is going to produce positive results?" asked Deeanne. "Is it possible that she wants to work with Andy simply because she doesn't enjoy recess? And why isn't she doing better with her own schoolwork? If she can help Andy, why doesn't she help herself?"

"I've given this a lot of thought over the last couple of days. I don't have the answers to all of these questions," Donald answered. "But I think that unless Sarah is given opportunities like the one with Andy, she is not apt to have much interaction with the other students. Additionally, Sarah doesn't value her role as a student. Her negative self-image as a learner has probably been reinforced many times. By contrast, her ability to help her younger brother has brought her praise from her mother."

"But Donald, you still have not addressed the tough questions," Betsy said. "If you start giving Sarah privileges and rewards that she really hasn't earned, are you going to be helping her? And, what about the other students who don't earn things? Are you going to give them the same opportunities?"

Again, Donald did not have answers to these difficult questions. He was disappointed that the meeting with his experienced peers had not provided answers. In fact, it only added questions about how he should work with Sarah in the future.

The Challenge

Put yourself in Donald's place. What course would you follow in trying to help Sarah?

ISSUES FOR FURTHER REFLECTION

1. Can a student's self-image really affect his or her academic achievement? Why or why not?
2. Assess the idea of constructing tasks for students that can easily be completed so that the teacher can provide praise. Is such a practice professionally defensible?
3. To what extent do you think that Sarah's relationship with her brother is relevant to this case?
4. Donald has concluded that Sarah should be achieving at a higher level because of her scores on group ability tests. Do you agree that teachers should make such judgments?
5. Is there a pedagogical or psychological basis for Donald's conclusion that Sarah's self-confidence increases when she is put in a position to help someone else?
6. Why is it important for a teacher to create a linkage between a student's personal effort and success?
7. Discuss the issue of busing students to different neighborhoods to achieve racial balance. What are the advantages and disadvantages for the students who are bused?
8. Do you think that it is good practice for Donald to meet with other fourth-grade teachers so frequently? Why or why not?
9. What is your opinion of the caution issued by Betsy Irons that teaming Sarah with Andy was not in Sarah's best interests?
10. Discuss ways that students like Sarah and Andy can develop social interaction with their peers.
11. Are social role expectations for fourth-grade girls significantly different from those for fourth-grade boys?
12. If you were Donald, would you have sought advice from persons other than the other two fourth-grade teachers? If so, from whom would you seek this advice?
13. What is the difference between self-esteem and self-confidence?
14. Are there dangers associated with making students "feel good" in an attempt to raise their self-esteem?
15. What are the advantages and disadvantages of peer tutoring among preadolescent students?

SUGGESTED READINGS

Beane, J. (1991). Sorting out the self-esteem controversy. *Educational Leadership, 49*(1), 25–30.

Belle, D., & Burr, R. (1991). Why children do not confide: An exploratory analysis. *Child Study Journal, 21*(4), 217–234.

Black, S. (1991). Self-esteem sense and nonsense. *American School Board Journal, 178*(7), 27–29.

Black, S. (1992). In praise of judicious praise. *Executive Educator, 14*(10), 24–27.

Byrd, D. (1990). Peer tutoring with the learning disabled: A critical review. *Journal of Educational Research, 84*(2), 115–118.

Canfield, J. (1990). Improving students' self-esteem. *Educational Leadership, 48*(1), 48–50.

Cooley, J. (1985). To be someone special. *Principal, 65*(2), 32–33.

Coultas, V. (1989). Black girls and self-esteem. *Gender and Education, 1*(3), 283–294.

Dembo, M. (1994). *Applying educational psychology in the classroom* (5th ed.). New York: Longman (see chapters 4, 5).

Dewhurst, D. (1991). Should teachers enhance their pupils' self-esteem. *Journal of Moral Education, 20*(1), 3–11.

Emmer, E. (1987–1988). Praise and the instructional process. *Journal of Classroom Interaction, 23*(2), 32–39.

Good, T., & Brophy, J. (1990). *Educational psychology: A realistic approach* (4th ed.). New York: Longman (see chapters 5, 17, 18).

Gwin, J. (1990). Self-esteem vs. academic excellence: Are the two on a collision course? *Crisis, 97*(10), 16–18, 21.

Henson, K. (1993). *Methods and strategies for teaching in secondary and middle schools* (2nd ed.). New York: Longman (see chapter 12).

Madden, L. (1988). Do teachers communicate with their students as if they were dogs? *Language Arts, 65*(2), 142–146.

Madhere, S. (1991). Self-esteem of African-American preadolescents: Theoretical and practical considerations. *Journal of Negro Education, 60*(1), 47–61.

Marchant, G. (1991). A profile of motivation, self-perception, and achievement in black urban elementary students. *Urban Review, 23*(2), 83–99.

Reasoner, R. (1992). Pro: You can bring hope to failing students. What's behind self-esteem programs: Truth or trickery? *School Administrator, 49*(4), 23–24, 26, 30.

Scales, P. (1992). From risks to resources: Disadvantaged learners in middle grades teaching. *Middle School Journal, 23*(5), 3–9.

Stevenson, H. (1992). Con: Don't deceive children through a feel-good approach. What's behind the self-esteem programs: Truth or trickery? *School Administrator, 49*(4), 23, 25, 27, 30.

Streitmatter, J. (1988). School desegregation and identity development. *Urban Education, 23*(3), 280–293.

Tang, T., & Sarsfield-Baldwin, L. (1991). The effects of self-esteem, task label, and performance feedback on task liking and intrinsic motivation. *Journal of Social Psychology, 131*(4), 567–572.

Modeling

PREPARING TO USE THE CASE

Background Information

One of the most effective instructional approaches that a teacher can use is modeling. On a daily basis teachers serve as role models, showing enthusiasm for learning, sharing beliefs about appropriate behavior, shaping students' attitudes, and nurturing values. Teachers can also model cognitive skills by organizing brainstorming activities, demonstrating creative-thinking skills, encouraging divergent thinking, or by providing opportunities for problem solving. Procedures associated with step-by-step low-level skills can be illustrated by teachers. Such illustrations are particularly effective in teaching motor skills, from learning to speak to learning to walk.

Modeling is central to social learning theory. A substantial amount of learning occurs as a result of imitating others' actions. Children learn to imitate those who are important to them—a parent, a relative, a friend, a teacher, a minister, a star athlete, a movie star, a television celebrity. By having mental images of the mannerisms of another person, children imitate their behavior. By observing the behavior of others, we learn how to act appropriately in a variety of settings and situations—at a church service, a museum, a theater, a wedding, a funeral, and at school.

Advocates of social learning theory argue that effective learning may occur through interactions among cognitive, behavioral, and environmental determinants. They note that both behavior and environment can be changed.

In this case a group of teachers are at odds as to the way to organize children for instruction. The veteran teachers are convinced that the traditional and rigid grouping by ability is the most effective strategy. Yet in the case of one child, they readily admit that grouping had little impact on either his behavior or his achievement. Because of the peer pressure for ability grouping, the first-year teacher organizes children in this fashion. Gradually, she has more difficulty accepting this organization, particularly as her children become more aggressive toward one another, based on their grouping. After several playground incidents, she tries another approach to resolve the conflict and encourage all her students to achieve.

Topics for Reflection
1. Cognitive development
2. Individual differences
3. Instructional planning
4. Instructional strategies
5. Learning theory
6. Low-ability students
7. Peer relationships
8. Problem solving
9. Teacher values and beliefs

THE CASE

"I've found the neatest stickers for my reading and math groups," Ginger Halcom began, as she pulled samples from her purse. "Look. Bluebirds for the middle group, eagles for the high flyers. And crows for the slow learners."

"Those are prettier than your old ones. And fuzzy," Bryan King observed, as he examined the stickers.

"You aren't really going to use those, are you?" Celeste Mecham inquired.

"Of course I am," Ginger responded, somewhat indignantly. "I've used stickers every year of the 14 years I've taught."

"I do too," Bryan King agreed. "except I like to use flowers—roses for the brightest children, violets for the middle group, and daisies for the slowest."

"Don't the children feel funny being identified that way?" Celeste Mecham asked.

"No," the other two teachers replied in unison.

"They love it," Ginger chided.

"It helps them identify. Know where they stand," Bryan King added.

The bell rang, ending the lunch period. The three teachers returned to their classrooms. The teachers have 28 children in their self-contained classrooms. The children reflect a social and intellectual balance—a wide range of academic abilities and economic backgrounds.

Celeste Mecham was in her third week at Comstock Elementary. Each week she had become more distressed by the behavior of her planning team members— an instructional-planning group implemented in her school by the principal. The lunchtime conversation added to her anger. From the first time the team met she had felt at odds. Initially, she thought it was probably due to age and teaching experience.

Together, Ginger Halcom and Bryan King represent a half century of classroom practice. They are alike in many ways. Both are single, claiming to have devoted their lives to teaching. Both are hard-working teachers who care deeply about their students, and both are graduates of an eastern liberal arts college. They share an emphasis on reading, writing, and arithmetic. They believe that the development of the mind is the primary, overriding purpose of teaching. The development of most other goals, they agree, is better left to parents. They share the view that children should be taught at their level of ability.

In some respects, they differ. Mr. King has been teaching for three more years; he specialized in science and mathematics; he enjoys traveling, and lists gourmet cooking and playing the piano as hobbies. In contrast, Ms. Halcom is a member of the Daughters of the American Revolution and relishes history. She is an avid reader, appreciates art, and rarely travels. She has never ventured beyond 127 miles from her birthplace.

Ms. Mecham is a neophyte, beginning her first year. A graduate of a top-rated teacher-training institution in the Midwest, she feels well prepared for her first job. She had participated in a special undergraduate program that doubled the number of field experiences she had and integrated the disciplines in organized blocks of time. During her junior year she spent a semester abroad, working in a British infant school. She feels well grounded in recent research on effective teaching. Creativity and a mature understanding of instructional theory and its application to practice are strengths in her training.

On nearly every issue she and the two veterans disagreed. The most serious disagreement among the team members began before the start of the school year. During the two workdays before classes began, the three team members shared information on the children they would be teaching. Mr. King talked about the children he had had in first grade the year before who were now assigned to Ms. Mecham's second-grade class. Because Ms. Mecham was new, he also told Ms. Halcom what he knew about the third-graders he had had in class two years before. More than half of one day was devoted to sharing stories about the children and their families, and assigning the youngsters to reading and mathematics groups. For the new children in the classes, the teachers examined and discussed "criterion-referenced" tests traditionally used in the school for diagnosing ability levels.

Ms. Mecham was shocked by the personal matters the teachers discussed. She was particularly troubled by Mr. King's lengthy discussion of the Blane family as the "dredges of society."

"You had better keep an eye on that Eddie Blane," he had warned Celeste. "He's a thief, liar, and brute. He's the worst kid we've ever had here. Just like his father, Ben Blane."

"Can't agree with you more," Ms. Halcom chimed. "Ben was an absolute beast. No wonder he's been in jail for the last seven years."

Although she had wanted to stay out of the conversation, she had been drawn into it. "Why has he been in jail for so long?" Celeste asked.

"Murder!" Mr. King replied. "He molested a seventh-grader, then strangled her."

Startled, Celeste sat quietly, listening to the rest of the details of the crime, which Mr. King and Ms. Halcom seemed to enjoy describing.

"The Blane's other two boys—Eric and Sam—were little devils, too. Not violent, just disruptive," Mr. King continued.

"Yes, they never really hurt anyone," Ms. King said. "But you could always count on one of them to disrupt the class, putting chewing gum in someone's hair, sharpening a pencil until it was so small it could not be used, throwing an eraser, spitting, tripping. You name it, the Blane boys did it."

"I wonder which group you put Eddie in," Mr. King wondered aloud.

"Probably a group of his own," Ms. Halcom chortled.

While Celeste was uncomfortable making assignments without knowing the children, she was astounded by the details that Mr. King and Ms. Halcom had shared. Based on her studies in the teacher education program at City University, she had become suspicious of the value of ability grouping. At one point in the discussion she asked the teachers why they used ability grouping.

The teachers responded with disdain. "It has always been done this way at Comstock," they said. "It works!"

She had felt devastated that they would not even listen to her views on the subject.

Reluctantly, she had implemented ability grouping in her second-grade class-room. For the most part, the same children were assigned to the low groups in both subjects. To her surprise, she found that ability grouping with the high-achieving groups in mathematics and reading had been somewhat successful. Individual progress had been more rapid than she had expected. She had been worried that her negative attitude toward ability grouping might prove to be a self-fulfilling prophecy—that her students would not do well because of her atti-tude. Although achievement for the high-ability students had progressed favorably, she was bothered by some problems that had arisen.

On three occasions during the first two weeks, Celeste Mecham had to break up fights on the playground between children from the low-ability groups and the high-ability groups. In many cases the children who worked together in the ability groups tended to congregate and play together during recess. The high-ability students tagged the slower children as "dummies." The low-ability children had retorted with "brats" and "weirdos." Celeste's lectures about cooperating and respecting differences had gone unheeded. Grouping children in other ways during other instructional activities and games had had little impact.

Ms. Mecham had become increasingly concerned about the low-ability chil-dren. Early in the year some of them had impressed her as energetic, thoughtful, and attentive. But once they had been labeled, they seemed to slip into a more passive, listless role. She noticed that they had become less willing to participate in activities, tended to make more errors, gave up sooner on tasks, and had become more attached to other members of their group. In the classroom, when asked to work with other children from middle- and high-ability groups, they rebelled the loudest and the strongest. Children in low-ability groups in both reading and mathematics behaved similarly.

As she might have expected, but had not wanted to anticipate, Eddie Blane was always at the center of controversy. He was the first to shout an obscenity, push another child, or strike out. He was the last to complete an assignment, often refusing to do the work required. Homework assignments sent home with him never seemed to get finished or returned.

She had tried to contact Mrs. Blane by phone on several occasions. On the fifth try Mrs. Blane answered.

"Hello," She said.

"Mrs. Blane?" Celeste asked.

"Yes," she responded.

"This is Celeste Mecham. Eddie's teacher," Celeste said.

"What do you want?" Mrs. Blane said gruffly.

"I'd like to talk with you about problems I'm having with Eddie," Celeste said.

"I don't have time," Mrs. Blane interrupted.

"I just want a minute of your time," Celeste pleaded.

"Look, I live alone. Have to do everything. Eddie has no father," Mrs. Blane rapidly fired, just before hanging up.

"Hello? Hello? Mrs. Blane?" Celeste asked.

Celeste dialed again, but received the continual beep of a busy signal.

The day following her meeting with the other teachers Celeste went through the motions of teaching, but her thoughts drifted back to the conversation in the faculty lounge. When she went home at the end of the day, Celeste Mecham still felt troubled and tried to call Dr. Marsha Wellington, a professor of educational psychology at City University, who had taught a child psychology class that was a required course in the teacher preparation curriculum. Dr. Wellington had visited on the first day of class and had told Celeste to call her at work or at home if she needed to talk.

"I've got to get out of this mess," Celeste thought to herself. "I can't go on grouping these children this way. I don't believe in it, and I'm unhappy."

She dialed Dr. Wellington's number. It rang four times before the professor answered.

"Wellington's residence," she answered.

"Hi, Dr. Wellington. This is Celeste Mecham," she said.

"Celeste—how is teaching?" Dr. Wellington replied.

"That's why I'm calling," Celeste responded. "I'm having a terrible time right now."

"Tell me about it," Dr. Wellington said.

For about an hour Celeste described the events that had led to her discomfort. She painstakingly provided details regarding Eddie Blane and the veteran teachers.

Toward the end of the conversation, Dr. Wellington said: "Do you still have your educational psychology text?"

"Yes," Celeste answered.

"Reread the section on social learning theory. Pay particular attention to applications. Ask yourself what you can do to model the kind of social and academic behavior that you want your children to exhibit. Use children who exhibit the behaviors as models as well."

The Challenge

You are Ms. Mecham. How will you model the behaviors that you want the children to exhibit? How will you have children model the behaviors you want them to exhibit?

ISSUES FOR FURTHER REFLECTION

1. What is social learning theory?
2. How might it be applied in this case?
3. What specific ways might the teacher model behavior that is desired for social purposes? For academic purposes?
4. Which children might be used for modeling behavior?
5. What specific ways might the teacher use children for modeling behavior desired for social purposes? For academic purposes?
6. How might modeling be used to try to alter Eddie's behavior?
7. If she would cooperate, how might Mrs. Blane be enlisted to model behaviors aimed at improving Eddie's social interaction? His academic performance?
8. Given that she has established a pattern of instructional organization, what steps must Ms. Mecham take to introduce the approach to modeling? How successful do you believe she would be?
9. Do you believe the behaviors exhibited in Ms. Mecham's class are serious enough to warrant giving up ability grouping? Defend your answer.
10. How do you believe the other teachers would react to any changes that Ms. Mecham might make in regard to ability grouping? Should she be concerned about their reactions? Explain.

SUGGESTED READINGS

Bandura, A. (1989). Regulation of cognitive processes through perceived self-efficacy. *Developmental Psychology, 25*(5), 729–735.

Bandura, A. (1990). Selective activation and disengagement of moral control. *Journal of Social Sciences, 46*(1), 27–46.

Bean, J. (1991). Sorting out the self-esteem controversy. *Educational Leadership, 49*(1), 25–30.

Belle, D., & Burr, R. (1991). Why children do not confide: An exploratory analysis. *Child Study Journal, 21*(4), 217–234.

Bjorkland, D. (1992). Development differences in the acquisition and maintenance of an organizational strategy. *Journal of Experimetnal Child Psychology, 54*(3), 434–448.

Canfield, J. (1990). Improving students' self-esteem. *Educational Leadership, 48*(1), 48–50.

Cohen, E. (1989). Can classrooms learn? *Sociology of Education, 62*(2), 75–94.

Dembo, M. (1994). *Applying educational psychology in the classroom* (5th ed.). New York: Longman (see chapters 2, 3, 4, 5).

Dewhurst, D. (1991). Should teachers enhance their pupils' self-esteem. *Journal of Moral Education, 20*(1), 3–11.

Ferguson, E., & Houghton, S. (1992). The effects of contingent teacher praise. *Educational Studies, 18*(1), 83–93.

Good, T., & Brophy, J. (1990). *Educational psychology: A realistic approach* (4th ed.). New York: Longman (see chapters 6, 7, 8, 9).

Grusec, J. (1992). Social learning theory and developmental psychology: The legacies of Robert Sears and Albert Bandura. *Developmental Psychology, 28*(5), 776–786.

Henson, K. (1993). *Methods and strategies for teaching in secondary and middle schools* (2nd ed.). New York: Longman (see chapters 9, 13).

Marsh, H. J. (1986). Self-serving effect (bias?) in academic attributions: Its relation to academic achievement and self-concept. *Journal of Educational Psychology, 78*(3), 190–200.

Moyer, J. (1986). Child development as a base for decision making. *Childhood Education, 62*(5), 325–329.

Pasch, M., Sparks-Langer, G., Gardner, T., Starko, A., & Moody, C. (1991). *Teaching as decision making: Instructional practices for the successful teacher*. New York: Longman (see chapters 4, 5, 6, 7).

Reid, D., & Stone, C. (1991). Why is cognitive instruction effective? Underlying learning mechanisms. *Remedial and Special Education, 12*(3), 8–19.

Schmida, M. (1987). Ability grouping and students' social orientation. *Urban Education, 21*(4), 421–431.

Wigfield, A. (1988). Children's attributions for success and failure: Effects of age and attentional focus. *Journal of Educational Psychology, 80*(1), 76–81.

CASE **10**

Are Facts Enough?

PREPARING TO USE THE CASE

Background Information

Those preparing to be teachers are exposed to a number of clinical or field-based experiences that are designed to provide a picture of reality. Through activities such as observations and participation, teacher-education students are able to see firsthand how real classrooms function; in so doing, they quickly discover that teachers do not approach their work in the same ways.

Planning and instructional strategies are affected by a teacher's personal and professional philosophical frameworks. That is to say, each teacher possesses values and beliefs about people, learning, and teaching that direct decisions made in the classroom.

There are multiple theories related to learning that often are broadly categorized into three groups: (a) behaviorists' theories, (b) cognitive theories, and (c) humanistic theories. Behaviorists argue that environmental stimuli and rewards are critical to learning. In essence, these theorists believe that behavior is learned, and the teacher is expected to control conditions to maximize learning. Cognitive theories of learning focus more on the structuring and processing of information. Emphasis is often placed on building connections between prior knowledge and new information. Humanists contend that learning is associated with the uniqueness of the individual. Feeling, thinking, and acting are seen as important variables in the learning process. To complicate matters further, there are multiple theories in each of these categories.

If teaching were simply a matter of applying a prescribed method of instruction for a given subject, professional practice would be far less complicated. In reality, teachers need to understand various theories of learning, and they are expected to use this knowledge to make informed choices about instructional strategies. A teacher who is inflexible, that is, one who always teaches in the same manner to all students, will eventually incur difficulties. The needs of students, subject matter and course purposes, and school-community expectations exemplify critical variables that influence decisions about instructional planning and teaching strategies.

In this case, a beginning teacher is proud that his students have acquired basic facts about government. But when a state senator visits the class, it becomes apparent that the students struggle to apply this information to the processes that are associated with the operations of government. In other words, they appear to have memorized information that seems to have little practical meaning to them.

The experience with the state senator spawns questions in the mind of the teacher. He searches for meaning and begins to question the effectiveness of his teaching strategies. Central to this introspection are questions about learning theory.

Topics for Reflection
1. Learning theory
2. Cognitive development
3. Critical-thinking skills
4. Problem-solving skills
5. Relevance of subject matter in social studies

THE CASE

As Tony Fretta sat on the bank of a farm pond holding his fishing rod and staring at his bobber, he thought about the seven months that had just passed. He had arrived in Lyleville full of enthusiasm and looking forward to teaching Spanish and social studies at the high school. The transition from college student to professional teacher had been exciting—especially in the first few months. Tony had his own apartment; he was making money; he bought a new car; and his students respected his position and knowledge.

By early November, however, Tony started to experience what a former professor had called, "the realities of being a teacher." Decisions that had to be made on a day-to-day basis were not all that easy. Students, especially the seniors, were prone to challenging what he said in class. And there were all the little management tasks that took precious time from his primary duties.

Tony's recollections of the school year were sparked by growing self-doubts about his effectiveness as a high school teacher. He wondered if his students were really learning the right things, and he asked himself if they would have learned more from an experienced teacher. Most of all he questioned whether his class would eventually make the students better citizens.

As the warm, spring Saturday wore on, Tony focused on a particular incident that was largely responsible for his recent doubts. He had invited Ross Bannister, a state senator, to speak to his government class. This occurred in late February after the two had met at a public forum on state government held in Lyleville.

Tony told the senator that he taught two sections of a government class at the high school, and suggested that the senator's visit with the students would be a positive addition to his instructional program. Senator Bannister noted that he was always eager to meet with future voters.

Of his five classes, three of which were in Spanish, Tony was proudest of the students in his fourth-period government class. They were mostly seniors who showed interest in finding out about local, state, and federal governmental agencies. He had the least amount of discipline problems with this class, and their performance on quizzes and tests indicated that they were absorbing the course content. On a 100-point semester examination, the lowest score in the class was 78. Thus Tony was confident that Senator Bannister would be impressed with what the students knew about the functions of government. He was so sure that he even invited Virginia Taylor, the principal, to attend class on that day.

When Tony issued the invitation to Senator Bannister, he failed to be specific relative to his guest's role. He surmised that like most elected officials, the senator would use the opportunity to talk about himself, his initiatives, and state government. It did not take long after introducing his guest to discover that he was only partly correct.

"Good afternoon," the senator began. "When Mr. Fretta invited me to visit this class, I agreed without hesitation. My job is quite hectic and time consuming, but an opportunity to exchange ideas with young adults like you is simply too attractive to pass up. Now, you are probably sitting there saying to yourselves that this guy is going to be boring and talk about himself or what he wants to see in state government. Well, I'm not going to do that. Rather, I want to spend most of the time listening. I want you to tell me what you know about state government. And, I'm especially interested in your ideas about how we can improve the way we do things. I hear so much today about how our young citizens are not learning anything in school." The senator paused and a smile came across his lips, "I want to find out if it is true."

The principal and Tony could see by the looks on the students' faces that they too had expected something different from their visitor. They had anticipated a speech and they thought they would be passive audience members.

"To start, who can tell me how our state legislature is structured?" Senator Bannister asked.

About 12 hands shot up, and he pointed to Jane in the second row.

She stood and answered, "The state legislature has two parts, the House of Representatives and the Senate. The House is composed of 100 members and the Senate of 50 members."

"Good. Now who can tell me if there are requirements that one must meet to be a legislator in this state?"

Again, the senator saw about a dozen hands go in the air. He selected a young man who correctly responded that a legislator had to be a legal resident of the state and at least 21 years old.

The senator asked four or five more questions about the structure of state government and elections, and each time a number of students were able to provide a correct answer. Tony sat in the back of the room and he could hardly contain his pride. His students had been confronted by a surprise examination, and they were able to provide the right answers—and in front of the principal no less!

But then Senator Bannister shifted direction and asked a different type of question, "One of the problems we have in this state, and in our federal government, is getting legislation passed. It seems that every time we get a new governor, he or she has a very difficult time getting new ideas to be accepted. Who can tell me the causes of this problem?"

This time there were no volunteers to provide an answer. After about 30 seconds, the senator concluded that no student was going to respond, so he asked another question.

"Who can tell me how a piece of legislation is promulgated? That is, how does a policy idea eventually become a law?"

Again, no hands were raised. The senator walked over to a student and looking down at him asked, "How about it son? You want to take a crack at my question? Don't be afraid to be wrong."

The young man answered cautiously, "I don't remember reading about that in our text. And I've never seen the legislature operate. My guess is that the governor decides what becomes law."

It was clear to all that the mood in the classroom had changed. Students who moments ago were competing to answer factual-type questions were now exhibiting nonverbal behaviors that suggested they wanted to become invisible. The students became even more anxious as they realized that the senator was not going to cease asking questions just because students were no longer volunteering to answer.

"In our state, a bill must be passed by both the Senate and House and be approved by the governor to become law. You all should know that. Often compromises are necessary to get things done. For example, you may want to pass a bill increasing scholarships for college students and I want to pass a bill setting higher requirements for graduation from college. Assume that we do not support each other's bills. How might we compromise? And would it be legal and ethical to strike a deal?"

This time, Tony tried to encourage his students to answer, but it was to no avail. Again there were no volunteers. Growing impatient after three of his questions went unanswered, the senator started to give the students a lecture.

"For our state government to be effective, we must have an informed citizenry. In that regard, each of you has a responsibility to understand how your government operates and to become an active participant in the process. I never cease to be amazed by people who call or write and say that they oppose taxes or a specific piece of legislation; and yet, they have no idea about how our law-making process functions. They act as if I can change things alone. Now, I have to be honest with you. You seem to know a lot of facts about government, but you are not really sure how the political system functions. You appear to know what you read in your books; but as we have seen here this afternoon, that information alone does not provide you with a perspective of how our government operates. You seem to have given little thought about how processes could be changed—how they can be improved. Before long, some of you will be in positions where you can influence the directions our state will take. But you can't do that if you don't know how the system works. Take some advice. Take your facts and apply them to the real world. Talk about problems; discuss better approaches; suggest solutions. You may find that the things you read in your books will be more meaningful.''

Tony was devastated. He took the senator's lecture to be a direct attack on his teaching. It took all of his fortitude to rise from his chair and thank Senator Bannister for taking the time to visit the class. The senator shook Tony's hand, thanked him and Principal Taylor for the opportunity, and left without saying another word. Mrs. Taylor looked at Tony and said, "Interesting class." Then she left as well. Tony stood in the doorway frozen, the bell rang, and the students left without commenting on the class session.

Immediately after school that day, Tony visited Mrs. Taylor. He told her that he was deeply troubled by his students' inability to respond more appropriately and by what his guest had said. He asked the principal, "Do you think Senator Bannister was being fair? It was almost as if he wanted to keep asking questions until the students could not answer."

Mrs. Taylor had visited Tony's class on three previous occasions—each time as part of the mandatory evaluation program. Her observations led to positive assessments of his teaching performance.

"Maybe we both learned something today," she answered. "If you are going to invite a political figure to class, you ought to have a good idea of what he is going to do. I think it was a bit unfair for him to have done this. You know, many of these politicians complain that our students don't do well on tests; and yet, when the students know the facts, they're told that it isn't good enough. Let's just hope that he forgets about this experience."

Tony was a little surprised at her response. He posed another question,

"The more I think about what he said, the more I find that it made sense. Maybe we should be taking our students to the legislature to see how it operates. Maybe we should spend more time talking to people who are part of the political process. Maybe we should focus more on problems, process, and solutions."

This time the principal did not answer; she simply shrugged her shoulders to indicate that she wasn't sure. She then told Tony she had to get to a meeting at the central office and left.

In the six weeks since the incident, Tony has been haunted by the comments of Senator Bannister. He thought about what he was teaching in his government class. Was it what the students really needed to learn? He thought about his teaching methods. Was he really being an effective teacher by merely transferring facts to them? He thought about his own learning experiences. What classes did he find to be most helpful in high school and college, and how were these classes taught?

Even escaping to a secluded farm pond on a warm spring Saturday failed to eradicate from Tony's mind the weighty comments made by Senator Bannister. As he stared aimlessly at his bobber, which now had started to jump up and down in the water, Tony sat motionless and asked himself repeatedly if he was a good teacher.

The Challenge

Determine the significance of this case from the perspective of learning theory. Assume that Tony is your friend. What would you advise him to do?

ISSUES FOR FURTHER REFLECTION

1. Why do you think the students were able to answer questions that involved facts but were unable to answer process-type questions?

2. What do you think was the content of Tony's tests in this class?

3. What is your impression of the principal in this case?

4. Do you believe that the senator's criticisms and concerns about the class are valid? Why or why not?

5. What do you believe should be the major purposes of a high school class in U. S. government?

6. Identify several ways that course content can be associated with contemporary problems in social studies classes.

7. Do you think that Tony's approach to teaching this government class was typical?

8. What is a concept? What is the relationship between facts, perceptions, concepts, and behavior?

9. How can examples and nonexamples strengthen a student's comprehension of a concept?

10. In an information-based society, technology has provided access to vast amounts of information. Do you think this capability should affect the way social studies classes are taught? If so, in what ways?

11. As learners become older, do you believe that they demand greater relevance in learning activities? Why or why not?

12. One common experience in social studies that many students share is the memorization of the 50 state capitals. Discuss whether this activity is beneficial for students in today's society.

13. Discuss how each of the following techniques could be used to enhance learning among high school students: (a) simulation, (b) case studies, (c) community service, (d) mentorships.

14. Assigning desirable tasks to students based on their performance is associated with what types of learning theories?

SUGGESTED READINGS

Atwater, T. (1991). Critical thinking in basic U. S. government classes. *PS: Political Science and Politics, 24*(2), 209–211.

Barber, B. (1989). Public talk and civic action: Education for participation in a strong democracy. *Social Education, 53*(6), 355–356.

Brandhorst, A. (1990). Teaching twenty-first century citizenship: Social psychological foundations. *Theory and Research in Social Education, 18*(2), 157–168.

Court, D. (1991). Teaching critical thinking: What do we know? *Social Studies, 82*(3), 115–119.

Dembo, M. (1994). *Applying educational psychology in the classroom* (5th ed.). New York: Longman (see chapters 2, 3, 4, 5).

Ferree, G. (1988–1989). Schools as agencies of social criticism. *Michigan Social Studies Journal, 3*(1), 11–18.

Good, T., & Brophy, J. (1990). *Educational psychology: A realistic approach* (4th ed.). New York: Longman (see chapters 6, 7, 8, 9).

Gursky, D. (1991). The unschooled mind. *Teacher Magazine, 3*(3), 38–44.

Henson, K. (1993). *Methods and strategies for teaching in secondary and middle schools* (2nd ed.). New York: Longman (see chapter 3).

McPhie, W. (1987). Citizenship education and the public schools. *Southern Social Studies Quarterly, 13*(1), 34–42.

Neeper, A. (1991). Teaching for transfer: A simple method to upgrade lesson plans. *Social Studies Texan, 7*(3), 58–60.

Newmann, F. (1990). Qualities of thoughtful social studies classes: An empirical profile. *Journal of Curriculum Studies, 22*(3), 253–275.

Parker, W. (1988). Thinking to learn concepts. *Social Studies, 79*(2), 70–73.

Philips, E., & Tieger, H. (1981). Changing student attitudes toward social studies requires changing teachers' approaches. *Social Studies Review, 20*(3), 33–40.

Rakow, S. (1992). Six steps to more meaning. *Science Scope, 16*(2), 18–19.

Reid, D., & Stone, C. (1991). Why is cognitive instruction effective? Underlying learning mechanisms. *Remedial and Special Education, 12*(3), 8–19.

Wineman, S., & Hammond, R. (1987). Citizenship education through the webbing approach. *Social Studies, 78*(4), 169–172.

CASE 11

A Teacher Uses Metacognition

PREPARING TO USE THE CASE

Background Information

In a recent Gallup poll (Elam et. al., 1992), both the teachers and the public rated "developing the ability to think creatively, objectively, and analytically" near the top of a list of goals for education. Being a contributing citizen in today's society requires nothing less (Rowe, 1990). Today's citizens also demand well-rounded students, that is, students who have many interests and abilities. As Hoerr (1992) has said, "If we are not careful, we can define intelligence too narrowly and how we define intelligence makes a philosophical statement about what we value in education." (p. 67)

Another force is pressuring teachers to focus on standardized test scores. Throughout the country, education reform is occurring in every state. The ultimate goal of this movement is simple: school boards are demanding high test scores. Both communities and school administrators want their schools to place in the top half of the national range. Parents want their children to perform well on these tests.

The results of these forces can be an oversimplification of the processes called *learning* and *education*. Like the old TV show *Dragnet,* with Sergeant Friday who just wanted the facts, "Just the facts, ma'am," when teachers teach mainly for content coverage and high test scores, students, too, get an oversimplified sense of the purpose of education. Stefanich (1990) has said that students view learning only as the mastery of knowledge.

But as Glickman (1991) has said, "The measure of school worth is not how students score on standardized achievement tests but rather the learning they can display in authentic or real settings." (p. 8)

At the 1991 meeting of the American Educational Research Association, principal Deborah Meier was later quoted (Bracey, 1992) as saying, "We learn best when we are in a position to make sense of things—especially to make sense of things we are interested in. Human beings are by nature meaning-makers, trying to put the puzzle together from the moment of birth until death—this is our preeminent mode. Schools rarely capitalize on it." (p. 265)

Topics for Reflection

1. The effects of metacognition on learning
2. The effects of the emphasis that educational reform programs put on achievement test scores
3. Metacognition strategies that work
4. The effects of student involvement with metacognition on their levels of motivation

THE CASE

Mapledale Village is a working-class community embedded in one of the seven largest populated urban areas in the country. In the 1930s, Mapledale grew rapidly because of the steel mills. Most residents had blue-collar jobs that required little formal education. According to the 1940 census, the average educational level of the residents of "the Village", as it was commonly called, was seventh grade. Almost everyone who lived in the Village either worked in the mills or operated one of several small businesses that served the mill workers.

During the late 1930s and early 1940s, the community expanded at a steady rate as a flow of newcomers moved in to be close to their jobs. The mill was unionized in the early 1950s, bringing higher wages and attracting laborers from the South who left their nonunion jobs in the textile mills to accept better paying jobs in Mapledale Mills.

Although the mills offered better wages, Mapledale was never a heaven of bliss. Alcohol abuse has always been common among the mill workers. In general, the few social clubs (as bars were called) were unsafe in the daytime and a clear risk to life itself at nighttime.

America's entrance into World War II in late 1941 produced an immediate need for more weapons and ammunition. The open-hearth furnaces of the mills were perfect for making the steel which would be shipped elsewhere to be made into guns, tanks, and ships. The only finished products made locally were the hulls for 105-mm and 155-mm Howitzer shells, and even these were shipped away to be loaded.

The urgent need for increasingly more ammunition and supplies offered unusual opportunities for the mill workers to make good money. Overtime was common, and as the quotas set in all departments were reached and passed, bonuses were given for extra production.

When the war ended, the mill was converted back to traditional peacetime production. The per capita income for the area remained at a comfortable level until the early 1950s when gas furnaces replaced the open-hearth models. Because of the age of the mill, its owners concluded that the cost of converting to the new furnaces was prohibitive. The smelting department, which consisted of 60 percent of the mills, was closed.

Since the mid-1950s, the community has been on a steady decline. Those who remain have stayed because they own homes in the village. Most workers have retired.

The Public Schools in Mapledale Village

All schools need support, both personal and financial. The Maple County Schools had survived for a quarter century on a shoestring budget. Without strong support from the mills, and with an aging population who would not and could not give strong financial support, this school district had learned to be satisfied with mere survival. New state education reform laws sounded great to those who taught in wealthy districts, but the Maple County Schools could not afford to go beyond daydreaming about reform.

Schools also need the support of parents. Without it, significant academic achievement is unlikely to occur. Terry Bell (1993), who formulated the panel that wrote the first school reform report, *A Nation at Risk,* a decade later said: "Education must become everyone's responsibility, and we must transform the total culture so that it nurtures learning inside and outside the school." (p. 596)

The School

Of the twenty schools in the district, Maple Middle School is the poorest. The school building is an eyesore even to the impoverished community. Having already experienced three decades of steady deterioration, the physical appearance of the school plant quickly worsened last year when the ceiling tiles were removed to rid the building of asbestos. Without the funds required to replace the tiles, the administration had no choice but to leave the ceilings open, giving the building the appearance of a warehouse.

The classrooms at Maple Middle reflect the building's general appearance; most are devoid of supplies beyond the basic necessities. Even the chalkboard trays are filled with chalk dust and only a few short stubs of chalk. Cloths are found on most of the trays, replacing the erasers that have long since worn out and been discarded. Few rooms have overhead projectors or screens, and the few screens scattered throughout the building are torn.

The Parent-Teacher Association has all but disappeared. About the only contact the Maple Middle School teachers have with the parents is when students are arrested for drugs or when severe discipline problems occur.

The Teacher

Brad Wideman is beginning his third year on the Maple Middle School faculty. Having grown up in the Village and attended only Mapledale schools, he has never thought much about these austere conditions. On the contrary, the day he landed a job at Mapledale was one of his happiest days. Like many students, Brad chose to major in education because of the job itself and also because it afforded him the opportunity to work in his hometown, if he were lucky enough to get a job there. Many of his friends have stayed in the community. His fellow teachers would be the first to say that Brad is well liked by everyone, largely because of his easy-going disposition and his ability to take everything in stride.

But Brad's lackadaisical style disappears when he enters his classroom. His teacher-education program was responsible for this change. If you were to ask him, he would tell you that his college was one of the best in the country. Beyond that, he was just plain lucky to have been assigned to a team of professors and teachers whose main research efforts were in metacognition. The college had a laboratory school where students were assigned extensive pre–student-teaching classroom experiences. A new technology grant has equipped the teacher-education building with two new computer laboratories. Each laboratory is fully equipped with 30 new computers, a laser printer, and a software server.

Three of the required education courses had classroom observation and participation components in the lab school. These classes were: EDF 200: Introduction to Education; EPY 300: Human Growth and Development; and EPY 400: Learning Theory.

Each wing of the laboratory (elementary, middle, and high school) has a new computer lab. All are equipped exactly the same as those in the College of Education. The best part is that all 110 computers in these labs are fully networked so that a piece of software can be shown on all of the computers simultaneously.

Brad had enjoyed his education courses, especially the foundations course, the human growth and development course, and the learning theory course, because each of these courses required participation in the laboratory school classrooms. Some classes required him to develop lessons using software and then implement these lessons. Students were encouraged to plan a variety of metacognitive strategies into mini-lessons, later to be tried out in the laboratory school classroom.

Another distinct advantage of working at this laboratory school was the high caliber of teachers with whom Brad was privileged to work. Furthermore, he had opportunities to work on a variety of projects with different teachers. At first, Brad was reluctant to join a research team which had members from this faculty and professors of teacher education. But his mind changed when he read that the following values accrue from being involved in research and metacognition.

"The research on the effect of studying one's own thinking strategies has been mounting. Many teachers are conducting their own investigations. Several benefits accrue when teachers conduct research studies in their classrooms. Some of the most recognized benefits include:

1. Improves research skills of the teacher.
2. Improves teachers' instructional decision-making skills.
3. Affects their lesson planning.
4. Improves teachers' abilities to evaluate new methods of instruction.
5. Clarifies teachers' theories and beliefs.

6. Promotes collegial interaction.
7. Infuses excitement into teaching.
8. Increases students' interest in learning." (Henson, 1993, pp. 119–120)

In one of his professional association's journals, Brad read an article titled, "Teachers as Researchers" written by Linda R. Cooper (1991). The article listed the following advantages that result from teacher involvement with research:

Teacher-Research programs provide an opportunity for:

* reflecting about the teaching experience.
* developing formal inquiry from informal inquiry.
* doing research rather than merely reading about it.
* compiling findings that can be immediately applied to each teacher's classroom.
* increasing knowledge and skills.
* enhancing teacher self-esteem.

Not bad, Brad concluded. All this just from being involved in a classroom research project.

Brad had found the research itself to be totally nonthreatening, nothing like he feared it would be. Furthermore, he found working with this caliber of teachers exciting, rewarding, and just plain fun.

The Incident

To say the least, Mapledale was different from the lab school, especially in appearance. Most of the faculty members were content just to complete the day. Yet a few seemed to stay on "the cutting edge" of their disciplines. Several were attending evening classes and were using ideas learned in these graduate classes to design materials and activities for school.

Although these teachers were friendly enough, Brad had been unsuccessful in trying to interest them in metacognition; therefore, he pursued his own research by himself.

During the past two years Brad had experimented with several cognitive approaches, one at a time. One of the most gratifying lessons was an experiment that he had conducted with advance organizers. The experiment had involved three separate lessons, each purposefully different. In one lesson he used a videotape. Prior to showing the tape to one of his classes, Brad identified four concepts that he wanted students to notice. In a second lesson he used as many mnemonics as he could.

In a third class, Brad purposefully made several assignments to assure success for all students so that he could use reinforcements. He was interested in learning what effects a lesson so rich in reinforcements might have on the students.

For each of these lessons, Brad used another class as a control group. Although he did not record the results, from observing each class he concluded that the experimental lessons clearly resulted in more learning.

Brad considered all of these lessons as "trial" lessons. The students did not display the level of enthusiasm for inquiry as had his students at the university laboratory school. Now he was ready to incorporate these strategies into a lesson that would be appropriately recorded and conducted in an acceptable research project.

Brad wanted to improve this lesson further by having the students discover the pertinent concepts for themselves, rather than having them pre-identified. But he wasn't quite sure how he could use advance organizers and also have the students discover the concepts. He also wanted to introduce both an individualistic approach and cooperative learning. This paradox was, to say the least, perplexing, yet the literature he had read supported both individual learning (i.e., accommodating the individual styles of learners) and learning cooperatively.

The lesson Brad chose to incorporate these strategies was a surprise to the students. He began by grouping the students, assigning five students to each group and purposefully grouping the extroverts together to prevent them from dominating their groups. He also grouped the introverts together to force participation among the members of these groups.

The chairs in each group were assembled in a tight circle around an empty desk. On the desk, in the center, Brad placed a small cloth bag with a drawstring. Students in each group were to empty the contents on the table. From each bag came a match, a paper clip, a few sunflower seeds, and a small calendar. Before giving the command to empty the bags, Brad turned on a strobe light and a record player with a record of electronic music.

With their items in front of them, the students were told that they were to use their imaginations and describe what they saw. They would be allotted 30 minutes to write their story. Those who preferred could discuss or "talk out" their perceptions, and those who preferred to write alone without discussing their views could do so.

The second part of the lesson would involve a totally different assignment, the black box puzzle. Students were given a black box containing one moveable object. They were to conduct such investigations as shaking the box, inverting it, smelling it, and even dropping it. They were to listen to the box and weigh it. In summary, they were told to use their senses to solve the mystery of the unknown contents. Each student was permitted to ask three investigative questions.

For this activity, the entire class worked as individuals. The objective was to be the first to correctly identify the contents. Brad wondered whether the competition for this activity or the cooperation in the former activity would be the stronger stimulus.

During the hour, Brad moved about the room carefully monitoring the students. He offered no advice, but he responded to each question that students directed to him.

Some of the students found both of these activities challenging and exciting. Others, who always seemed withdrawn, were content to remain passive. Some groups got a little loud, but the noise level subsided each time Brad moved near the noisy groups. Brad was more concerned over the withdrawn students than he was over the noise level. He wondered whether the teacher's role is to ask questions or to answer questions.

The Challenge

Suppose you were in Brad's position. How would you alter this lesson to produce more creativity and learning?

ISSUES FOR FURTHER REFLECTION

1. How might the Mapledale Village community affect students' reactions to an open lesson such as this? How might Brad prepare these students to be more receptive?
2. Were there any advance organizers in this lesson? What role should/can they play in an inquiry type of lesson?
3. What evidence do you find that Brad is aware of the differences among students' preferred learning styles, and how might he adjust this lesson to further accommodate their styles?
4. Do you believe Brad's grouping the reserved students with other reserved students was a wise choice? Why or why not?
5. Do you believe that allowing the students to choose whether they wished to perform the first assignment with others or individually was a good decision? Can you cite literature or research to support your answer?
6. Suppose you were teaching this lesson and the principal, who pressed hard to raise student achievement test scores, asked you to refrain from ''wasting'' time on this type of lesson. How might you convince this principal of the value of such a lesson?
7. Consider Mr. Bell's statement about ''a nurturing community,'' and explain how you think Brad might garner the support of the Mapledale parents.
8. Explain what you believe caused the major differences in the level of support given by the laboratory school parents and the Mapledale parents.
9. How could Brad apply his college experience with technology to stimulate creativity and problem solving in his classes at Maple Middle School?
10. How could Brad use his experience with mnemonics in these lessons?
11. In such an austere environment, if you were given $100 to buy any equipment you chose to buy, how would you spend that money?
12. Brad is well received by his fellow teachers. How might he convince them to help him get the community's support for this school?
13. Individuals can improve their ability to think logically if they understand how they currently think. At the conclusion of this lesson, how might Brad best help students analyze their approaches to solving the black box problem?
14. How might Brad use reinforcement in these lessons?
15. In addition to using reinforcement, how might Brad help these students improve their self-concepts?
16. The writing activity had no stated goals. What are some justifiable objectives of such an activity?

17. Brad was careful to avoid interfering in these lessons. How involved and how unobtrusive should a teacher be during such assignments?

18. Brad monitored the class. Is this good or bad? Why?

SUGGESTED READINGS

Alberto, P., & Troutman, A. C. (1990). *Applied behavior analysis for teachers: Influencing student performance* (3rd ed.). Columbus, OH: Merrill.

Bell, T. H. (1993). Reflections one decade after "A Nation at Risk," *Phi Delta Kappan, 74*(8), 592–597.

Bonds, C. W., Bonds, L. G., & Peach, W. (1992). Metacognition: Developing dependence in learning. *The Clearing House, 66*(1), 56–59.

Cooper, L. R. (1991). Teachers as researchers. *Kappa Delta Pi Record, 27*(4), 115–117.

Dembo, M. (1994). *Applying educational psychology in the classroom* (5th ed.). New York: Longman (see chapter 3).

Elam, S. M., Rose, L. C., & Gallup, A. M. (1992). The 24th Gallup poll of the public's attitudes toward the public schools. *Phi Delta Kappan, 74*(1), 41–53.

Etscheidt, S. (1991). Reducing aggressive behavior and improving self-control: A cognitive behavioral program for behaviorally disordered adolescents. *Behavioral Disorders, 16*(2), 107–115.

Frymeier, J. (1988). Understanding and preventing teen suicide: An interview with Barry Garfinkel. *Phi Delta Kappan, 70*(4), 290–293.

Glickman, C. (1991). Pretending not to know what we know. *Educational Leadership, 48*(8), 4–9.

Good, T. L., & Brophy, J. E. (1990). *Educational psychology: A realistic approach* (4th ed.). New York: Longman (see chapter 10).

Henson, K. T. (1993). *Methods and strategies for teaching in secondary and middle schools* (2nd ed.). New York: Longman (see chapter 7, appendix E).

Hoerr, T. R. (1992). How our school applied multiple intelligence theory in our school. *Educational Leadership, 50*(2), 67–68.

Keating, D. P. (1990). Adolescent thinking. In S. S. Feldman & G. R. Elliott (Eds.), *At the threshold: The developing adolescent* (pp. 54–90). Cambridge, MA: Harvard University Press.

Marshall, C. (1991). Teachers' learning styles: How they affect student learning. *The Clearing House: 64*(4), 225–227.

Richardson, J. L. (1989). Substance use among eighth-grade students who take care of themselves after school. *Pediatrics, 84*(3), 556–566.

Rowe, J. W. (1990). To develop thinking citizens. *Educational Leadership, 48*(3), 43–44.

Stefanich, G. P. (1990). Cycles of cognition. *Middle School Journal, 22*(2), 47–52.

CASE 12

When Planning Doesn't Pay Off

PREPARING TO USE THE CASE

Background Information

One of the greatest challenges for beginning teachers is instructional planning. This is especially true for secondary school teachers who are assigned to teach several different courses. Not only do these individuals end up having to do multiple preparations (i.e., having to prepare for several different courses), but they also are likely to face a wide range of student abilities. And unlike elementary school teachers who spend a good part of their day with the same pupils, secondary teachers often instruct as many as 150 different students in five or six different classes.

Basically, there are three critical elements related to instructional planning: (1) knowing how to plan, (2) knowing what to plan, and (3) knowing when to plan. Each is multifaceted. For example, the act of planning requires good organizational skills, but it also requires the ability to develop appropriate relationships among objectives, activities, and evaluation. Yet one could understand the process of planning quite well and still have difficulty because of uncertainty about content and the proper sequencing of content. And even when process and content are solid, improper timing can create serious problems.

As students, you probably have been in classrooms where each of these difficulties was present. Have you had a professor or teacher in high school who failed to tie one class to another? Did each class seem totally unrelated to the previous one? Or have you had courses in which the instructors addressed material already covered in other courses? Have you had a teacher talk about a concept before he or she provied basic information that would permit you to understand the concept?

In this case, you are exposed to the frustrations of a mathematics teacher in a middle school who is struggling with one of his classes—an applied mathematics class for eighth-grade students. Despite efforts to motivate the students and to create daily lesson plans, many of the students continue to do poorly on quizzes and tests.

Often teachers working with low-achieving students find motivation to be a key consideration. Here the teacher tries different tactics to excite the students— to create an awareness of the importance of mathematics in their daily lives. They go on field trips; they have guest speakers in class; and they are given unique projects to complete.

As you read this case, focus on the teacher's planning efforts. Do they make a contribution? Or do they just make matters worse? Think about the relationships among the content of the course, the lesson plans developed by the teacher, and student outcomes. Make some judgments about whether this teacher is using instructional time productively. Finally, think about the teacher's objectives— both in the cognitive and affective realms.

Topics for Reflection
1. Making decisions about what to teach
2. Unit planning
3. Setting instructional objectives
4. Developing lesson plans
5. Integrating motivational techniques with instructional planning
6. Working with low-ability students
7. Affective and cognitive goals

THE CASE

Bob Kimball had decided to become a teacher in his junior year of college. He wasn't quite sure what had convinced him to change his major from business administration, but it was clear that he wanted to work with young people. Fortunately, his first two years of college consisted mainly of general education courses, and after seeing an academic adviser, he was able to switch his major to mathematics education.

Bob was active in his social fraternity and was a member of the student government association. It was through such campus-based activities that he got his first exposure to working with adolescents. His fraternity worked with the local YMCA to sponsor a junior football league for underprivileged boys, and Bob volunteered to coach one of the teams. He found it to be one of the most gratifying experiences he had ever had.

Teaching, Bob concluded, would allow him to combine two things that were personally rewarding. First, he had always been a good mathematics student, and he found this subject to be personally challenging. He recognized that he did much better in mathematics than most other students. Second, holding a teaching post would make it possible for him to continue coaching—a job he had come to love.

His aspirations were reinforced when he did his student teaching in the fall of his senior year at a high school near the university. He was assigned to work with the head football coach who was a mathematics teacher. He was exposed to two geometry classes and two advanced algebra classes. Given Bob's interest in coaching, his supervising teacher was all too happy to have him help out with the team. The fact that the team won 10 games and made the state play-offs became yet another bonus in what had been an extremely positive experience.

Just prior to graduation, Bob had interviews with six school districts. This culminated in three job offers. He decided to accept a position at Burtonville Middle School. There he would teach five classes of mathematics and coach the eighth-grade football team.

Burtonville is a suburban community that is continuing to grow. The middle school, which contains grades 6, 7, and 8, has an enrollment of just under 900 students. For the most part, the students come from middle-class families.

Bob was assigned to teach three sections of seventh-grade mathematics, an algebra class (taken by selected eighth-grade students), and a section of applied mathematics (a remedial-type class for eighth-grade students). This meant that Bob had to prepare for three different classes and coach football—a somewhat difficult assignment for a new teacher.

After just two or three weeks of school, it was clear to Bob that teaching the algebra class was the easiest assignment he had. The students were all bright; they were highly motivated. By contrast, his applied mathematics course was a real challenge. Increasingly, he found himself devoting more of his planning time to this course.

In observing students in the five classes assigned to him, Bob deduced that those in the applied class were far less motivated than the others. Clearly, he had some students in his seventh-grade classes who were not highly motivated either, but they were a small portion of the class.

As the school year moved into October, Bob decided that his traditional approaches were not effective with the applied mathematics class. He was relying on the textbook to sequence instruction, and his teaching methodology consisted largely of lecturing on a concept and then having students do exercises or homework on the material he covered. Of the 22 students in this class, probably no more than five or six seemed to be paying attention at any given time. Often homework assignments were not completed, or they were done incorrectly. Weekly quizzes were serving to verify Bob's observations. Only a handful of students seemed to be mastering the material.

Pondering ways that he could improve his performance, Bob remembered two experiences from his college classes. One related to a teaching methods class in which the professor stressed the importance of developing daily lesson plans. He also recalled a video presentation in one of his educational psychology classes that showed how motivation was a key factor, especially with special-needs students. It featured an alternative school in California that was able to get students excited about learning. To do this, the teachers took risks; they strayed from traditional teaching methods and materials. For example, students were able to start their own company that specialized in removing graffiti from city property (a topic many of the students knew a great deal about). In doing this, they learned mathematics in a very practical way. And not only did they learn, they actually became excited about going to school.

Although Bob had been sketching out what he intended to do in each class, he really did not consider this to be detailed lesson planning. When he started the school year, he figured he would cover the content in the textbook over the course of the year (applied mathematics was a two-semester course). There were 17 chapters in the book, and Bob thought that he would do one chapter approximately every two weeks.

Bob decided to change his teaching tactics to assure that: (1) he would do more detailed planning, and (2) he would make the learning experiences more relevant for the students. He recognized that to do the latter, he might have to become far less reliant on following his textbook. That might mean jumping around from working with fractions to working with multiplication to working with decimals. At this point, he decided that getting his students excited about learning mathematics was more important than following a prescribed path.

One of the first things that Bob did to pursue his new course of action was to develop a list of potential resource people and activities that he could integrate into his applied class. The list included the following:

- Invite a car dealer to talk to the class about how people finance cars. This will lead to a discussion of loans and interest rates.
- Invite a sports writer from the local paper to discuss how baseball batting averages are calculated.
- Invite an owner of a boutique to discuss basic financial concepts related to operating a small business (e.g., calculating overhead expenses, estimating profits).
- Take a field trip to a manufacturing plant to see how workers are required to use mathematics in their jobs.
- Have the students create their own candy company so that they could manage funds.
- Study how much it costs to operate a car on an annual basis (e.g., cost of insurance, gasoline).

Each night before a scheduled activity, Bob detailed a plan of how he would spend each of the 47 minutes of class time. He wanted to make sure that the time would be used wisely. For the activity with the car salesman, for example, he decided that three class periods would be needed. His daily plans for the three sessions are listed below.

Monday, November 2

10:00–10:05 Introduce Jack Davis of Burtonville Buick and outline for the students what he will be discussing that day

10:05–10:35 Mr. Davis talks about the cost of new and used automobiles

10:35–10:47 Time for student questions

Give students the following assignment: If a person earns $15,000 per year and buys a used car for $6,300, what percent of his annual income does he spend on this one item?

Tuesday, November 3

10:00–10:05 Discuss assignment from previous day

10:05–10:35 Mr. Davis discusses how car prices are determined (e.g., the value of options, the concept of depreciation)

10:35–10:47 Time for student questions

Give students the following assignment: If a person buys a new car that has the following price breakdown: base price = $9,200; options = $3,100; dealer preparation costs = $410; sales tax = $460. What is the total price of the car? What percent of the total cost is due to options? What percent of the cost is due to dealer preparation and sales tax?

Wednesday, November 4

10:00–10:10 Discuss assignment from previous day

10:10–10:40 Mr. Davis discusses how cars are financed and the meaning of interest on loans

10:40–10:47 Time for student questions

Although students reacted positively to sessions such as those with Mr. Davis, subsequent quizzes and tests failed to show that student progress had improved. By mid-November, Bob was truly concerned. His principal had come to observe his teaching only once. He visited the algebra class in late September for 20 minutes and subsequently sent Bob a note saying, "Keep up the good work."

Mathematics at the school was in a combined department with science; and the chair of the department, a science teacher, had never even asked Bob how his classes were progressing. Feeling that he was pretty much on his own, he turned to a friend and colleague in the mathematics department, Sarah Allen. Although Sarah was only in her second year of teaching, she already acquired a reputation as an outstanding instructor. And besides, the third full-time mathematics teacher in the department was Mr. Chambers, who kept to himself; Bob had barely gotten to know him.

After listening to Bob explain his difficulties with the applied mathematics class, Sarah asked if the same problems were evident in his four other classes. Bob said that they were not. It was his observation that the other students were responding well to his traditional approaches to teaching—especially the students in the algebra class.

"Although I think I have gotten the students more excited about mathematics, I'm not sure they are learning enough," Bob explained.

Sarah inquired, "What units are you covering during the first semester?"

"I started out following the chapters in the textbook; however, when I decided to try to liven things up for the students, we started jumping around a bit. I do plan my lessons daily. But I try to take advantage of whatever math skills are associated with the activity," Bob explained.

Having said that, Bob reached into his briefcase and pulled out a folder containing the three lesson plans that involved Mr. Davis, the car salesman. Sarah read each one and then asked, "What specifically were you trying to teach with these lessons?"

"Well, we were able to look at problems involving division and the students got exposure to interest and interest payments."

Sarah asked yet another question, "But how does that fit into your overall plans for instruction during this semester?"

"Right now my main objective is to find out what excites these students. I'm convinced that once they see that math is so necessary to their lives, they'll be more willing to learn." Bob paused and asked Sarah, "Do you think I am approaching this in the right way? Is there something I should be doing that I'm not? Now that football season is ending, I'll be able to devote a little more time to this class, and I want to make sure that I'm going in the right direction."

The Challenge

Put yourself in Sarah's position. What advice would you give to Bob?

ISSUES FOR FURTHER REFLECTION

1. Do you agree with Bob's judgment that he has to use motivational techniques to get these students interested in studying mathematics? Why or why not?

2. In your opinion, does Bob have a good perspective with regard to what he hopes to accomplish in this class? What evidence did you use to arrive at your answer?

3. What is the relationship of daily lesson plans to unit lesson plans? From what you read in the case, does Bob have unit plans?

4. What are performance objectives? From what you read in this case, does it appear that Bob has established educational (performance) objectives?

5. Evaluate Bob's daily lesson plans for November 2, 3, and 4. Are they complete? If you do not believe that they are complete, what would you add?

6. Do you classify Bob's activities as an attempt to use "discovery learning?" Why or why not?

7. Is Bob being impatient? Is he expecting results too quickly?

8. How do you assess Bob's decision to turn to Sarah for help? Should he have asked someone more experienced (e.g., the principal)? Do beginning teachers often feel alone, not knowing where to turn for help?

9. Is there any evidence in the case that Bob is concerned about educational objectives in the affective domain of learning?

10. Do you think that the problem Bob is encountering results from inadequate instructional-planning skills? From not understanding low-achieving students?

11. What is your opinion of Bob's total assignment at the school? Is this typical for a beginning teacher in a middle school?

12. Should low-achieving students be placed in one class? Would these students do better if they were dispersed among the other eighth-grade students?

13. Are students with low achievement levels typically less motivated than other students? Defend your response.

14. As a parent, would you object if your child were placed in remedial-type courses?

SUGGESTED READINGS

Borko, H., & Livingston, C. (1989). Cognition and improvisation: Differences in mathematics instruction by expert and novice teachers. *American Educational Research Journal, 26*(4), 473–498.

Choate, J. (1990). Study the problem. *Teaching Exceptional Children, 22*(4), 44–46.

Ciscell, R. (1990). A matter of minutes: Making better use of teacher time. *The Clearing House, 63*(5), 217–218.

Clark, R. (1982). Antagonism between achievement and enjoyment in ATI studies. *Journal of Educational Psychology, 17,* 92–101.

Dembo, M. (1994). *Applying educational psychology in the classroom* (5th ed.). New York: Longman (see chapter 6).

Fuchs, L., & Deno, S. (1991). Paradigmatic distinctions between instructionally relevant measurement models. *Exceptional Children, 57*(6), 488–499.

Good, T., & Brophy, J. (1990). *Educational psychology: A realistic approach* (4th ed.). New York: Longman (see chapter 11).

Griffin, G. (1983). The dilemma of determining essential planning and decision-making skills for beginning teachers. In D. Smith (Ed.), *Essential knowledge for beginning educators* (pp. 16–22). Washington, DC: American Association of Colleges for Teacher Education.

Henson, K. (1993). *Methods and strategies for teaching in secondary and middle schools* (2nd ed.). New York: Longman (see chapters 3, 4).

Jonassen, D., & Hannum, W. (1986). Analysis of task analysis procedures. *Journal of Instructional Development, 9*(2), 2–12.

Jongsma, K. (1991). Grouping children for instruction: Some guidelines. *Reading Teacher, 44*(8), 610–611.

Levine, D. (1991). Tips for beginners. *Mathematics Teacher, 84*(6), 454–456.

Martin, B. (1989). A checklist of designing instruction in the affective domain. *Educational Technology, 29*(8), 7–15.

Martin, B. (1990). Teachers' planning processes: Does ISD make a difference? *Performance Improvement Quarterly, 3*(4), 53–73.

Miller, L., & Beattie, J. (1992). Line up a plan. *Teaching Exceptional Children, 24*(4), 54–55.

Montague, M., Bos, C., & Doucette, M. (1991). Affective, cognitive, and metacognitive attributes of eighth-grade mathematical problem solvers. *Learning Disabilities Research and Practice, 6*(3), 145–151.

Moore, B. (1988). Achievement of basic math skills for low performing students: A study of teachers' affect and CAI. *Journal of Experimental Education, 57*(1), 38–44.

Pasch, M., Sparks-Langer, G., Gardner, T., Starko, A., & Moody, C. (1991). *Teaching as decision making.* New York: Longman (see chapter 3).

Peterson, J. (1989). Tracking students by their supposed abilities can derail learning. *American School Board Journal, 176*(5), 38.

Smith, L. (1989). Lesson complexity, student performance, and student perception in mathematics. *Journal of Experimental Education, 57*(3), 219–227.

Szubinski, G., & Enright, B. (1992). Organize the facts. *Teaching Exceptional Children, 24*(3), 58–59.

Tennyson, R., & Rasch, M. (1988). Linking cognitive learning theory to instructional prescriptions. *Instructional Science, 17*(4), 369–385.

Williamson, R., & Osborne, D. (1985). *Instructional planning and beginning teacher assessment: Taking the anxiety out of accountability.* (ERIC Document Reproduction Service No. ED 286 856)

CASE 13

The Problem with Packaged Planning

PREPARING TO USE THE CASE

Background Information

Beginning teachers often cite instructional planning as one of their most difficult tasks. But this does not mean that their problems are necessarily identical. For some, the mere act of planning is arduous (perhaps they never learned good planning skills). For others, difficulties are related to properly sequencing course content or setting appropriate instructional objectives. And for still others, individualized planning is seen as unnecessary (e.g., teachers who rely entirely on a textbook to guide their practice).

Often inexperienced teachers are tempted to use commercially produced curriculum packages either because they feel insecure about instructional planning or because they are unwilling to devote adequate time to the process. The use of such materials, in and of itself, is not necessarily a problem. Difficulties typically emerge when teachers use such materials exclusively. There is no integration of current issues or supplemental materials (e.g., visual teaching modules) that serve to make the content more interesting and cogent to the students' personal lives.

Inadequate instructional planning often is related to, or results in, measurement and assessment problems. That is to say, when teachers are poorly prepared to associate their classroom activities to specific objectives, unit plans, and daily lesson plans, they are prone to err in making judgments about student learning. Deciding to use a commercially produced test that comes with a textbook, for example, is likely to provide only a single measure of student growth—but it may be highly reflective of teaching effectiveness.

This case centers around a first-year teacher whose primary interest is coaching basketball. Teaching is treated as a rather routine task; as a result, little thought is given to the purposes or goals of teaching a civics class. Additionally, the teacher relies almost entirely on the lecture method of teaching—an instructional approach that many students find boring. During each class, students sit passively and listen as the teacher simply outlines the content of the textbook.

As you read this case, a number of questions about instructional goals, student aspirations, instructional practices, and planning are likely to emerge. For example, to what extent does this teacher know what he is trying to accomplish? Do the students have any sense of what is expected of them? Does the teacher really understand measurement and grading? You also may have some questions about this teacher's motives for selecting his profession.

All of us prefer to be in situations where we know the rules—we want to know what is expected of us. This is true regardless of whether we find ourselves in the role of student (knowing what our teacher expects) or the role of teacher (knowing what our principal, students, and parents expect). When direction is missing, behaviors become less predictable. In reading this case, think of what it must have been like to be a student in this teacher's class.

Topics for Reflection
1. Instructional planning
2. Making decisions about what to teach
3. Setting appropriate objectives
4. Associating student interests and needs with curriculum and instructional techniques
5. Evaluating pupil progress

THE CASE

"Maynard Buckles Named Basketball Coach at KHS," read the headlines in the Klutchville newspaper in early July.

Hiring a beginning teacher to be head basketball coach is rare; but then again, Klutchville has a long-standing reputation for doing things a little differently. Located in a rural area of a mid-Atlantic state, it is a very small high school. With an enrollment of only 110 pupils in four grades, it is part of the state's second smallest (in terms of enrollment) school district. Over the past 20 years, there have been numerous attempts by neighboring districts to force consolidation, but each time, Klutchville officials were able to retain their independence. Local residents fear that if the school district becomes part of a larger unit, the town itself will virtually die.

For the past 14 years, Edison Jones has served as principal of Klutchville High School, and during this period he has hired three basketball coaches. This time, he would have preferred employing a more mature and experienced teacher for this visible position, but such individuals were not exactly standing in line to take a job at a small school where talent was usually very limited. Mr. Jones called friends across the state asking if they knew of an ambitious assistant coach seeking an opportunity to be a head coach. His efforts proved fruitless. Finally facing the reality of the situation, he made the unprecedented move of hiring a 23-year-old, inexperienced teacher to direct the school's major athletic team.

Maynard Buckles is enthusiastic, extroverted, and a risk taker. He is the sort of person who always volunteers at magic shows to get hypnotized or sawed in half. Unfortunately, his zest for adventure was not matched by his performance as a student at Haslow College. School was always somewhat a challenge for Maynard, but university study was especially difficult. In fact, were it not for his basketball talents in high school, and the athletic scholarship that those talents produced, he probably would never have been granted admission to Haslow—a liberal arts college with an enrollment of about 1,400 students.

When he enrolled at the college, Maynard selected prelaw as his major, but after only three semesters he started having doubts about this decision. He surmised that because of his grades he would have difficulty getting accepted by any law school. Accordingly, he decided to pursue a less financially lucrative, but for him a far more exciting career—that of basketball coach. After seeing a counselor at Haslow, he learned that schools do not hire persons just to be coaches. To reach his new objective, he would have to enter a curriculum in teacher education. He decided to major in physical education and minor in political science (only because he had already taken three classes in government).

The summer after changing his major, Maynard was involved in a serious motorcycle accident that shattered his left knee and ended his career as a basketball player. He feared that as a result, he would lose his scholarship. But largely due to the intervention of his coach, Frank Day, Haslow officials agreed to let him keep his scholarship. In return, however, Maynard was obligated to work with Coach Day as a student assistant. With the change in majors, his accident, and low grades, Maynard found himself struggling to raise his grade point average to a level required for student teaching and graduation. He finally managed to do so in his fifth year of enrollment at Haslow.

Maynard's teaching assignment at Klutchville High School includes three classes of physical education and one class of government. Without question, he found teaching in a classroom to be more difficult than supervising physical activities in the gym. There were 17 students in the government class, and they included sophomores, juniors, and even two seniors.

The athletic director at the school, Roger Piper, had a vested interest in seeing Maynard succeed. He had played a part in Maynard's employment, and it was he who recommended the dismissal of the previous coach. Roger realized that failure on Maynard's part would reflect badly on him—and he liked being athletic director.

The school year started in late August, but Maynard moved to Klutchville in late June. This gave him an opportunity to meet with the athletic director on several occasions to talk about the basketball program. It was during one of these sessions that Maynard expressed some apprehension about having to teach the government class. He told Roger that he wished he could have had all physical education classes, but both of them knew that scheduling needs and faculty resources made this impossible.

"The key to keeping your head above water," Roger told him, "is to plan all your lessons before basketball season. That way, you won't have to worry about too much pressure on you at one time. If you do that, teaching the government class shouldn't be any more demanding than your other assignments."

"How am I going to do that?" Maynard asked. "I've never taught high school government before. My student teaching was completely in physical education. So, how am I supposed to develop all those lessons in just two or three weeks?"

"The text you are using—does it have an instructor's manual? If so, just follow it."

Maynard noted that there was an instructor's manual. In fact, even tests for evaluating pupil progress were included.

"There you have it, Maynard," Roger said. "All you have to do is make a master calendar and fit everything into your overall plan."

Having given this advice, Roger could see that Maynard wasn't really convinced that it was the route to follow. So he tried to reassure the inexperienced teacher. "Listen, this is the only way you can avoid getting bogged down once basketball season is here. Most teachers rely heavily on the instructor's guide. There's nothing wrong with that. Why do you think these guides are written?"

The meeting between the two occurred on August 10th. The very next day Maynard started following Roger's advice. By the time school opened on August 27th, he had created a file folder for each week of both semesters. Inside each were sheets listing the topics for daily classes; there were the dittos that would be used for homework assignments; and there were notes and objectives copied from the instructor's manual.

All during the month of September, Maynard viewed himself as a well-oiled machine. He would lecture for 40 minutes, give the students their assignments, and send them on their way. He decided that teaching government wasn't nearly as difficult as he once thought.

In early October, Maynard was approached by the principal in the lunchroom, "Maynard, I hear good things about you from my daughter who is in your government class. I asked her how you were doing as a teacher, and she says you come to class prepared. I like that in a teacher. Students know when someone's just talking off the top of their head. You keep up the good work—you hear."

Now Maynard was really sure that teaching wasn't as hard as a lot of people told him it would be. He was able to keep students in his physical education classes busy by having them engage in games such as basketball, softball, and soccer. That sure didn't take much planning, and because the students liked the activities, he rarely had discipline problems. To this point, the preplanning in the government class was paying dividends. Maynard found that all he needed to do was to look at his folder a few minutes before class and he was able to talk about the scheduled topics without much difficulty.

By the second week in October, students started asking questions in class. Some were starting to feel lost, because there was so little discussion following the lectures. At first, Maynard tried to answer the inquiring students; but as the questions became more frequent and complex, he became reluctant to respond.

He remembered how he and some of his pals at Haslow used to love throwing professors "off track" by asking them one question after another. These interruptions often made it difficult for the professor to discuss everything in his notes for that class session. At times, the questions would spark a discussion of a totally different topic. The students who engaged in this behavior believed that their efforts would reduce course content. Hence, they would have that much less to know for examinations.

Now Maynard was looking at student questions from a different perspective. Yet he took the narrow view that his students were trying to do to him what he had done to several former professors. He decided to beat them at their own game. Rather than answer the questions in class, he suggested that the students get together after class and help each other.

"I'll tell you what, if you don't understand something, talk to your classmates. See if they can help you. That way, you will be learning from each other. You shouldn't expect your teacher to give you everything."

Maynard also had a definite position on homework—he believed in giving students some every day. But it was mainly busy work that required little effort on his part. For example, he never graded assignments. Instead, he would often tell the students to read portions of the text and then answer questions on one of his ditto sheets or at the end of the book's chapters. Since he never collected this material, it did not take the students long to figure out that the assignments were just a formality. By the end of September, most ignored them.

Basketball practice officially started in mid-October, and KHS played its first game on November 16th. As he had guessed, coaching was taking up almost all of his time now. He saw first-hand how difficult coaching could be when he worked with Coach Day at Haslow. What he never realized was how emotionally draining the work could be most of the time—especially when you are losing. By February 1, the KHS basketball team had one win and 14 losses. Maynard started having dreams about what it would have been like if he had gone to law school!

But on that morning of February 1st, coaching abruptly became a secondary concern for this novice teacher. At 3:10 PM as he was changing clothes for basketball practice, Maynard heard the door to the coach's room burst open. Through it came a visibly angry Principal Jones.

His face as red as a ripened tomato, the principal yelled, "Buckles, what the hell happened in your civics class? I just saw your first semester grades: two B's, three C's, seven D's, and five F's. And my daughter, Melanie, the one who told me last September how great you were, she got a D. She's never had a D before. I want an explanation."

"Hey, Mr. Jones. Your daughter's grade is not exactly my fault. She's the one who didn't do well on the test."

"Oh yeah, that's another thing. When we were talking about what happened, she told me that you based the entire semester's grade on one stinking test. Is that true?"

Maynard knew he was in trouble. It was very difficult for him to think clearly with this angry authority figure standing in front of him. He tried to explain, "You remember how you told me that I was doing a good job. Well, I was following the teacher's guide that goes with the textbook for the government class. The lessons are all sequenced, and I didn't skip any. The students knew that we were going to have only one test at the end of the semester. They also knew that their grades would be based on that test. I don't think it is that unusual to have a grade based on a test at the end of a semester. I had several professors in college who graded that way.''

Principal Jones seemed unaffected by Maynard's explanation. "Did you have any idea of whether these students were understanding what you were trying to teach? Do you know what you were trying to teach? And how do you know your test was fair?''

"I know it was fair, because I used the test that came with the teacher's guide." Maynard went on to explain, "So you see, the material was all there and the test was designed for the material. Is it my fault that the students didn't study or pay attention? Is it my fault that they didn't do their homework?''

"Speaking of homework," the principal responded. "My daughter said you never even collected it and therefore had no idea whether it was being completed. As I see it, much of this mess is your fault. You should have paid more attention to what the students were learning. Why, I asked Melanie how she could have gotten a D in your class, and she just couldn't give me an answer. The poor child's been crying ever since I told her what grade she was getting. You know she has four A's and one B in her other classes. And I have to tell you, Maynard, she doesn't think you're such a great teacher anymore.''

Maynard stood silently not knowing what to say. He had only followed the advice of an experienced teacher. He had gotten nothing but praise up until now. He followed the instructor's manual religiously. How could this be happening? he asked himself.

Seeing that Maynard was at a loss for words, Principal Jones spoke again. "You are going to reconsider these grades. What's more, you're going to give students quizzes every week this next semester. I see now that I have to pay a lot more attention to you. You can expect me to visit your class regularly for the rest of the school year. With your basketball record, you're in no position to be a lousy teacher.''

The next day, Maynard went to see Roger Piper and seek his advice. When he entered Roger's office, he was greeted with more hostility.

"Thanks a lot, Buckles. I tried to help you, and you got me in trouble with Jones. Don't you know better than to base your entire semester's grade on one test? Don't you know that students are not going to do homework that isn't collected by the teacher? I thought you were smarter than that. I've got enough to worry about with your coaching performance. With each additional loss, my phone calls from unhappy taxpayers increase. No, I'm not going to be responsible for your teaching. Go find somebody else to help you iron out your problems with teaching.''

The Challenge

Critique Maynard's performance as a beginning teacher. Describe the planning and evaluation errors you believe were made in this case.

ISSUES FOR FURTHER REFLECTION

1. Should Mr. Piper have given Maynard advice about teaching?
2. What is your perception of the principal in this case? Is this a principal that you would want as your supervisor? Why or why not?
3. What is your assessment of the homework assignments in Maynard's civics class?
4. Do you think that students knew what was expected of them in this civics class? What evidence leads you to your conclusion?
5. From the material in the case, do you believe that Maynard knew what he wanted to accomplish in teaching the civics class?
6. Do you believe that the reaction to this situation would have been different had Maynard given mostly A and B grades to the students? Why or why not?
7. What is the importance of the teacher knowing the students' needs and interests in this case?
8. Do you think Maynard would have taught the civics class differently if he was not coaching? What factors lead you to your answer?
9. Is the principal being fair with Maynard? Why or why not?
10. If you were Maynard's friend, what would you advise him at this point about the principal's demands and future instructional planning?
11. In what ways could an induction program or the assignment of a faculty mentor have been of assistance to Maynard?
12. Should grades reflect progress made during the course or a level of final performance? Justify your response.
13. Do you think many high school students are motivated by grades?
14. Do you think that this incident will make Maynard a better teacher?
15. Think of what you have learned about instructional planning. How do you see this information helping you in your first year of teaching?
16. Do you think that one's professional image of teaching is important with regard to instructional planning?

SUGGESTED READINGS

Ball, D., & Feiman-Nemser, S. (1988). Using textbooks and teachers' guides: A dilemma for beginning teachers and teacher educators. *Curriculum Inquiry, 18*(4), 401–23.

Conn, S. (1988). Textbooks: Defining the new criteria. *Media and Methods, 24*(4), 30–31, 64.

Dembo, M. (1994). *Applying educational psychology in the classroom* (5th ed.). New York: Longman (see chapter 6).

Good, T., & Brophy, J. (1990). *Educational psychology: A realistic approach* (4th ed.). New York: Longman (see chapter 11).

Harris, M., & Collay, M. (1990). Teacher induction in rural schools. *Journal of Staff Development, 11*(4), 44–48.

Heath-Camp, B., & Camp, W. (1990). What new teachers need to succeed. *Vocational Education Journal, 65*(4), 22–24.

Henson, K. (1993). *Methods and strategies for teaching in secondary and middle schools* (2nd ed.). New York: Longman (see chapters 3, 4).

Hills, J. (1991). Apathy concerning grading and testing. *Phi Delta Kappan, 72*(7), 540–545.

Hipple, T., & Bartholomew, B. (1982). What beginning teachers need to know about grading. *English Education, 14*(2), 95–98.

Jongsma, K. (1991). Rethinking grading practices. *Reading Teacher, 45*(4), 318–320.

Ohanian, S. (1984). What will you bring to your students this year? *Learning, 13*(1), 16–17, 19–20, 25.

Pasch, M., Sparks-Langer, G., Gardner, T., Starko, A., & Moody, C. (1991). *Teaching as decision making.* New York: Longman (see chapter 4).

Raths, J., Wojtaszek-Healy, M., & Della-Piana, N. (1987). Grading problems: A matter of communication. *Journal of Educational Research, 80*(3), 133–137.

Schell, L., & Burden, P. (1985). Working with beginning teachers. *Small School Forum, 7*(1), 13–15.

Shick, J. (1990). Textbook tests: The right formula? *Science Education, 57*(6), 33–39.

Snelbecker, G. (1988). Instructional design skills for classroom teachers. *Journal of Instructional Development, 10*(4), 33–40.

Waters, S., & Morehead, M. (1989). Teacher induction: A solution for rural schools. *Journal of Rural and Small Schools, 3*(3), 2–5.

Wilson, R. (1990). Classroom processes for evaluating student achievement. *Alberta Journal of Educational Research, 36*(1), 4–17.

Using Planning
to Overcome Inertia

PREPARING TO USE THE CASE

Background Information

Since 1983, when the president's National Commission on Excellence in Education released the report, *A Nation at Risk,* the media and over 300 special-interest groups learned that they could get attention for their organizations and themselves through bashing the public schools. Obviously, the administrators, teachers, and other school personnel took the brunt of this criticism. A decade and over 300 education-reform reports later, former Secretary of Education Terrel Bell (1993), who established the Commission on Excellence in Education, wrote:

> We have foolishly concluded that any problems with the levels of academic achievement have been caused by faulty schools staffed by inept teachers—and that by fixing the schools we can attain the levels of success we so desperately need in this decade. (p. 595)

Mr. Bell concluded his article by saying:

> After 10 years of trying to make our schools more effective, we are learning at last that we must begin with bright, dynamic, and persuasive school leaders. It is futile to even begin to try to improve a school if the leadership lacks luster. We also know that teacher leadership of and involvement in school improvement must become a more integral part of our plans. (p. 597)

As Mr. Bell implies, generally teachers have been left out of the national and state education-reform programs. Ironically, for reform to succeed, teachers are the ones who must implement it.

The public has tended to accept the reform rhetoric. This affects teachers both positively and negatively. One positive result of the reform reports is increased parental support. For example, parents now believe that more homework should be assigned. One negative effect of the reform reports is that laypeople often over-simplify the education process and the solutions to its problems. For example, most parents believe that increased homework will improve grades, but few realize that this is true only for high school students, less true for middle school students, and generally untrue for elementary students; even for older students, there is no evidence to support the common belief that the more homework, the better.

As you enter the teaching profession, be prepared to cope with some colleagues who will work against the system. Embittered by feeling neglected and over-worked, these teachers will lack the level of enthusiasm and dedication required to stimulate their students to reach their maximum potential. Many of these same frustrated individuals have given years, some even decades, of their best effort to teaching. But all professions have members who oppose innovations.

Successful teachers learn to focus their attention and planning to their own classes. As you read the following case, think about ways that you can improve your own planning strategies. Only through planning can you control the level of success of your classes. Finally, if your planning is to succeed, you must use research-proven strategies. You can begin testing your knowledge of effective planning by reading and getting further involved in the following case.

Topics for Reflection
1. Long-range planning and daily planning
2. The effect of homework on achievement
3. The role of concepts in planning and learning
4. Using anticipatory set, modeling, guided practice, and closure
5. Using planning to remain enthusiastic in a negative environment
6. Planning strategies that motivate students

THE CASE

"Heaven on earth." That's what Coastal Shores is, if you can believe the Realtors, for that is exactly how they advertise it. If you like year-round sunshine, blue skies, white beaches, and palm trees, and if you have plenty of money, you might not find this description far off target.

The area is a metropolis of over 20 small townships. Some are like many inner-city communities, full of drugs and violence. In fact, on a segment of "60 Minutes" the police commissioner advised residents to buy handguns and learn how to use them if they want to protect themselves and their families. But just blocks away are communities that are unsurpassed in beauty and wealth.

The School District

Lincoln County School District is among the 20 largest school systems in the country. During the period of rapid school population growth in the early 1970s, Lincoln County had almost 200 schools. Its southern coastal location has made Lincoln County School District unique in two important ways. First, when rapid school enrollments peaked for the rest of the country, redistricting and busing laws caused Lincoln's enrollment to increase. A second unique aspect of the Lincoln County area is its reputation as a retirement heaven. The warm climate, clear blue skies, and the white sandy beaches attract a constant flow of middle-age and senior citizens from the northern states. Because these residents have no school-age children, most of them are reluctant to vote for any proposal that would give support to the schools. Most harbor the "We've done our share" attitude. And because most of these older residents are on a "fixed" income, many of them really cannot afford the tax increases needed to operate a quality school district.

The School

Coastal Shores High School is located in an affluent suburban community, one of the wealthiest in the country. Here property in both business and residential zones is appraised not by acreage but by linear footage. A single vacant residential lot often sells for hundreds of thousands of dollars. Throughout the 1950s and 1960s this plush community was the home of some of the wealthiest people in the country. Many older residents moved to the area decades ago when the land sold at a small fraction of its current value; others moved there from other sections of the country. Strict building codes and high prices shielded the residents from the rest of the world.

During the 1950s and 1960s the student body at Coastal Shores High was made up mostly of children of local families who could afford to live in the area. Wealthy northerners who insisted on having the very best schools available for their children boarded their children in the town to enable them to attend this outstanding school. Coastal Shores High had a national reputation as one of the best high schools in the country. The administrators and teachers proudly announced that their students won more academic scholarships and national awards than any other students. After each standardized test was administered, the newspaper ran a full center-page spread with a chart listing all the standardized achievement test scores of each of the more than 200 high schools in the state. The chart also contained the national mean achievement scores, enabling residents to compare their local schools with the nation as a whole.

But the school busing laws of the 1960s and 1970s finally penetrated the walls that shielded Coastal Shores from the rest of the population. Suddenly, the student body experienced a rapid shift from a population of very wealthy Anglos to a balanced mix of students representing more than fifty cultures, the majority from low-income families. Predominant minority groups included African Americans, Cubans, Bahamians, Haitians, and Jamaicans. The faculty and student body of Coastal Shores experienced total fragmentation. The faculty's sense of pride was replaced by indignant feelings of: "How could this happen to us?" or "Why did they do this to our school?"

The Teacher

Unlike the majority of college students who either change their majors one or more times (and those who do not select a major until their second or third year at college), Amy Worley has always known that she wanted to teach. Her teacher education program has reassured her that she was destined to become not just a teacher, but a great teacher.

Fortunately, since she began kindergarten, Amy has mostly had good teachers. Even when they were not so good, Amy managed to enjoy them and to benefit from their instruction. Among the group were some really excellent teachers who were always prepared and who kept their students involved in a variety of enjoyable tasks. Amy's personal goal was to develop a repertoire of strategies that would involve her students meaningfully and enthusiastically in every lesson, and she had worked hard to develop the skills needed to accomplish this goal.

The Incident

Just prior to graduation, Amy received a teaching position in a school that had distinguished itself nationally. A social studies major, Amy welcomed the opportunity to work with students from so many cultural backgrounds. Her assignment included two sections of tenth-grade social studies and three sections of eleventh-grade American history. Like most first-year teachers, Amy had developed many lesson plans that she wanted to "try out." In her American history class she was especially eager to experiment with some simulations and games that she had personally developed in her methods classes.

Right away, Amy noticed among her students a sense of complacency; she also observed several behavioral patterns that she had not expected. Many of the students seemed to be isolating themselves in their own individual worlds. Most of the complacent students usually sat near the back of the room. When called on to participate, they seldom had any idea of what was happening in the class, and their factual knowledge of the work was dismally poor. Also, several students in each of her classes seemed particularly rude to their classmates. For example, each time a girl sharpened her pencil, the boys would often whistle and make exaggerated nonverbal gestures to draw attention to the girl's hip movements. The behavior of some of the girls was no better.

But Amy felt that she could handle these distractions. She knew that many of the students just wanted more attention, and she had many excellent student activities planned into her future lessons. In all, she felt optimistic; and having recently made the transition from student teacher to real teacher, Amy was thankful for the opportunity to have her own classes.

Each school day was so busy—even hectic—that Amy looked forward to her planning period. This was a time to reflect on her classes and a time to share her new experiences with her fellow teachers. For the first few weeks she did just that; each planning period was spent in the teachers' lounge. After a few weeks had passed, Amy noticed something that she had not been aware of in the past. Each day she had been so excited that she had spent every minute she was with her colleagues talking about her classes, her students, and some of the simulation games she had recently discovered. Amy's enthusiasm for her assignment and her confidence in her own ability to turn these students around and make them more studious were reflected in her comments. As she discussed the games that she had selected, she displayed so much enthusiasm that her colleagues expected her to begin teaching the games to them at any moment. Undaunted and determined to overcome any criticism and the current state of inertia that seemed to characterize all students at Coastal Shores, Amy was confident that she could develop a plan that would reverse this negative state of affairs.

Having learned in her methods classes that simulations and games are effective strategies for motivating student interest, Amy was planning to introduce a game called *Conflict,* which focuses on a crisis that erupts in 1999. This game instructs students that the nations of the world have developed three international councils with an international policy for peace. Amy hoped that the game would increase the level of motivation of her apathetic students while making them sensitive to the need to work together cooperatively.

Another game Amy had prepared to use in her social studies classes is called *Politica,* which presents a major international crisis set in Latin America and involves large-scale global conflicts. If for some reason her students failed to relate to these games, Amy had identified a backup strategy, a game entitled *Yes, But Not Here.* This game presents an urban conflict over a possible location for a condominium for the elderly. Amy had also chosen a special game for her American history class. *Simulation of American Government* places students in roles found in various branches of the U.S. government.

For each game, Amy wrote two or three objectives that were tied to the long-term goals in her six-week teaching-learning unit. Each objective had action verbs that expressed what she wanted the students to be able to do. Amy assigned some homework to all students, but not much. The fact that she seldom checked it and never assigned homework grades reflected the low priority with which she held homework.

In addition to having stated objectives for all of her lessons, Amy always singled out major concepts that she thought were important to understand the lessons. She used these concepts at the beginning of each period to establish cognitive (or anticipatory) set. She purposefully modeled attitudes that she wanted her students to share, especially her love for exploring new information.

At the end of each lesson, Amy summarized the major concepts, never ending the lesson without asking the students whether they understood all of the concepts and then asking them if they had any questions about the lesson.

Amy wondered whether she should even mention to her fellow teachers her plans to use these games. She feared it might cause resentment toward her and her level of enthusiasm. For the first time, Amy realized that she had not been giving her colleagues an opportunity to discuss their own classes.

When she finally slowed down enough to listen, Amy discovered that her fellow teachers were saying things about their students and about the school that she did not want to hear. Mr. King, an English teacher, and Mrs. Holland, a psychology/physical education teacher, were rapidly approaching retirement. Their topics of conversation vacillated between discussions about the good old days when the students respected their elders, and particularly their teachers, and a more recent concern over the pending legislation that would encourage early retirement. Mr. Arnold and Mrs. Huff, both physical education/health teachers, were critical of some of the other teachers who had begun an experimental drug-abuse prevention program. A common attitude among these four teachers was what they perceived as a current state of hopelessness, a condition that they blamed on modern society, the current laws, and a generation of apathetic students and parents. In all of their comments, Amy heard a clear message of pessimism. Some of the teachers were still openly bitter and resentful over the changes that they had seen happening in the school without their having had opportunities to provide any input. Each day, Amy talked less and listened more. Soon her fellow teachers began to ask her to agree with their views. Amy wanted to be friends with the other teachers, but she abhorred their negativism. She wondered what she should do.

The Challenge

Amy must make some decisions. Her choices could affect her future in the Lincoln County School District. Put yourself in her place as you consider the following issues.

ISSUES FOR FURTHER REFLECTION

1. To what extent must teachers let the climate of the school affect the climate in their own classes?
2. Like Amy, many beginning teachers are very enthusiastic. What problems can this cause?
3. What possible results can occur when a teacher hears negative comments each day from other teachers?
4. What additional information is needed before deciding on a course of action?
5. How do you feel about the low priority that Amy assigns to homework?
6. How does a teacher know which concepts are important?
7. Should Amy assign a grade to homework? Why or why not? If so, how frequently should she check it?
8. What do you remember about Amy's objectives that contributed to their clarity?
9. Can you think of a variety of ways to put excitement into the introduction of a lesson?
10. Can you improve on Amy's lesson closure?
11. Can you suggest further types of lessons that Amy can include in her repertoire?
12. Which of Amy's strategies would you most prefer to have in your own repertoire of lesson plans? Why?

13. With an ample number of daily lesson plans, why are unit plans also necessary?

14. How can Amy convince her principal of the value she sees in such indirect instruction as playing games?

SUGGESTED READINGS

Bell, T. H. (1993). Reflections one decade after *A Nation at Risk, Phi Delta Kappan, 74*(8), 592–597.

Dembo, M. (1994). *Applying educational psychology in the classroom* (5th ed.). New York: Longman (see chapters 8, 9, 10, 11).

Good, T., & Brophy, J. (1990). *Educational psychology: A realistic approach* (4th ed.). New York: Longman (see part 6).

Gronlund, N. E. (1991). *How to write and use instructional objectives* (4th ed.). New York: Macmillan.

Harrison, C. J. (1990). Concepts, operational definitions, and case studies in instruction. *Education, 110*(4), 502–505.

Henson, K. T. (1993). *Methods and strategies for teaching in secondary and middle schools* (2nd ed.). White Plains, NY: Longman (see chapter 13).

Lewellen, J. R. (1990). Systematic and effective teaching. *The High School Journal, 63*(1), 57–63.

Means, B., & Knapp, M. S. (1991). Cognitive approaches to teaching advanced skills to educationally disadvantaged students. *Phi Delta Kappan, 73*(4), 282–289.

Means, B., & Knapp, M. S. (1991). Introduction: Rethinking teaching for disadvantaged students. In B. Means, C. Chelemer, and M. S. Knapp (Eds.), *Teaching advanced skills to at-risk students* (pp. 1–26). San Francisco: Jossey-Bass.

Peterson, P. L., Marx, R. W., & Clark, C. M. (1978). Teacher planning, teacher behavior, and student achievement. *American Educational Research Journal, 15*(4) 555–565.

Walter, L. J. (1984). A synthesis of research findings on teaching, planning, and decision making. In R. L. Egbert & M. M. Kluender (Eds.). *Using research to improve teacher education* (pp. 54–63). Lincoln, NE: American Association for Colleges of Teacher Education.

VanGulick, R. (1990). Functionalism, information, and content. In W. G. Lylcan (Ed.), *Mind and Cognition.* Cambridge, MA: Basil Blackwell.

CASE 15

Questioning in the Classroom

PREPARING TO USE THE CASE

Background Information

Educators agree that developing thinking skills in students is an important educational objective. How to accomplish this goal is a matter of debate.

One point of view holds that teaching thinking skills is easier to accomplish in some subjects. From this view it is argued that the method of inquiry in the sciences may lend itself naturally to increasingly complex levels of thinking. In contrast, a more didactic approach to learning traditional grammar may inhibit such thinking. A second view notes that it is the instructional approach that most critically affects learning. Some forms of instruction, such as simulations, games, and discussions are more readily used to promote higher-order thinking than a classroom lecture. A third view suggests that the learner is the key to enhancing thinking.

From this perspective, the aptitude, interest, maturation, readiness, and other such learner characteristics will determine how successful the teacher may be in improving students' thinking skills. Another view points to the environment or setting in which teaching and learning takes place as most critical. Physical factors, such as heat, color, sound, furniture, and texture can be either stimulating or detracting. A final view suggests that all of these factors are interrelated and that for each learner, knowing how these combined factors affect performance is the best indicator for success.

Regardless of the view supported, it is clear that teachers often work in settings (physical environments) to which they are assigned, with little control over them other than how furniture and instructional equipment may be arranged. Similarly, teachers more often than not must teach in a heterogeneous classroom setting, where there is wide variation in race, ability, maturation, interest, and other student characteristics. Teachers tend to have more control in their selection of teaching materials and instructional methods.

As teachers make judgments about which materials and methods they believe will be most successful, they consider a variety of factors based on: (1) personal beliefs about content and instruction; (2) learning theory; (3) knowledge of the subject being taught; (4) classroom experience; for example, what has been most successful in the past; and (5) the backgrounds and abilities of their students.

This case is about a beginning teacher who attempts to implement a teaching strategy to improve students' thinking skills. Excited about the use of questioning techniques as a result of his attendance at an in-service meeting, the teacher develops a set of questions related to a lesson he is teaching in a social studies course. The case revolves around a problem that arises as he incorporates questioning techniques into the lesson.

Topics for Reflection
1. Developing higher-order thinking skills in students
2. The effects of instructional strategies on encouraging higher-order thinking
3. The relationship between instructional planning and student outcomes
4. Interfacing attributes of students—motivation, interest, ability, readiness—with instructional planning

THE CASE

As they rode back to their school, the four Belmont teachers compared notes on the afternoon in-service session.

"Professor Brooks really knew her stuff," Jayne Broderick remarked enthusiastically. "I'm not easily impressed by in-service workshops, but there were several activities I observed today that I can integrate into my science teaching."

"What made it for me was the way she used those three teachers from Cranston to illustrate questioning techniques. That made it so much more realistic," commented Jessie Crane. "And the fact that one of them was a home economics teacher like me made it even better."

"I understand that Professor Brooks has been working with the teachers at Cranston for several months. Some kind of grant from the state department of education," Henry Carlyle added.

"I had forgotten about Sanders's *Classroom Questions* [1966] and Bloom's *Taxonomy* [1956]. They've been collecting dust in my bookcase at home since I finished my social studies methods class. I'd forgotten how useful they could be," Robert Benson said.

"We used them, too, in my English methods course at Tech," noted Mr. Carlyle.

"In an NSF summer institute a few years ago, I remember having to prepare instructional goals and related questions using the taxonomy," Mrs. Broderick said.

"I'm going to take another look at some of the materials I have at home on questioning techniques," Mr. Benson said, as he steered the car into the Belmont parking lot.

"Thanks for driving today," Mrs. Broderick said.

"Yes, we appreciate it," Mrs. Crane agreed. "First-year teachers don't always get stuck driving."

The teachers laughed.

Robert Benson parked his car and let the other teachers out. As they departed, each offered the others wishes for an enjoyable weekend.

Benson pulled from the parking space, drove out of the lot, and headed toward his apartment a few miles away. As he drove, he thought about his seven weeks of teaching at Belmont. He recalled how surprised he had been, when he interviewed for the job, that seven native languages are spoken by Belmont students. Having grown up in a small, rural town and attended a school that enrolled 656 students in grades 7–12, he had been awed by the 2,227 students at Belmont and the massive, block-long brick complex that housed them. He had been shocked by plainclothes security guards in the school.

As he had come from a nearly all-white community, Robert Benson had viewed teaching in a racially mixed school composed of 62 percent black, 26 percent Hispanic, 7 percent Asian, 4 percent white, and 1 percent Native American students with both excitement and fear. In a short time, however, he had become comfortable working in a multiethnic school in an urban community. He felt there were so many cultural advantages to teaching in such a setting.

Four of his five teaching assignments had gone well. He felt fortunate to have three preparations—two in different periods of American history and one in geography. Although he considered his classes to be large from his own school experience, having classes of 30–35 students is common in basic subjects at Belmont.

The geography class presents the most difficulty, even though Benson feels he can communicate effectively with the 31 students. The student composition of the class reflects that of the school. There are 18 black, 7 Hispanic, 4 Asian, and 2 white students in the class. The class is an elective at Belmont, but it is used to meet graduation requirements. The range of abilities in the class is wide. A quarter of the students are B+ to A students in all course work. More than half are C students. The remainder are D students. Generally, the students are well behaved.

Finding instructional resources is no problem. Benson has been able to find a varied selection of films, filmstrips, slides, and other materials concerning climate, imports and exports, transportation systems, and social, economic, and political conditions of the countries being studied. "The students are attentive. I just can't get them to think," he mumbled aloud. "Perhaps attending the conference was a good omen," he thought as he pulled into the parking lot next to the apartment complex where he lived. "Maybe I should spend more time on questioning and less time on lecturing and using audiovisuals."

He got out of his car, locked the door, and walked to apartment 3B. He inserted his door key, grabbed three letters from his mailbox, opened the door, and entered his apartment. He nudged the door shut with his foot while glancing at the mail. "Just more bills," he grumbled, as he tossed the letters on top of the desk. He unzipped his jacket, took it off, and threw it on the couch. He undid his tie as he walked to the kitchen. As he opened the refrigerator door with one hand, he tossed his tie onto the kitchen table. He pulled out a diet soda, snapped open the top, and sipped from the can. As he continued drinking, he walked back into the living room to a bookcase.

"I know they're here somewhere," he thought. Spying a tattered paperback copy of Bloom's *Taxonomy of Educational Objectives* near the top of the shelf, he pulled it out.

"If I were organized, I'd find Sanders's book close by," he mused.

"Ah, here," he said aloud, as he noticed the book on the bottom shelf between *Yeager* and *Collected Short Stories of Mark Twain.* He walked to his desk, put his drink down, and began leafing through Sanders's *Classroom Questions: What Kinds?* An excerpt from page 7 caught his eye.

"The taxonomy of questions helps to clarify "learning by doing" by demonstrating that a child can be sitting quietly at a desk and yet be vigorously engaged in any one of a number of kinds of mental activities."

"Just the opposite of my geography class," he thought. "They sit quietly at their desks but aren't really engaged mentally."

He took a sharp pencil and legal-sized yellow pad from the desk drawer and took notes. In short order he opened Bloom's text. He skimmed over introductory remarks, a discussion of purposes for developing the taxonomy, to the appendix.

"Here it is," he remarked.

He copied the levels of the taxonomy on a second sheet of paper. He closed Bloom's book and reopened the Sanders text, went back to the first sheet of paper, and continued writing.

During the weekend, Benson reworked his lesson plan for his fifth-period geography class. He reviewed notes on a 20-minute UNESCO film on the economic system of Mexico. Then he drew a grid of the taxonomy with each level noted down the left-hand margin of the paper. As he went back over his notes, he wrote questions for each level of the taxonomy. On Monday morning, after getting dressed and eating breakfast, he reworked the questions for a last time, realizing there would not be time during the day to do more planning for the class.

Thirty minutes before the first bell, Benson packed his materials, left the apartment, and drove to Belmont. Up to the fifth period, the day went smoothly. Students in each of his classes had been attentive. The level of student participation was higher than usual, particularly for a Monday. He anticipated the geography classes with confidence and enthusiasm.

The Problem

He had spent several hours preparing questions and was excited about trying his sequenced approach to questioning. The fifth-period bell rang, and the students took their seats. Benson looked over the names in his grade book and glanced around the room. All the students were present.

For the first five minutes of the class he reviewed Friday's lesson, which had covered the political system in Mexico. After summarizing major points of the political system, Benson set the stage for the class's activity. "For the remainder of the period," he continued, "we will explore the economic system of Mexico."

"To introduce the topic I have printed five key terms on the chalkboard. Please put these in your notes."

"As you view the short film I will show in a minute," he continued, "each of these terms will be defined and discussed. Please define the terms in your own words in your notes. Some of the terms you should recognize. We've used them before."

He then repeated the key terms aloud: "*Currency. Gold standard. Inflation. Balance of trade. Consumption.*"

"Mona, please turn off the lights," Benson said as he motioned to a student to ready the room for the film.

After the film, he turned off the projector and flipped on the lights. Take the next couple of minutes to finish your notes, while I rewind the film and put it in its canister," Benson instructed the class.

Three minutes later, armed with questions he had prepared over the weekend, Benson began the discussion.

"You will recall that when we studied other countries, we talked about the fact that a country's currency serves as the foundation for its economic system. What is a currency?"

None of the students responded. He waited. After a half-minute of silence, he said impatiently:

"Come on, we've covered this in three other South American countries in the past two weeks. What is a currency?" Meekly, one of the students offered a response.

"That's a good start," Benson replied reassuringly. "Who can build on what Lois has said?"

For the next 30 minutes Benson struggled to get students to respond. He stumbled through the grid of questions, noticing that students seemed reluctant to offer answers and had trouble moving up the taxonomy to higher-order questions. Out of frustration he ended the discussion early.

"We'll continue this tomorrow. Until the end of the period, I want you to read pages 123 to 130, your assignment for tomorrow," Benson concluded.

He walked to his desk, sat down, and retraced his steps through the questioning process. He reviewed his list of questions. "What did I do wrong?" he wondered.

After class, Benson went to the teacher's lounge, a place he often went to plan, grade papers, or discuss teaching strategies with Dolores Whitney, a 43-year-old social studies teacher whom he considered his mentor. He had met Dolores at a state social studies conference while he was student teaching a year earlier. She was already in the lounge, putting grades in her grade book. As Benson entered, Dolores greeted him: "Hello, Bob. How are you?"

"Not so good," Benson responded glumly.

"It shows," Dolores said. "About class?"

"I'm not sure what the trouble is. But, yes, the geography class last period was difficult. Especially after all the work I did this weekend to prepare."

"Tell me about it," Dolores remarked.

Benson related his excitement about the Friday in-service course, explained the preparation he had made for the class, and reviewed what had happened. Benson appreciated the fact that Mrs. Whitney was a patient listener. He had come to respect her for her unwillingness to give him immediate advice and for her insistence that he think of alternative solutions for the instructional problems he faced. Accordingly, he was not surprised when she asked, "What are you going to do?"

The Challenge

What can Benson do to make the use of higher-order questions a more constructive, successful activity?

ISSUES FOR FURTHER REFLECTION

1. Do you believe higher-order thinking skills can be taught? Defend your answer.

2. Assume Benson's role. From the information given, what reasons might be provided for the lack of success in using higher-order questions in the geography class?

3. What can Benson do to salvage his effort to use questioning techniques to get his students to engage in higher-order thinking? Describe potential consequences of changes in his attempt to use questioning techniques to improve the level of thinking in his class.

4. Describe the merits of Benson's use of questioning techniques with visual material. Did the fact that the students had studied the concepts earlier in text materials help or obstruct Benson's efforts in using questioning techniques? Explain your answer.

5. Some educators argue that the appropriateness of instructional strategies varies from one subject area to another. In this view, could it be argued that using questioning techniques to encourage higher-order thinking would be more appropriate in a social studies class than in an art class? Take a position on this issue and defend it.

6. In what ways might an understanding of *motivation* contribute to improving Benson's use of questioning techniques to encourage higher-order thinking? An understanding of *learning styles*?

7. Can you recall a time when one of your teachers tried an instructional activity aimed at promoting higher-order thinking? Describe the experience. How successful was the experience? What enhanced its success? What inhibited its success?

8. There are domains other than the *cognitive* that have been described in the education literature, such as Harrow's *psychomotor* domain, Krathwohl, et al's *affective* domain, and Kohlberg's *moral* domain. Read about each of these domains. In what ways do you view these domains as helpful in increasing the level of students' performance in these areas? In what ways might a domain restrict a teacher's view of what can be expected from student performance?

9. What relationships exist among the domains? How can teachers use these relationships to plan more effectively for student learning?

10. A number of educational programs have been developed in order to teach critical-thinking skills. Name one and describe the elements of the program.

SUGGESTED READINGS

Bloom, B. (1956). *Taxonomy of educational objectives. Handbook 1: Cognitive domain.* New York: David McKay.

Carlsen, W. (1991). Questioning in classrooms: A sociolinguistic perspective. *Review of Educational Research, 61*(2), 157–178.

Check, J. (1985). Fielding and initiating questions in class. *Clearing House, 58*(6), 270–273.

Ciardiello, A. (1986). Teacher questioning and student interaction: An observation of three social studies classes. *Social Studies, 77*(3), 119–122.

Clarke, M. (1990). A critically reflective social studies? *History and Social Science Teacher, 25*(4), 214–220.

Dean, D. (1986). Questioning techniques for teachers: A closer look at the process. *Contemporary Education, 57*(4), 184–185.

Dembo, M. (1994). *Applying educational psychology in the classroom* (5th ed.). New York: Longman (see chapters 3, 4).

Dillon, J. (1984). Research on questioning and discussion. *Educational Leadership, 42*(3), 50–56.

Fairborn, D. (1987). The art of questioning your students. *Clearing House, 61*(1), 19–22.

Farrar, M. (1986). Teacher questions: The complexity of the cognitively simple. *Instructional Science, 15*(2), 89–107.

Felton, R., & Allen, R. (1986). Building questioning skills. *Social Education, 50*(7), 544–548.

Gall, M. (1984). Synthesis of research on teachers' questioning. *Educational Leadership, 42*(3), 40–47.

Good, T., & Brophy, J. (1990). *Educational psychology: A realistic approach* (4th ed.). New York: Longman (see chapters 11, 13).

Harris, P., & Swick, K. (1985). Improving teacher communications: Focus on clarity and questioning skills. *Clearing House, 59*(1), 13–15.

Harrow, A. (1972). *A taxonomy of the psychomotor domain: A guide for developing behavioral objectives.* New York: McKay.

Henson, K. (1993). *Methods and strategies for teaching in secondary and middle schools* (2nd ed.). New York: Longman (see chapters 4, 5).

Hunkins, F. (1989). *Teaching thinking through effective questioning.* Boston: Christopher-Gordon.

Johnson, B. (1992). Concept question choice: A framework for thinking and learning about text. *Reading Horizons, 32*(4), 263–278.

Kohlberg, L. (1976). Moral stages and moralization. In T. Lickona (Ed.), *Moral development and behavior: Theory, research, and social issues.* New York: Holt, Rinehart, & Winston.

Krathwohl, D., Bloom, B., & Masia, B. (1964). *Taxonomy of educational objectives. Handbook II: Affective domain.* New York: McKay.

Nessel, D. (1987). The new face of comprehension instruction: A closer look at questions. *The Reading Teacher, 10*(7), 601–606.

Pasch, M., Sparks-Langer, G., Gardner, T., Starko, A., & Moody, C. (1991). *Teaching as decision making: Instructional practices for the successful teacher.* New York: Longman (see chapter 4).

Perez, S. (1986). Improving learning through student questioning. *Clearing House, 60* (2), 63–65.

Rogers, D. (1990). Are questions the answer? *Dimensions, 19*(1), 3–5.

Sanders, N. (1966). *Classroom questions: What kinds?* New York: Harper & Row.

Sheingold, K. (1987). Keeping children's knowledge alive through inquiry. *School Library Media Quarterly, 15*(2), 80–85.

Wilen, W. (1991). *Questioning skills for teachers: What research says.* Washington, DC: National Education Association.

CASE 16

Taking Sides

PREPARING TO USE THE CASE

Background Information

Helping students become critical thinkers is one of the most important objectives in teaching. Complex tasks, ambiguous information, and competing views on issues all require the ability to analyze, synthesize, and evaluate.

Beyond the classroom value of assisting students to become more critical, the value to the individual lies in the ability to make more informed choices as a consumer and worker. As important, such instruction is directly related to preparing students to contribute productively to democracy. There are valuable, long-term political benefits from insuring that students leave school able to make critical judgments.

Several approaches are available to the teacher to encourage more critical thinking. One is to provide assignments that have several correct solutions— some being better than others—and to require each student to explain why a particular solution was chosen. A second approach is to provide opportunities for discussion and debate on controversial issues that are important to students. A third involves the use of case studies in which students must wade through problems posed to arrive at a resolution that they must defend. A fourth approach is to share films and documents designed to persuade people to support a particular program or action and have students conduct in-depth research on the presentations. Many other similar activities can be planned to force students to think in more diverse ways.

While there is no denying that teaching critical thinking is vital, and that an array of ways to do so are readily available to the teacher, the fact is that any effort to accomplish this objective will be shaped by other factors. Cultural perspectives may affect how students from different racial and ethnic groups interpret and judge the information presented. The socioeconomic status of the students will shape the values and understandings with which they approach tasks. Level of maturity, the extent to which personal problems may consume their thinking, the ability to read and comprehend information, the amount of parental support—a number of factors beyond the control of the classroom teacher—will affect how successful the teacher will be in enabling students to think more critically.

In this case, a first-year teacher becomes enraged by a policy decision made by the high school principal. She uses the incident as a way to involve her students in a critical analysis of the conflict between First Amendment rights and a recent court decision. Beyond engaging her students in the debate, she enlists the support of teachers in considering how the principal's decision might be overturned.

Topics for Reflection
1. Critical thinking
2. Parental influence and involvement
3. Peer relationships
4. Problem solving
5. Legal requirements
6. Values and beliefs
7. Teacher decision making
8. Ethical concerns

THE CASE

"I can't believe it. I can't believe it," Susan Raines, journalism teacher at Eastwood High School, mumbled aloud.

An empty feeling came to her stomach, and a tear slid down her cheek. "I can't believe it!" she shrieked. She pressed the "off" button on the remote control, and the television screen went dark.

"Five to three. Incredible," she thought. "I've got to respond."

She went to her desk, pulled a yellow pad and a pen from the drawer, and sat down. An hour later she stopped writing, folded the letter, placed it in an envelope, addressed it, and put a stamp on it. Then she went to her car and drove to the post office. As she dropped the letter into the box, she said angrily, "You may think you can censor my kids, but you can't censor me!"

The next evening she leafed through the local newspaper, the *Eastwood City Press.* When she came to page 8 she exclaimed, "They printed it!"

Slowly, focusing on each word, she read her letter to the editor:

Congress shall make no law respecting an establishment of religion, or prohibiting the free exercise thereof; or abridging the freedom of speech, or of the press; or the right of the people peaceably to assemble, and to petition the Government for a redress of grievances.

(Amendments to U.S. Constitution, Article I)

She had remembered these words from her social studies class in her junior year of high school. Her teacher had stressed the importance of freedom of expression. In the same year she read *1984* and *Fahrenheit 451* and learned why the right to free speech had to be protected.

One of the most difficult events of her life also occurred that year. Ms. Allison Johnson, her high school newspaper adviser, was fired. Thoughts of the tension and pain associated with the dismissal of a teacher who had meant so much to her had weighed heavily over the years. Those events profoundly influenced Susan's decision to become a journalism teacher. Ironically, she now found herself in a similar situation.

Ms. Raines has four journalism classes and nearly 82 eager students. They work hard to find interesting, sometimes controversial stories of concern to other students. They research issues, conduct interviews, write feature and news stories, always seeking to be fair and accurate.

The Supreme Court case of *Hazelwood School District v. Kuhlmeier* upheld the principal's right to censor the student newspaper—in this case to prevent the publication of an article on student pregnancies and one on the effects of divorce on young people.

Now, after this decision, will my students be free to express their ideas? Will they be allowed to write about teenage pregnancy? Drug abuse? Suicide? An inadequate curriculum? Incompetent teaching? Unfair grading?

The Supreme Court has spoken. But only three justices have spoken for my students and me.

During the evening, several friends called, praising Susan for writing the letter. She felt somewhat redeemed. Having the letter published was cathartic. She slept comfortably.

When she arrived at work the next morning, Susan was met at the school entrance by Mary Reeves, the drama teacher at Eastwood High.

"Susan, hurry—you've got to check your mail," she said excitedly.

"Why?" Susan asked.

"Look at this," she responded, handing a memo to her.

It read:

January 15, 1989
TO: Mrs. Reeves, Drama Teacher
FROM: Mr. Marlin Erlick
RE: Theater Performances
As of this date, before any play or other theatrical performance can be performed publicly, the script must be submitted to me for review by my administrative staff. This procedure is being implemented not to censor or obstruct student performance. It is being set in place to assure that selections appropriate for the public are performed.

"I was afraid this would happen," Susan said.

They walked hurriedly toward the main office. Susan went in, gathered her mail, and returned to the hall, where Mary was waiting.

"Looks like I got one too," Susan remarked waving a piece of paper. "Mr. Erlick wants to see the student newspaper before it goes to the printer."

Before the first bell rang, Susan and Mary learned that the choral director, the band instructor, the art teachers, and the librarian had received similar letters. As the two teachers parted to teach their first-period classes, Mary said, "We've got to get together and do something."

"What should we do?" Mary asked.

"You get in touch with Mr. Carter, Mrs. Grimes, and Ms. Keene. I'll talk to Ms. Bertrand and Mr. Munoz. Can we use your room? I'll have students in mine, working on the next issue of the paper," Susan said.

"I have the same problem. Students are rehearsing scenes for *Sweet Charity.* Mrs. Grimes is working with the musicians for the performance. Mr. Carter has his room tied up with the students practicing the vocal parts. And Bertrand and Munoz have students working on flats," Mary responded.

"That leaves Ms. Keene. Maybe we can use one of the conference rooms. I'll check on it. See you at lunch."

Enraged, Ms. Raines went to the copy room and made copies of the principal's memorandum to distribute to students in each of her classes. She gathered the copies and walked hurriedly to her first-period class. As she entered the classroom, students were visiting informally, talking about their weekend experiences. The mood was light and friendly.

The atmosphere was quickly broken as Ms. Raines slammed the door behind her. Student conversation ended abruptly. She slammed the copies of the principal's letter on her desk, pulled out her chair, slumped in the chair, and began to cry.

Several students came to her desk and asked what was wrong.

Regaining her composure quickly, she apologized: "Look, I'm sorry."

"It has something to do with your letter, doesn't it?" one student inquired.

"Are they trying to fire you?" another asked.

"No," Ms. Raines replied. "No one has threatened to fire me. Don't worry, I'm not in any trouble."

"Then, what's wrong?" a third student asked.

"Please. Take your seat. We'll talk about this," Ms. Raines said.

During the remainder of the first period, Ms. Raines involved the students in a rousing discussion about First Amendment rights and the implications of the *Hazelwood* case. She initiated the discussion by telling about her experience in high school, reading the letter she wrote to the newspaper, and distributing a copy of the memorandum she had received from the principal. Once she had set the context for discussion, she tried to personalize the debate by asking questions: "What right do you have to say what you want to say?" and "Does your right of freedom of expression change when you walk through the door to your school?"

While the majority of students argued that they had the right to say whatever they wanted to say and that the right included any expression of speech while in school, a few students challenged the position.

One student argued: "We're not old enough and mature enough to know the right decision to make, a lot of times. We need adults to guide us in making tough decisions."

A second noted: "The school administration is ultimately responsible for what happens. I don't think we should do anything that makes them or our school look bad."

A third said: "My mother read your letter, Ms. Raines. She said you should worry more about teaching us and obeying the law."

A fourth argued: "Rules are good. Order is established. People know what they can and cannot do. I think it's great our principal is going to read our stuff before it gets printed. It really just means he is more interested. Besides, he's a nice guy. He's never stopped us from printing our stories in the past."

Agreeing, a fifth student added: "Yeah, just let Erlick do his job."

A final student argued: "I don't think anything should be said at school or presented at school that is offensive to any religious or racial group. And bad language shouldn't be tolerated at any time."

During the lunch period, Susan and Mary met again. Susan explained that she had altered her lesson plans for the day. She gave a detailed description of what had happened in her first three classes.

"I'm astonished," Mary said. "It's really gutsy for a first-year teacher to take on an issue like this."

"I'm not a novice," Susan responded tersely. "I went through something much worse than this while I was a student in high school." She proceeded to tell Mary about the story of her high school journalism adviser's dismissal. As she finished, she asked: "Have the other teachers agreed to meet?"

Everything was set. The conference room was reserved. All the teachers had agreed to meet at 4:00 PM.

"Was there any reluctance to meet?" Susan asked.

"None, the teachers see Erlick's memo as an insult to their professional judgment. Not surprising, is it?" Mary asked.

"No. How did Bill, Marla, and Ms. Keene respond?"

"Bill and Ms. Keene are fine. So is Marla . . . really. Bill's concerned about her, since this is her first year also. But Marla believes as strongly in this as we do."

"I knew we could count on Ms. Keene," Susan said.

It was critical for the teachers to get the support of Ms. Keene, the librarian. No one remembered her ever being called by her first name. She was always called "Ms. Keene." She is known as the "Grand Lady of Eastwood," wears the finest clothes from Saks, Gucci, Bloomingdale's, and Neiman-Marcus, and lives in an antiques-stocked colonial house listed in the National Registry. She belongs to the Daughters of the American Revolution, does volunteer work at the Eastwood Hospital Auxiliary, and regularly attends the Main Street Presbyterian Church. She is as much a leader in the community as she is in the school.

"Her presence demands respect," Susan added.

"What do you think about Marla? Should we leave her out of this?" Mary asked.

"Look, a new teacher can't ride the fence. She has to sink or swim on her own. She's old enough to teach. She's old enough to make up her mind," Susan responded matter-of-factly.

"Do you really think she has much choice? Surely she feels pressure from us."

"It's her decision. We'll make that clear to her," Susan stated. "And Bill?"

"I think he mentioned Marla as a way of projecting his own feelings of insecurity. He's not real strong. He also said he didn't think you should get involved."

"I don't understand. He has tenure. He's been here for eight years," Mary replied. "What's his problem?"

"He's taking heat. Replacing Carol Middleton has been tough. The choral groups have never won the awards or performed as superbly as when Carol was the director. He feels like he's being pressed to leave. He doesn't feel he gets the financial support or the best students. He thinks it's intentional," Susan said.

"Well, there's no problem with Carlos and Lisa. They're union advocates and they believe that the principal's edict on censorship is, at best, an item that must be negotiated. They want to file a grievance," Mary remarked.

During the two class periods after lunch, Ms. Raines repeated the same approach that she had followed in the morning classes. The outcomes were much the same, with the majority of students supporting the freedom of speech at almost all cost, even while at school. A few students marshaled competing arguments in support of the principal's decree.

At 4:00 PM Mary and Susan headed for the library conference room. The other teachers were seated at the table when they arrived.

Susan assumed leadership of the group. She first summarized the circumstances leading to the meeting, including how she had involved students in all of her classes in the debate, and then she said, "I believe we must do something. That's why I wanted us to meet."

"I don't mind meeting to talk about what we might do," Bill said. "But I must tell you, Susan, that I think it was inappropriate for you to bring your students into this."

"Getting my students to think critically is the most important challenge I face, particularly in a journalism class," Susan shouted angrily. "Furthermore, it's none of your business!"

The Challenge

Should Ms. Raines have involved her students in a critical analysis of the principal's policy decision? What should the teachers do?

ISSUES FOR FURTHER REFLECTION

1. To what extent could you argue that engaging students in a critical analysis of the principal's memorandum was an appropriate teaching strategy?

2. To what extent do you believe the way Ms. Raines organized the discussion was appropriate? How might she have improved the organization of the discussion?

3. Ms. Raines posed two questions to her class: "What right do you have to say what you want to say?" and "Does your right of freedom of expression change when you walk through the door to your school?" If you had been in her class, how would you have responded to each question?

4. Share your answers openly with other students in your class. Rank the responses in terms of critical analysis. Which answers show a high level of logical, insightful examination? Which do not? What are the characteristics of more critical and analytical answers?

5. Six students gave opposing views to that which Ms. Raines most likely hoped to hear. Take each of those views. In the same way that you ranked the responses of your peers in question 4, rank the six responses from students in Ms. Raines class in the same way. Similarly, which of the six responses showed the highest level of logical, insightful examination? Which showed the least?

6. Under what circumstances should teachers openly share their feelings about an issue? To what extent does showing emotion influence how freely students may feel they can share their own points of view?

7. At what point does a teacher's sharing personal feelings border on indoctrination? Defend your position by giving an illustration.

8. What specific actions should the teachers take?

9. What reasons can you give in support of the actions recommended?

10. What are potential consequences of these actions?

11. What rights do the teachers have?

12. What rights do the students have?

13. What rights does the principal have?

14. Ultimately, in this case, whose rights are the most likely to be protected? Explain your answer.

SUGGESTED READINGS

Adams, J. (1986). Districts "jump the gun" on prior restraint rules. *Communication: Journalism Education Today, 19*(4),19–20.

Court, D. (1991). Teaching critical thinking: What do we know? *Social Studies, 82*(3), 115–119.

Dean, D. (1986). Questioning techniques for teachers: A closer look at the process. *Contemporary Education, 57*(4), 184–185.

Dembo, M. (1994). *Applying educational psychology in the classroom* (5th ed.). New York: Longman (see chapters 3, 4).

Donelson, K. (1987). Censorship: Heading off the attack. *Educational Horizons, 65*(4), 167–170.

Farrar, M. (1986). Teacher questions: The complexity of the cognitively simple. *Instructional Science, 15*(2), 89–107.

Felton, R., & Allen R. (1986). Building questioning skills. *Social Education, 50*(7), 544–548.

Flygare, T. J. (1986a). Supreme Court restricts damages for constitutional violations. *Phi Delta Kappan, 68*(4), 246–248.

Flygare, T. J. (1986b). Teachers' First Amendment rights eroding. *Phi Delta Kappan, 67*(5), 396–397.

Good, T., & Brophy, J. (1990). *Educational psychology: A realistic approach* (4th ed.). New York: Longman (see chapters 10, 19).

Henson, K. (1993). *Methods and strategies for teaching in secondary and middle schools* (2nd ed.). New York: Longman (see chapters 5, 6).

Johnson, D., & Johnson, R. (1979). Conflict in the classroom: Controversy and learning. *Review of Educational Research, 49*(1), 51–70.

Jurenas, A. (1987). A delicate balance—a familiar dilemma. *American Secondary Education, 16*(1), 28–30.

Madden, L. (1988). Do teachers communicate with their students as if they were dogs? *Language Arts, 65*(2), 142–146.

Merrill, M. (1987). Authors fight back: One community's experience. *Library Journal, 112,* 55–56.

Splitt, D. A. (1987). School law. *Executive Educator, 9*(1), 5.

Managing Mistakes: Using Reflective Thinking to Solve Problems

PREPARING TO USE THE CASE

Background Information

Most teaching candidates feel some nervousness as they approach their first teaching positions. A degree of stress is natural; it can even be motivating. But excessive stress can cause problems and damage.

Beginning teachers can reduce this stress. They need to understand that teaching is a complex, interpersonal activity. At any moment, things can go wrong. Therefore, teachers must monitor the entire classroom at all times. Teachers can learn about methods of dealing with stress through attending stress-prevention workshops and reading such books as the Gold and Roth (1993) book cited in the Suggested Readings. No single strategy is a more effective stress controller than planning an effective lesson.

All these steps can be taken and all can help reduce the teacher's probability of making mistakes. But even with all these precautions, teachers will still make mistakes. So in addition to developing and using a strategy to reduce mistakes, teachers should also be prepared to deal with problems when they do occur.

One strategy that is worth considering is turning the mistake into a positive experience. The following case shows how one teacher does this. As you read it, observe how this teacher manages to avoid a catastrophe and molds it into a positive learning experience.

Topics for Reflection
1. Preparing students to reflect
2. Planning reflective thinking into lessons
3. Managing mistakes

4. Planning to avoid mistakes
5. Managing stress
6. Teacher development

THE CASE

Wilson Heights was named for former president Woodrow Wilson. For awhile it was the socially fashionable suburb of a major city. Then gradually the city's downtown area grew until it absorbed Wilson Heights. Many of its early residents moved further out into newer suburbs. Parts of the area were rezoned, and the once beautiful, showcase community deteriorated into a landscape of warehouses and factories. After several decades the community was like any other urban ghetto.

The School

Wilson High is located in the middle of Wilson Heights. From any part of its campus the only outside view is rows of dilapidated tenement housing. Above the rooftops the horizon is peppered with smokestacks, most bellowing out white smoke.

Wilson High School encompasses grades 7 through 12. The two-story building is the workplace for 50 teachers and is the educational environment for about 2,000 students.

The Teacher

Jean McCarthy had enjoyed her college experience. Most of her courses had proven helpful. Even some of the courses that she doubted would ever be useful for anything had proven to be good resources during her student teaching. The student-teaching experience had been a climax of her program. She finally felt that she was being rewarded for all the studying she had done. But most of all, she enjoyed the status of being a quasi-teacher. She knew that her university still considered her a student, but out there where it really counts, in her own classroom, she was a teacher.

Throughout her student-teaching program, Jean remained receptive to criticism. In fact, she actively sought her cooperating teacher's advice. During her lunch hour and planning period, she purposefully initiated conversations with other teachers to learn their perceptions and practices. This open, investigative attitude had paid off. Her increased level of maturity during the student-teaching semester was remarkable.

Having enjoyed her student-teaching program and knowing that she had progressed well, it is no surprise that Jean looked forward to her first year as a full-time teacher. Jean was glad that she lived in a state that provided a full year of internship experience for all teachers. She entered it with the same perspective she had held toward her student teaching, seeing the coming years as an opportunity to experiment, inquire, and improve.

Jean was excited as she drove to Wilson High School for her first week of internship. She arrived in time to check with the office and be escorted to her room. The office was humming with students and teachers. The hallways were almost as noisy. Jean thought about this high energy level. Channeled in the right direction, there should be no limits on achievement.

Jean's first day was exciting. She enjoyed meeting all the students and giving them their first assignments. At 3:00 p.m. she sat and mused over each group and each period. Clearly, the day could be declared a success. But Jean was never completely satisfied. She always wanted to learn how to improve everything she did. So she made careful notes to herself of specific ways to improve her work with each class. She had learned through student teaching that all classes have their own personalities. This is what makes teaching so much fun, she thought. Each class is different, and even the same class differs from one day to the next.

During her introduction-to-education course, *Educational Foundations 200,* Jean learned that teachers develop over a period of several years, passing through some definite stages of professional growth.

Armstrong Henson & Savage (1989) describes the induction stage of professional development:

> The induction phase of a teacher's career is that period following the beginning of the first teaching position when the teacher gradually develops the confidence and competence of the professional teacher. The induction phase is a transition time. At the beginning, it is common for the teacher to still think of himself or herself as a "prospective" or "beginning" teacher. At the end, the teacher sees himself or herself as a "real" teacher . . . .
>
> The beginning of the induction stage is the start of a teacher's first year of teaching. Ryan (1986) points out that many teachers experience what he calls the "shock of the familiar" at this time. Much of what they must do bears a certain resemblance to what they experienced during student teaching. But, for the first time, they alone are responsible for the classroom. Many beginners are surprised at the sheer volume of activity required, the paperwork that must be completed, and the number of meetings that must be attended. Consequently, feelings of great stress and incredible fatigue are very common . . . .
>
> In some states, Kentucky and Oklahoma are examples, the first year of teaching is regarded as a continuation of the teacher preparation program. There are attempts to provide some continued assistance to beginning teachers to help them respond to the many challenges associated with their new roles. There may continue to be some involvement of college and university education specialists. Within some schools, support groups consisting of other new teachers have been organized. Another common plan is the designation of mentor teachers to assist newcomers. Mentor teachers are experienced professionals who are thought to be particularly sensitive to newcomers' problems as they adjust to the profession.

Jean looked forward to her second day wondering what unexpected experiences she would encounter. The day's lesson involved baking a batch of very simple cookies. All students watched attentively as she demonstrated. As this experimental batch reached a desired amber glow, Jean carefully removed them from the oven. When she set the hot pan of cookies on the butcher's block, she noticed that the bag of brown sugar that she had brought especially for this activity was unopened. Jean felt a chill of fear as she realized that she had forgotten to include perhaps the most important ingredient in any cookies—sugar. And she had planned to have the students sample them. Quickly, she wondered how to handle this situation. "After all," she thought, "I am the teacher, and the teacher shouldn't make such mistakes." She had planned a student critique of her work as each student sampled a cookie. Now they were ruined. And it was almost time to begin cleaning up in preparation for the next class. There was not enough time left in the period to bake another batch.

Immediately, Jean explained to the class what had happened. She then introduced the major concepts in the lesson, "texture" and "taste." But she altered the original intent, which was for the students to *develop the proper techniques* for attaining correct texture and taste. Now she emphasized *the importance* of texture and taste in cooking. She ended the lesson by having each student sample a cookie and describe both its texture and its taste. A good discussion was conducted as the students sampled the goods. Jean raised further questions such as, "How do you think the texture and taste would be altered if we used unrefined sugar? How would these characteristics be affected if other ingredients were omitted? What additional ingredients could be added to improve the texture? Could the texture be improved while worsening the taste, and vice-versa?" The students enjoyed the latitude provided by these open-ended, divergent-type questions. Realizing her omission, Jean chose these types of questions because they stimulate students to be creative. Each time a student hesitated or provided an incorrect response, Jean provided hints that led the student to make the correct responses.

As the lesson ended, Jean looked around to see her internship supervisor, Dr. Evans, standing in the door. She had dropped by to see how things were going. Dr. Evans greeted Jean with a pleasant smile, asked to see a copy of her lesson plans for the day, and asked for a conference during Jean's planning period.

Dr. Evans began this first conference by giving Jean a copy of the evaluation guide (Figure 1) which would be used to grade her internship experience. Jean was glad to receive this guide at the beginning of the program.

Dr. Evans began the conference with a few pleasantries, gradually guiding her comments toward the lesson she had observed and toward Jean's lesson plans.

"I noticed that you displayed a lot of flexibility in your lesson this morning, and I want to compliment you for turning a possible disaster into a successful lesson. I also noticed that your poise and self-confidence were transmitted to the students. Of course, our ultimate goal is to improve students' knowledge and skills.

"Your establishing a comfortable atmosphere that permits mistakes and capitalizes on the mistakes will contribute significantly to both of these goals."

Jean smiled as she continued to listen to this expert observer's opinions.

LESSON COMPONENTS

TEACHER BEHAVIORS

Treatment		
	1. states/defines lesson component	
	2. explains component clearly	
	3. demonstrates component	
	4. provides guided practice	
	5. provides independent practice	

TEACHER BEHAVIORS   DURING INSTRUCTION

Communication		
	1. cues students	
	2. uses emphasis	
	3. uses challenge/task attractions	
	4. uses sarcasm/negative affect	

Questioning Techniques		
	1. asks academic questions	
	2. asks multiple questions	
	3. allows call-outs	
	4. does not provide wait time	
	5. guides reciter	
	6. does not guide reciter	
	7. asks procedural questions	
	8. asks unrelated questions	

Responses		
	1. acknowledges student responses	
	2. rephrases/amplifies student responses	
	3. corrects/clarifies student responses	
	4. does not correct/clarify responses	

Praise		
	1. uses specific academic praise	
	2. uses general academic praise	
	3. uses group academic praise	

Management		
	1. uses specific conduct-related praise	
	2. stops misconduct positively	
	3. stops misconduct negatively	
	4. does not stop misconduct	
	5. manages overlapping events	

Time		
	1. minimizes management time	
	2. mismanages instructional time	

REFLECTION:

FIGURE 1 Internship Evaluation Guide

"I do want to give you two suggestions during this initial conference. Notice on the evaluation form that there is space following each lesson for reflections. I want you to write a brief paragraph about each lesson, explaining specific changes you can make to improve the lesson the next time you teach it. It is best to complete these reflections as you go. By this, I mean use your planning period each day to write the reflections on those lessons that precede the planning period, and after school is out, write your reflections for the remaining periods of the day."

Dr. Evans asked Jean if she had any questions about the reflection part of the evaluation. Hearing Jean's confident negative response, Dr. Evans continued:

"I noticed that some of the questions you asked were divergent questions. I like that because such questions encourage students to be creative. For example, "How do you think the texture and taste would have been affected by omitting other ingredients?" "What additional ingredients could be added to improve the texture?" etc. I also noticed that these questions focused on the major concepts in the lesson. This is important since it uses the time to develop those major concepts.

The next time I visit you, I would like to see you repeat this practice. Be careful to focus your questions on the major concepts in the lesson, as you did today. Now, do you have anything that you want to ask or tell me?"

Jean thanked her for her helpful suggestions and assured her that she looked forward to her next visit.

The Challenges

Sometimes the major concepts in a lesson are difficult to identify. How can Jean know which concepts are the major concepts in each lesson?

- —The lesson objectives are the best clues for identifying the major concepts in the lesson.
- —Each objective in each lesson should have one or more corresponding major concepts.
- —The major concepts are those main content generalizations that are essential to understanding the lesson.

How should "reflections" be written?
Reflections should always:

- —Be written as soon after the lesson ends as feasible.
- —Be written in terms of specifics. Specifically, what types of changes can improve this lesson?
- —Focus on the lesson's major objectives.
- —Include more effective ways to improve students.

ISSUES FOR FURTHER REFLECTION

1. Should teachers always be so honest with students?
2. Should all lessons be constructed around a few major concepts?
3. Was the teacher wrong in straying from the original lesson?
4. Is it wise to involve students during the lesson as these students were involved through testing these cookies?
5. Is inquiry learning an appropriate method for all subjects? If so, why? If not, why?
6. Should teachers attempt to involve students in every lesson?
7. What might be the results if a supervisor saw a beginning teacher using mistakes to teach?
8. Does a principal have a right to insist on seeing a teacher's lesson plan?
9. This teacher saw an opportunity to use her inquiry skills to turn a potentially disastrous lesson into a rich learning experience. Should teachers purposefully plan inquiry lessons to have students explore their subjects?
10. Teachers are frequently reminded of the need to cover all of their subject content so that their students will be prepared for the next year; yet the inquiry approach is a very inefficient and slow method. Is it realistic to think that teachers really have time to use the inquiry method?
11. What does the research say about the purpose of reflection?
12. How does reflection help teachers relate new information to old knowledge?
13. How can teachers use reflection to help students relate new information to previously learned concepts?

SUGGESTED READINGS

Armstrong, D. G., Henson, K. T., & Savage, T. V. (1989). *Education: An Introduction* (3rd ed.). New York: Macmillan.

Bonds, C. W., Bonds, L. G., & Peach, W. (1992). Metacognition: Developing independence in learning. *The Clearing House, 66*(1), 56–59.

Boschee, F. (1992). Small-group learning in the information age. *The Clearing House, 65* (2), 89–92.

Dembo, M. (1994). *Applying educational psychology in the classroom* (5th ed.). New York: Longman (see chapter 10).

Farber, B. A. (1991). *Crisis in education: Stress and burnout in the American teacher.* San Francisco: Jossey-Bass.

Glatthorn, A. A. (1990). *Supervisory leadership: Introduction to instructional supervision.* Glenview, IL.: Scott, Foresman/Little, Brown.

Gold, Y. & Roth, R. A. (1993). *Teachers managing stress and preventing burnout.* Washington, DC: Falmer.

Gold, Y. (1992). *Psychological support of mentors and beginning teachers: A critical dimension, in mentoring: Contemporary principles and issues.* Reston, VA: Association of Teacher Educators.

Good, T., & Brophy, J. (1990). *Educational psychology: A realistic approach* (4th ed.). New York: Longman (see chapter 13).

Henson, K. T. (1993). *Methods and strategies for teaching in secondary and middle schools* (2nd ed.). New York: Longman (see chapter 5).

Oliva, P. F. (1993). *Supervision for today's schools* (4th ed.). New York: Longman.

Ross, D. D., Bordy, E., & Kyle, D. W. (1993). *Reflective thinking for student empowerment.* New York: Macmillan.

Ryan, K. (1986). *The induction of new teachers.* Fastback No. 237. Bloomington, IN.: Phi Delta Kappa Education Foundation.

Sugarman, L. (1985). Kolb's model of experiential learning: Touchstone for trainers, students, counselors, and clients. *Journal of Counseling Development, 64*(4), 264–268.

Wilson, B. G. (1985). Using content structure in course design. *Journal of Educational Technology Systems, 14*(2), 137–147.

Young, D. B. (1993). Developing thinking skills: What teachers can do. *National Association of Laboratory Schools Journal, 17*(3), 32–52.

CASE **18**

Experimenting with New Teaching Methods

PREPARING TO USE THE CASE

Background Information

For at least a couple of centuries, Americans assumed that the major difference between good and poor teachers was that good teachers were born that way. But recent research findings challenge this assumption. During the past 30 years, research on teaching has grown at a rapid rate, and much of that research links good teachers with what are considered effective teaching behaviors.

Many states now have education-reform programs that require teachers to have a knowledge base to support their practices. The National Council for the Accreditation of Teacher Education (NCATE) now requires all accredited teacher education colleges to use a knowledge base to set policy and make operational decisions. The Association of Teacher Educators is currently revising its *Handbook of Research on Teaching.* Certainly teachers are now expected and required to have a knowledge base that they can comfortably discuss.

Another responsibility shared by today's teachers is the need to make lessons stimulating and inviting to *all* students. In the past, teachers have frequently explained low achievement by saying that the low achievers just don't care. This explanation no longer works. Today all teachers are being held accountable for the performance of all students on state-administered achievement tests. Nor can today's teachers blame student complacency on their ethnic or socioeconomic backgrounds. Contemporary teachers are held accountable to inspire all students, regardless of their backgrounds.

The following case concerns a student teacher who works desperately hard to motivate his students only to have his enthusiasm backfire and get him into trouble with his college supervisor.

As you read this case, think about the need today's teachers have to motivate their students and to use sound (proven) techniques. These two goals may appear mutually exclusive, but they are not. Think about how you can use the research and literature to plan lessons that will motivate the interests of your future students.

Topics for Reflection
1. Motivation strategies
2. The relationship between motivation and planning
3. Basing instruction on research and the literature
4. The role of politics in teaching
5. Student-centered instruction

THE CASE

State University evolved first from a normal school to become a teachers college with a superb K–12 laboratory school on its campus, a university where teacher education dominated the other colleges and departments with its size, prestige, and teacher-education mission. Comprehensive University has a different first mission—research. At Comprehensive University, teacher education is one of a dozen colleges, and its level of prestige does not begin to rival that of the colleges of engineering, medicine, or architecture, or the departments of mathematics, chemistry, or physics.

Getting A Student-Teaching Assignment

As an undergraduate student at Comprehensive University, David Brown had known and cared very little about the university's mission. Even as a first-year intern, his only concern was to become the best biology teacher in the state. Having grown up in a rural setting and having attended a small rural high school that had only about 200 students in seventh through twelfth grades, David was relieved to learn that the university's policy permitted interns to perform their first year of teaching in distant, rural communities. Because out-of-town placements require additional travel time for faculty members to supervise these assignments, any intern who requests such a placement is responsible for persuading a professor to volunteer to perform the supervisory responsibilities.

David thought that he should be granted permission to teach in the high school from which he graduated because that was precisely the type of school in which he hoped to secure a permanent position. In fact, he had dreams of getting a position at his old alma mater when he completed his teacher-internship program.

David was a little bewildered to learn that his advisor, who supervised all of the science teachers, did not share David's enthusiasm about choice of schools. It wasn't the school that bothered his advisor; rather, it was the fact the school was located almost 200 miles from Comprehensive University. The science advisor, Dr. Ahrens, was already having difficulty finding the time he needed to conduct research and publish the results. Under the university's new policy, failure to produce research, grants, and publications resulted in a loss of merit pay and delayed promotions. Because Dr. Ahrens was an associate professor, and some of his younger colleagues had attained full-professor status, he was becoming more sensitive to the issue.

Unaware that Dr. Ahrens was facing this embarrassing situation, David felt a degree of success when Dr. Ahrens reluctantly agreed to supervise him in David's hometown school.

The School

Asbury High School is housed in a large two-story brick building. The building predates the lunchroom which was added on several years ago. On the opposite side of the lunchroom is the old high school building which has now become the new junior high building.

Counting grades 7–12, Asbury has about 700 students and 60 faculty members. A learning resource center has films, videotapes, audiocassette tapes, and about a dozen professional journals to which the school subscribes for the teachers to use. Like most faculties, this one has a few teachers who are standing ready to implement new, innovative curricula. Unfortunately, it also has a few teachers who work hard to dodge any responsibilities. The majority of the faculty just wait until they are sure that the new innovations are going to work. They don't want to squander their energy and time only to discover later that everything has gone up in smoke.

Mr. Bob Smith who was to be David's on-site mentor was an easygoing, pleasant person who made Bob feel at ease. Now in his mid-forties, it is unlikely that Bob has ever gotten stressed out over anything. His two most common expressions are "Don't worry about it," and "It will work out fine." It was clear that Mr. Smith considered the first-year internship a growth experience. His expectations at this time were very moderate. David knew that he was fortunate to be assigned to Mr. Smith.

Getting Prepared

David's enthusiasm grew as he began thinking about and planning for his first lesson. In his methods course he had learned that a teacher's beginning sets the tone for the rest of the year. He wanted to make a good impression on his students but, even more, he wanted to provide a lesson that they would enjoy. From student teaching, he remembered that his cooperating teacher stressed the significance of developing positive rapport with all students.

They must know that you care before they care what you know.

David took this advice in balance; he believed that both knowledge and caring are important, and he wanted his lesson to show that he cared for all students and that he had the expertise required to deliver an information-packed lesson.

To make certain that he delivered such a lesson without making errors—which could happen with an unfamiliar lesson—he selected a lesson on plants. Having grown up in the country, David was familiar with most of the plants that he studied in his college biology courses. The few exceptions were plants that were not indigenous to the area. For example, Osage Orange was new to him, and he didn't know the differences among the palm trees. This is not to say that David thought he knew everything. In fact, he was fascinated to learn about many characteristics of those trees that he already had the ability to recognize.

The Student-Teaching Experience

When David arrived at his old high school, he was welcomed with open arms by the faculty, administration, and students. The school's remote location made the task of recruiting good teachers difficult. He had just arrived, and already the principal was planning a permanent slot for him on the faculty, with full expectation that following graduation, David would return to teach biology. Having a teaching intern was a new experience for the students in this school.

But no one was more excited than David. His enthusiasm was reflected in his lessons. On his first bi-weekly visit to supervise David, Dr. Ahrens saw a performance unlike anything he had witnessed in his 15 years of supervising teacher interns. The lesson topic focused on trees. David had gotten up at daybreak and gone into a wooded area to collect leaves. But what Mr. Ahrens saw was much more than a leaf collection. David had brought tree limbs–dozens of them–and the classroom looked like an arboretum.

The Lesson

Dr. Ahrens entered through the door at the back of the room and quietly sat down. As usual, he prepared to take notes and complete an assessment form, but he quickly became so surprised by David's activities that he forgot to complete the form. David was running from one part of the room to another, and then another, taking limbs and small trees with leaves and giving them to students to examine. First he had the students taste the sassafras leaves. Some comments about root beer were heard. Then David took a double handful of sweet-shrubs and crushed them. As he walked down each row of students letting every student smell them, the students "oohed" and "aahed," expressing their approval of the sweet aroma. Next David gave each student a leaf from a cherry tree. He asked them to break the leaves in half and sniff them to see who could tell him the type of tree these leaves came from. Some said that they smelled like a milkshake. Others said the smell reminded them of the chocolate-covered cherry candy that they get at Christmas. After a wisecrack guess that it was a Christmas tree, someone screamed "cherry."

Next David had some yellow roots. He asked each student to take a small hair of the root and taste it. They were as bitter as quinine. Students gasped in exaggerated disapproval of the bitter taste; some ran to the door and spat outside.

By the end of the period every student was grappling with a piece of sugarcane, twisting it and swallowing the sweet juice.

When the bell rang, the students applauded and commented about the lesson. Some said that this was the way school ought to be—fun. David was pleased that the students received the lesson so well.

Dr. Ahrens realized that he had become so engaged with observing the activities and so bewildered and upset at having seen something that didn't even resemble a lesson that he had failed to complete the rating instrument and was, therefore, unprepared for the assessment conference that was to follow. Nevertheless, he felt that he must give David some badly needed feedback, however general. He would spare no words for this young maverick.

Dr. Ahrens's first step toward resolving this perceived disaster was to meet with Mr. Bob Smith, David's mentor teacher. After sharing a few brief pleasantries, he fired the following questions at Mr. Smith.

"What do you think about this lesson?"

"The kids were really excited over it."

"Would you say that this was typical of David's lessons?"

"Yes, he always gets the students fired up."

"Do you think the lesson was well structured, well planned?"

"He obviously kept things moving at a good pace, and he didn't run out of material," Bob Smith answered.

"Does David usually give you a well-prepared lesson plan when he teaches?"

"David has the type of personality that enables him to move through the lesson well without a written plan. I think lesson plans are good if you need them, but they can handicap a natural teacher. David knows that as long as his lessons work, I really don't insist on seeing a written lesson plan," Bob Smith stated.

From this brief conversation Dr. Ahrens concluded that he would get little help from this lackadaisical teacher. In fact, he assumed that Mr. Smith was influencing David negatively by providing a loose, unstructured role model. Clearly, it was time to talk to David.

Dr. Ahrens began the session by asking David what he thought he was doing. He continued, "I drove 200 miles to watch you teach, and instead you provided a circus. My job is to help you raise the achievement scores in this class. From our pre–student-teaching seminar you learned that effective teachers give clear goals, hold high expectations, use direct instruction, and closely supervise all assignments. Instead of following this instructional model, you arranged for a disorganized, student-centered picnic, complete with refreshments. I am very disappointed. I will have to record these activities and place the report in your permanent records."

David was shocked. What could he do to salvage his student-teaching grade and his teaching career?

The Challenge

Put yourself in David's place. What would you do?

ISSUES FOR FURTHER REFLECTION

1. Is engaging students in activities such as sniffing leaves and eating sugarcane professional behavior?

2. What are some potential liabilities of providing such activities?

3. List some advantages of providing such student activities.

4. Can a teacher be too enthusiastic? Explain.

5. Is there evidence suggesting that David's selection of the school for his internship contributed to his problems? If so, how?

6. When teachers break away from the everyday routine way of teaching, such as changing the location of the class (field trips) or changing to different teaching methods, what types of precautions can they take to minimize the possible criticism?

7. In general, does increased teacher freedom imply increased teacher responsibilities? Explain.

8. What can teachers do to assure that students learn from experiential lessons?

9. Examine the following steps given in Porter and Brophy's model for effective teachers, and identify any steps that David omitted. According to Porter and Brophy (1988), effective teachers:

   a. Are clear about their instructional goals.

   b. Are knowledgeable about their content and the strategies for teaching it.

   c. Communicate to their students what is expected of them—and why.

   d. Make expert use of existing instructional materials in order to devote more time to practices that enrich and clarify the content.

   e. Are knowledgeable about their students, adapting instruction to their needs and anticipating misconceptions in their existing knowledge.

   f. Teach students metacognitive strategies and give them opportunities to master them.

   g. Address higher- as well as lower-level cognitive objectives.

   h. Monitor students' understanding by offering regular appropriate feedback.

   i. Integrate their instruction with that in other subject areas.

   j. Accept responsibility for student outcomes.

   k. Are thoughtful and reflective about their practice.

10. Exactly what, if anything, was wrong with the delivery of this lesson?

11. What kinds of positive messages did this lesson send to the students?

12. What kinds of negative messages did this lesson send to the students?

13. What evidence is there that students learn more when actually involved?

14. How would you describe the pace of this lesson. Was it too fast? Too slow?

15. What can you say about the goals for this lesson?

SUGGESTED READINGS

Armstrong, D. G., Henson, K. T., & Savage, T. V. (1993). *Education: An introduction* (4th ed.). New York: Macmillan (see chapter 11).

Berliner, D. C. (1989). Effective schools: Teachers make the difference. *Instructor, 99*(3), 14–15.

Cooper, H. (1990). Synthesis of research on homework. *Educational Leadership, 47*(3), 85–91.

Cooper, H. (1989). *Homework.* White Plains, NY: Longman.

Curry, L. (1990). A critique of research on learning styles. *Educational Leadership, 48*(2), 50–52, 54–56.

Dembo, M. (1994). *Applying educational psychology in the classroom* (5th ed.). New York: Longman (see chapter 9).

Good, T., & Brophy, J. (1990). *Educational psychology: A realistic approach* (4th ed.). New York: Longman (see chapter 12).

Henson, K. T. (1993). *Methods and strategies for teaching in secondary and middle schools* (2nd ed.). New York: Longman (see chapters 5, 6).

King, A. (1990). Reciprocal questioning: A strategy for teaching students how to learn from lectures. *The Clearing House, 64*(2), 131–135.

Lee, J., & Pruitt, J. W. (1978). Homework assignments: Classroom games or teaching tools? *Clearing House, 53*(1), 31–35.

MacDonald, R. (1991). Tutoring: An effective teaching tool. *Kappan Delta Pi Record, 28*(1), 25–28.

Manning, M. L., & Lucking, R. (1991). The what, why, and how of cooperative learning. *The Clearing House, 64*(3), 152–156.

Ramsey, I., Gabbard, C., Clawson, K., Lee, L., & Henson, K. T. (1990). Questioning: An effective teaching method. *The Clearing House, 63*(9), 420–422.

Snapp, J. C., & Glover, J. A. (1990). Advance organizers and study questions. *The Journal of Educational Research, 8*(5), 266–271.

Solomon, S. (1989). Homework: The great enforcer. *Clearing House, 63*(2), 64–66.

CASE 19

Teach to Please

PREPARING TO USE THE CASE

Background Information

A variety of instructional strategies are at the disposal of teachers. Strategies range from the more conventional lecture and discussion at one end of a continuum to more recently developed interactive, multimedia computer technology. Other points on the continuum include such strategies as cooperative learning, collaborative learning, case studies, discovery learning, simulations, games, and tutoring.

No one teaching strategy has been found to be effective in every instance to meet a desired goal. For example, a one-on-one tutorial situation where a teacher imparts specific information to the student, and the student has an immediate opportunity to demonstrate a level of achievement, followed by an evaluation of performance, offers the most personal, direct, and speediest way to measure a student's recall of knowledge. However, the use of interactive multimedia may be the most efficient and effective way to accomplish this goal, where the nonverbal cues of the teacher or other human factors may inhibit the student's desire to learn.

The most important point here is that the choice of an instructional strategy depends on a number of variables, including: the subject being taught, the organization of the material to be used, the level of learning to be accomplished, the readiness of the student to learn material being assigned, the availability of technology to deliver instruction, and the skill of the teacher to employ a particular strategy. The most important factor is the ability of the teacher in deciding on the most appropriate instructional strategy and the teacher's level of sophistication in employing the strategy.

Making decisions about instructional strategies and employing them effectively is a complex task. Not only is an awareness of all the available instructional possibilities a necessity, but it is also vital to understand the conditions in which particular strategies have been effective. In addition, recurring success with particular strategies—experience—plays a critical role in making decisions about instructional strategies. Most important may be the disposition that teachers have toward particular strategies. Simply, the strategies teachers enjoy and that are most related to their personality may be the ones they tend to use most often and most effectively.

In this case an art teacher takes a job in an alternative school where a variety of teaching strategies is encouraged. At the same time, students are expected to openly share their own wishes in regard to conditions for learning that they prize. A conflict ensues between how the art teacher wants instruction organized and how the students want it organized. Finding a suitable resolution to the conflict is the challenge.

Topics for Reflection
1. Cognitive development
2. Instructional planning
3. Instructional strategies
4. Motivation
5. Problem solving
6. Teacher interventions
7. Teacher values and beliefs

THE CASE

The School

The Westside Alternative School in Lake City is an oasis for students identified as potential dropouts or "pushouts." It is a place where students can vote on important issues during a weekly "Town Meeting." Students design many of their learning activities, and they can pursue independent study on almost any topic. When students' performance is evaluated, it is done through oral and written feedback. No letter grades are given. Everyone is on a first-name basis, even the principal, Nate Evans. Dress is relaxed. Most teachers and students wear jeans, T-shirts, sweatshirts, and casual footwear.

Decision making is shared widely. The curriculum of the school reflects the input of students and their parents. On occasion, students teach classes. Two National Merit semifinalists, who had studied for a summer in Russia, were assigned to teach an elective class on Russian novels. A variety of independent-study projects is available to students, taking advantage of the resources of the city. For example, one student spent two hours daily at WGN, a local talk-radio station. Another volunteered as a copy editor for a national magazine, whose main office was located six blocks from the school. Other students had completed projects in museums, art galleries, theaters, businesses, and government and social agencies.

Perhaps no decision illustrated the level of shared decision making more than the planning of commencement. Nate had empowered seniors to decide whether or not they even wanted to have a commencement. Only once in the school's history had there not been one. Where commencement was held and how it was organized were decisions that had become a tradition for seniors.

The most notable commencement was held in a major league baseball park. Parents and relatives sat in the box seats down on the first and third base lines. Nate stood on the pitcher's mound, next to a box containing diplomas. As each senior ran around the bases, Nate walked from the mound to home plate to greet him with a diploma. The owner of the park provided an organist and fireworks. The students had made all of the arrangements.

Nate started the school 17 years ago. He had been given this opportunity after a group of parents had petitioned the school board to offer an alternative program for students "turned off" by the traditional school experience. Given the success of this small, public school of 300 secondary students, the school was mandated by the board of education to remain at or below that number. Nate and his staff had become empowered to select teachers to replace anyone who left. An interview team was organized, composed of students, teachers, and parents. New teachers could be hired by majority vote. The hiring process was viewed as essential to maintaining a staff with similar interests and philosophies.

The Teacher

Kurt Kendrick had been somewhat intimidated by the interview process. He had been surprised by the thoroughness of the questions. Even more surprising was the fact that students and parents were involved. Having to teach a class while the interview team observed had tested his nerves. Yet he was ecstatic when he learned he had been hired. He felt he had been welcomed into a new family. There was a feeling of warmth, enthusiasm, and joy he had not sensed in other interviews he had had. He looked forward to teaching art at Westside.

"What we like most about you," Nate Evans told him, "is the fact you appear comfortable with teaching—relaxed, open, and caring."

Kurt felt lucky to land a job at Westside. There were five other alternative schools in Lake City, but none had the history or reputation of Westside. Located in a low-socioeconomic neighborhood near the industrial hub of this large, urban city in the Southwest, the school was housed in an abandoned warehouse constructed in the early 1920s. The building was filled with discarded furniture—overstuffed chairs, couches, tables, and assorted smaller pieces of every shape and size. This array of accumulated mismatched furniture resulted largely because students were permitted to bring their own desks and chairs to the school. Walls were filled with graffiti. These "extended chalkboards" reflected the changing moods of the school's inhabitants.

There is no newspaper or yearbook at Westside. "There's no reason for one," Nate claimed. "Students have free expression here, so they don't need another outlet."

Westside appealed to Kurt for several reasons. He was a maverick himself. He had studied violin for 13 years, and everyone in his family had expected him to become a professional musician or at least a music teacher. After his second concert, held the year before he enrolled at Central University, he had decided he did not want to do what others expected him to do.

Between his junior and senior year at Central he took a year off and worked his way through South America, moving from place to place as earnings permitted. This move had shocked his family as much as the earlier one. Upon Kurt's graduation, his father, a wealthy businessman in the East, had "reserved" a teaching and coaching position at a private academy in his hometown. Again, Kurt disappointed his family by not only moving 2,100 miles away but also by accepting a teaching position in a school which his father considered a "dilapidated jailhouse for juvenile delinquents."

Early during his first semester at Westside, Kurt discovered he was not as prepared for the free and unstructured environment as he thought. He had planned carefully for his art classes. Before school began he had borrowed a truck from a friend and collected scrap lumber, discarded metal, rubber tires, railroad ties, cardboard boxes, and plastic, and had purchased paints and oils he found on sale. A massive storage area in the school building had been converted into an art area. Large tubs, hot and cold water, and extensive cabinet space made the area nearly ideal.

On the first day of school his students were stunned to find no chairs in the art area, except a few surrounding a large work bench. Kurt greeted them saying, "I've put away the furniture, for now."

"Where are the chairs?" one student asked.

"I've put them up, temporarily," Kurt replied. "We can't have them in the area, while you renovate."

"Renovate?" another student asked. "Who is going to renovate this place?"

"You are," Kurt said. "And your friends."

"Right," another student said. "You're going to let us paint this place?"

"Seriously," Kurt said. "This is your art area. Make it what you want."

"Can we paint the ceiling, too?" a student asked.

"Sure, I don't see why you can't," Kurt encouraged. "But you'll have to bring the paint, brushes, and other supplies."

The remainder of the period he brainstormed with the students on different art concepts, history, and artists that they might study. During the last few minutes of the class, he allowed the students to talk more about "renovating" the art area.

He organized each class period around a specific timetable. For the first five minutes he reviewed what had been accomplished the preceding day. For the next five to ten minutes he lectured or "previewed" theories or principles underlying an art activity the students were expected to accomplish. On the first day of the week and on the last day of the week he tried to find a film, filmstrip, or other visual aid to illustrate the kind of product he wanted to inspire the students to create.

He repeated the same offer to students in the other art classes that day. For the remainder of the week, he helped students bring chairs to class. With two students from each class elected as a 12-member "planning committee" to organize the painting of the art area, he spent more than an hour each night overseeing the planning. By the end of the week, nearly every student had brought a chair of choice to the class. Plans were set for painting the area on Friday night and all day Saturday, so that by Monday of the second week the paint would be dry.

Plans for painting went smoothly. Students who had said they would bring supplies did so. Those who had indicated they would work at specific time periods on Friday night and Saturday during the day appeared on schedule and worked hard. By late Saturday night, the art area was ablaze with fluorescent colors reflecting the heroes, dreams, and images of his students.

On Monday, at the beginning of each period, Kurt thanked the students for their commitment to the painting project. He told them how proud he was of their effort. And he said, "I trust you will put the same kind of effort into the study of art the rest of this semester."

The Incident

Each day toward the end of the period before students put away their work, Kurt organized a brief discussion around a couple of students' efforts. Such "evaluation sessions," as he thought of them, were intended to build high expectations, cooperation, and creative thinking. While he used a variety of instructional methods, including demonstrations of his own work (he never asked students to do anything he would not do also), the routine was fixed.

He sailed smoothly through the first two weeks. It was during the third week that what seemed to be a well-oiled machine began to sputter. It started when Alicia Marsh approached him after his Wednesday morning, first-period class.

"Mr. Kendrick, may I talk to you?" she asked.

"Mr. Kendrick? Why don't you call me Kurt," he asked.

"You remember, I did, the first few days," Alicia said. "I just don't feel comfortable anymore."

"I don't understand," he said. "Have I done something to make you feel this way?"

"I just need to talk," she pleaded.

"Sure, but we'll need to hurry. I have another class coming in," he responded. "What is it?"

"Well, I don't know how to say this," she hesitated. "I like your class. You're a good teacher. And the other students in your classes like you too. But several of us are afraid things aren't going to work out."

"Why?" Kurt said with a look of surprise.

"Your classes are becoming monotonous," she said.

"I admit I'm organized, but I try to vary what we do," he responded. "And I allow students to choose the kinds of art projects they do."

"Maybe you're too organized. Give us some slack," she remarked.

The students in his next period class began to enter.

"Alicia, why don't you get some of the other students together after school today so we can talk about this. Is that possible?" Kurt said with concern.

"Sure," Alicia said. "Here in your room? 3:30?"

"Yes, that will be fine. See you later," Kurt responded.

After school, a dozen students came to Mr. Kendrick's room. Three of them were sophomores, two were juniors, and the rest were seniors. For 45 minutes they discussed their concerns about his teaching. Most of the students' comments focused on two points. One was that Mr. Kendrick seemed more rigid as a teacher than he had during the interview process. The second focused on the students' preferred approaches to being taught.

Some of the students said they needed to be left alone for longer periods of time to work on their projects. A few of the students indicated they wanted to work in pairs or teams. Other students suggested that he provide a variety of ways for students to learn in class. As one student said: "We want to choose what we study. That's why we came to Westside. Let us decide. All the other teachers do."

The Challenge

What should Mr. Kendrick do?

ISSUES FOR FURTHER REFLECTION

1. What are the responsibilities of the teacher for planning instruction?
2. How much freedom should students be given to make decisions about what is to be taught? About how it is taught?
3. Did Mr. Kendrick make a mistake by giving students too much freedom in the beginning, then placing more control on them during the second week? Explain.
4. To what extent might Mr. Kendrick's desire to have his students like him have affected the reaction of Alicia Marsh and other students he met who complained about his teaching?
5. Was the decision to meet with students to discuss their concerns about his teaching a good one? Defend your answer.
6. Are there times when teachers should not meet with students to openly discuss concerns they may have about their teaching?
7. How serious a problem do you believe Mr. Kendrick has? Explain your answer.
8. Does Mr. Kendrick have a responsibility to alter his instructional approaches based on students' concerns? Explain your answer.
9. What are possible positive outcomes from altering his instructional approaches?
10. What are possible negative outcomes?
11. Should Mr. Kendrick seek advice from someone else in the school? If so, who? And what kinds of advice should he seek? If he should not, why not?

SUGGESTED READINGS

Curtis, R. (1992). Taking AIM: Approaches to instructional motivation. *School Library Media Activities Monthly, 8*(8), 32–34.

Dembo, M. (1994). *Applying educational psychology in the classroom* (5th ed.). New York: Longman (see chapters 6, 7, 8, 9, 10).

Ellingson, S. (1991). A comparison of two approaches to preparing preservice teachers to manage classrooms. *Studies in Art Education, 33*(1), 7–20.

Good, T., & Brophy, J. (1990). *Educational psychology: A realistic approach* (4th ed.). New York: Longman (see chapters 12, 13, 19, 20).

Guskey, T., & Gates, S. (1986). Synthesis of research on the effects of mastery learning in elementary and secondary classrooms. *Educational Leadership, 43*(8), 73–80.

Hamblen, K., & Galenes, C. (1991). Instructional options for aesthetics: Exploring the possibilities. *Art Education, 44*(6), 12–24.

Henson, K. (1993). *Methods and strategies for teaching in secondary and middle schools* (2nd ed.). New York: Longman (see chapters 5, 7, 9).

Kane, P. (1987). Public or independent schools: Does where you teach make a difference? *Phi Delta Kappan, 69*(4), 286–289.

Kember, D., & Murphy, D. (1990). Alternative new directions for instructional design. *Educational Technology, 30*(8), 42–47.

Meier, D. (1987). Central Park East: An alternative story. *Phi Delta Kappan, 68*(10), 753–757.

Nathan, J. (1987). Results and future prospects of state efforts to increase choice among schools. *Phi Delta Kappan, 68*(10), 746–752.

Ornstein, A. (1993). How to recognize good teaching. *American School Board Journal, 180*(1), 24–27.

Rosenshine, B. (1986). Synthesis of research on explicit teaching. *Educational Leadership, 43*(7), 60–69.

Snelbecker, G. (1988). Instructional design skills for classroom teachers. *Journal of Instructional Development, 10*(4), 33–40.

Todd, R. (1990). The teaching and learning environment. *Technology Teacher, 50*(3), 3–7.

Van Horn, R. (1991). Educational power tools: New instructional delivery systems. *Phi Delta Kappan, 72*(7), 527–533.

No More Homework

PREPARING TO USE THE CASE

Background Information

Throughout the history of our schools certain beliefs about how teachers cause success to occur in their classrooms have endured. For example, most people believe that the teacher is a powerful determiner of whether or not students in their classrooms will succeed. But if you ask teachers, they will tell you that those students who do really well will succeed either with the help of good teachers or in spite of poor teachers. After almost three centuries of experiences with this issue, educators finally know that the research-based truth to this question is that indeed teachers are powerful determiners of student success.

But some of the beliefs that we have held for years about teaching and learning are wrong. For example, we are learning that competition among classmates is a far less important factor for motivating students than we once believed. Another hard dying "myth" that we hold about education is the role that homework plays in achievement. For example, for decades, we have commonly thought that "the more homework the better." But recent research has shown that this is not true, at least not for all classes.

As you prepare to enter the profession and move to a school, remember that wherever you go, you will not work alone. The days when teachers were isolated in their classrooms all day long every day have disappeared. You will be part of a school community and part of the community at large. In both of these communities you will find people who have powerful influences on what happens in your school. Some of these individuals will be people who harbor many false beliefs about what constitutes good teaching.

You will want to learn all you can about such important issues as planning, testing, using homework, and yes, even politics, especially the politics of working well with others. The following case concerns a teacher who is confronted with individuals who have not kept up with the research in education and who hold some outdated beliefs that affect the teachers at this school. As you read this case, think about the following issues:

Topics for Reflection
1. What the research is discovering about the effect of homework on achievement
2. The politics of working with individuals who hold onto myths
3. Ways of keeping informed on educational research
4. How grade level and age level affect the role that homework should play
5. Legitimate goals and illegitimate goals for using homework
6. Experiential education
7. How teachers deal with conflicting research findings

THE CASE

Capitol City is itself a fake name, but the city that it represents is real. In fact, it is one of our nation's oldest state capitals. Like many other state capitals, Capitol City is the home of a major university that has a well-known and well-respected college of education.

The School

During the 1970s the growth in population necessitated the building of a new high school. The enrollment of Capitol High School had reached well over 3,000, causing many problems. It had become clear that the once obvious answer to the problem (adding temporary classrooms) was no longer a viable option. Temporary classrooms had been tacked onto the existing structure until the entire physical plant looked like a patchwork quilt. Expressed diplomatically, Capitol High had lost much of its original charm. Put bluntly, Capitol High had become ugly.

Continuous increases in enrollment at Capitol High have caused emergency expansion that has resulted in dysfunctional physical facilities. Some departments are located on three different levels of the sprawling three-story building. Some of the newer types of programs have never found a central location for their departments.

Obviously, a new high school was the only sensible long-term option. The school board finally acted. Bonds were drafted and plans were soon underway to build a new high school that would rival Capitol High in size. But the new Capitol High East would be different; it would be carefully planned. Each department would be housed in its own building, strategically located according to the nature of the department.

The American Studies Program

Ironically, the teachers of history and American government were very concerned about moving into the new facilities. To these teachers a new building in a new location meant a loss in cultural heritage—a thread that runs deep throughout their courses. The teachers shared their concern with the chair of the secondary education department at the local university. Dr. Higgins, a social studies methods teacher and an expert in experiential education, has been on the local university faculty for the past 20 years. He has taught most of Capitol High's social studies teachers. As a former director of student teaching, Dr. Higgins has worked closely with Capitol High. When some of the Capitol High social studies teachers came to him for help, he rallied his own faculty to their cause, and began holding planning meetings. The results were an experience-based (experiential) American Studies program. Like all experiential programs, this program was loaded with meaningful hands-on student activities. All concepts and objectives were clearly identified, and each one had an activity that made its attainment easy. An old two-story, nineteenth-century jail was acquired to house the American Studies program. The building had been sitting vacant, inhabited only by the legendary ghost of a prisoner who had hanged himself from a large hook that still remained in one of the second-story rooms near the head of the stairs. A large, open area on the second floor has been turned into a replica of a nineteenth-century courtroom, where mock elections are held and mock court cases are tried. A large glassed-in case near the base of the stairs displays artifacts that students have taken from archaeological digs. During the city and county elections, students participate in planning and conducting elections, and after each election they continue helping by cleaning up the city, removing campaign posters and other postelection debris. Each year's program culminates with a trip to Washington, D.C., financed by donations from local businesses. In addition to a visit to the White House, this field trip provides students with opportunities to dine in some fine restaurants, which are chosen to represent the countries and cultures studied during this particular semester.

For over two decades, the experiential program has been offered to students on an optional basis. Ever since its inception, there has always been a list of applicants waiting to be admitted to the program.

The School Administration

Having been the principal of Capitol High for the past 25 years, Dr. Russel Wade feels a close identity with the program. His pride in the program and his perception of it as his program are no secrets. Last year was Dr. Wade's final year. His retirement speech focused on the American Studies program. He spoke about the success of the program and the national attention it had received in professional journals and textbooks. Dr. Wade's pride in the program was understandable: He had given it 20 years of solid support.

Last year after Dr. Wade was replaced as principal of Capitol High by Dr. Bob Gibson, several problems began to emerge. Randy Harper, a first-year social studies teacher, found himself in the middle of the worst of these problems. How or when he became so mixed up in the situation was a mystery to him. In late spring of last year when he interviewed for his current teaching position, the former principal promised him a free hand to experiment with new methods. Now, a year later, as he ponders his dilemma, Randy remembers his first few months at Capitol High. He was a graduate of the local university's department of secondary education, had taken an experiential secondary sophomore block (a six-credit-hour course taught by Dr. Higgins), and had been placed in the American Studies program for his pre–student-teaching field-experience assignment. Thus Randy was familiar with the program and was elated to have an opportunity to become a permanent Capitol High American Studies faculty member.

During those first weeks, Dr. Gibson attended a few of Randy's classes. Randy felt good about the visits because he interpreted them as evidence of Dr. Gibson's interest in the program. Soon it became obvious that Dr. Gibson's reason for visiting the program was to evaluate the program's effectiveness.

The Incident

Last Monday Dr. Gibson was visiting when Randy introduced a new six-week unit titled "The History of the American Studies Program." Randy began the instruction by telling the students that this unit would be completely experientially based. Students were to form investigative committees and interview people in the school and in the community to develop a history of the program. Some unique aspects of this unit included no reading assignments, no homework, and no written evaluations. Students would use tape recorders to gather the information. They would then make videotapes to transmit this information to Randy and to their classmates. The videotape presentations would be discussed by the entire class. Randy explained that this was an experimental approach. If it proved successful, he might pattern the rest of the year's units on this approach.

The next morning, Randy was summoned to Dr. Gibson's office, where he was chastised for his unorthodox approach. First, Dr. Gibson explained, "The other students will question the inequality of excusing entire classes of students from all homework assignments for an entire six-week period." Second, Dr. Gibson thought the plan was a bad idea because he is held accountable for the number of students who do poorly on the state competency exams. Third, the parents would question the absence of written assignments and homework, and especially the absence of written exams. And he noted that the school district suggests nightly homework assignments and requires a minimum of two exams during each six-week period.

Dr. Gibson explained, "You social studies teachers, of all people, should know that this country has become a major force because of competition. By basing grades on group projects and by replacing objective exams with presentations, you remove the competition and thereby destroy the students' motivation to succeed.''

Randy left Dr. Gibson's office feeling confused, embarrassed, and even a little angry. He was sure that he had read that there was little or no evidence that homework increases student achievement. He felt that this quandary had to be resolved. One way or the other, he needed to know whether homework affects cognitive gains and, if so, just what effect it has on achievement.

Randy's first step in resolving his dilemma was to go home and search through his class notes. When he found nothing there that showed the effects of homework on learning, he scanned his old textbooks. Bingo! There it was in an old text titled *Handbook on Formative and Summative Evaluation of Student Learning* by Bloom, Hastings, and Madaus (1971). This was the evidence Randy needed to show that his decision to dispense with the homework was a sound decision. Surely Dr. Gibson would understand when he saw this report on the effect of homework on achievement. Randy phoned a fellow teacher, Ms. Thames, to get her advice on how he should approach Dr. Gibson. After all, Ms. Thames had known Dr. Gibson for over a decade and had worked with him at another school. More importantly, Ms. Thames was a person of tact and diplomacy.

Randy was a little surprised at the level of support that Ms. Thames gave to his plans to confront Dr. Gibson.

"That's exactly what I think you should do. We are being encouraged to use the knowledge base to support our selection of content and methodology, and that's what you are doing. I think that later you would be disappointed in yourself if you didn't share this information with Dr. Gibson."

In concluding the discussion, Ms. Thames added:

"Since the research you are reporting is a little old, before seeing Dr. Gibson I think I would review the more recent research and see whether the results are the same."

The next Saturday, Randy drove over to visit the local university library where he ran a computer search on the topic, "Homework." Following is a summary of his discoveries.

In an article by Solomon (1989), Randy found these statements:

The purpose of homework is to prepare the student for his/her next lesson and/or reinforce concepts and skills learned in the previous lesson. (p. 63)

Teachers should encourage parents to: (1) set a definite time for study each day with a beginning and ending time and no interruptions; (2) provide the proper environment; (3) provide the materials needed, (4) require the student to organize school materials including books, notes, assignments, and papers; (5) require a daily list of homework assignments; and (6) provide support and guidance if the child becomes discouraged or frustrated. (p. 63)

Randy was becoming a little confused. If homework doesn't affect academic achievement, then why is this writer recommending more structured homework assignments? He continued scanning the article and to his surprise, there it was, a direct statement about the effect of homework on achievement.

A search of the literature proves that homework, assigned by a mentor for practice, participation, preparation, personal development, reinforcement, or as an extension of class study, will increase individual achievement. (p. 63)

What a contrast this report was compared to the studies presented in Randy's class. Randy continued his computer search. Next, he found an article by Cooper (1990) who had researched the effect of homework on achievement across grade levels. Cooper reported the following conclusions:

Homework has a positive effect on achievement, but the effect varies dramatically with grade level. For high school students, homework has substantial positive effects. Junior high school students also benefit from homework, but only about half as much. For elementary school students, the effect of homework on achievement is negligible.

The optimal amount of homework also varies with grade level. For elementary students, no amount of homework—large or small—affects achievement. For junior high students, achievement continues to improve with more homework until assignments last between one and two hours a night. For high school students, the more homework, the better the achievement—within reason, of course.

Cooper continued:

I found no clear pattern indicating that homework is more effective in some subjects than in others. I did conclude, however, that homework probably works best when the material is not too complex or completely unfamiliar. Studies comparing alternative feedback strategies revealed no clearly superior approach. (p. 88)

Randy found one additional article about homework that he thought worthy of recording. Although it was old and it did not directly address the effect of homework on achievement, it did give him some ideas for using homework in his classes. The article by Lee and Pruitt (1978) listed the following uses of homework:

1. Practice—designed to reinforce skills and information covered in class.
2. Preparation—given to prepare students to profit from subsequent lessons.
3. Extension—provided to determine whether a particular student can extend the concept of a skill learned in class to a new situation.
4. Creative—designed to require students to integrate many skills and concepts in producing some project. (p. 31)

This new information caused Randy to reconsider his planned visit to see Dr. Gibson. He wondered if Dr. Gibson might already be familiar with studies that support the use of homework to increase achievement. With all the recent pressure the school had been receiving to raise its students' achievement scores, Randy understood Dr. Gibson's concern for continuing homework assignments at Capitol High.

The Challenge

You are Randy Harper. How will you respond?

ISSUES FOR FURTHER REFLECTION

1. This is Dr. Gibson's first year at Capitol High. How might this affect his attitude toward the American Studies program?
2. This is Randy Harper's first year of teaching. How should this affect his reaction to Dr. Gibson's reprimand?
3. The American Studies program has over two decades of successful operation. Should this alone earn Randy the benefit of the doubt?
4. Randy's unit reflects the experiential "hands-on" quality that is basic to the American Studies program, and experiential education is a nationally acclaimed approach to teaching. Should this earn any credibility for this program?
5. The previous principal, Dr. Russel Wade, had perceived the American Studies program as his "pride and joy." What does this indicate relative to a teacher's need to understand the current principal's philosophy?
6. Through his secondary methods courses and pre–student-teaching field assignment, Randy has had previous experience with the American Studies program. He has chosen to further develop his expertise in experiential education by teaching in such a program. How far should a teacher go to defend teaching strategies?
7. During his previous visits to Randy's classes, Dr. Gibson gave no indication of his displeasure with Randy's teaching. Should Randy remind Dr. Gibson of this fact?
8. Can you think of ways to earn the administration's support of new programs and new teaching strategies?
9. How should teachers respond to conflicting research?
10. Can you think of other unproven assumptions that Americans hold about teaching, which may be wrong?

11. What is the teacher's role in teaching inquiry, and should teachers model inquiry?

12. What is the relationship between hands-on curricula and research-based curricula?

13. What does the research say about the effects of homework on the age groups that you plan to teach?

14. What are some legitimate uses of homework? What are some illegitimate uses?

15. What guidelines do we have for determining the types of activities we assign for homework? For example: hands-on activities versus reading assignments.

SUGGESTED READINGS

Armstrong, D. G., Henson, K. T., & Savage, T. V. (1993). *Education: An introduction* (4th ed.). New York: Macmillan (see chapter 11).

Bellon, C. B., Bellon, J. J., & Blank, M. A. (1986). *What really works: Research-based instruction.* Knoxville, TN: Bellon and Associates.

Berliner, D. C. (1991). Creating the right environment for learning. *Instructor, 99*(5), 16–17.

Berliner, D. C. (1989). Effective schools: Teachers make the difference. *Instructor, 99*(3), 14–15.

Bloom, B. Hastings, J. & Madaus, G. (1971). *Handbook on formative and summative evaluating on student learning.* New York: McGraw–Hill.

Bracey, G. W. (1991). Teachers as researchers. *Phi Delta Kappan, 72*(5), 115–117.

Brown, D. S. (1990). Middle level teachers' perceptions of active research. *Middle School Journal, 22*(2), 30–32.

Buckner, J. H., & Bickel, F. (1991). If you want to know about effective teaching, why not ask your middle school kids? *Middle School Journal, 22*(3), 26–29.

Bugler, K., & Fraser, B. (1990). *Window into science classrooms: Problems with higher-level cognitive thinking.* New York: Falmer.

Cooper, H. (1990). Synthesis of research on homework. *Educational Leadership, 47*(3), 85–91.

Cooper, L. R. (1991). Teachers as researchers. *Kappa Delta Pi Record, 27*(4), 115–117.

Cornett, C. E. (1986). *Learning through laughter: Humor in the classroom* (Phi Delta Kappa Fastback. No. 241.). Bloomington, IN: Phi Delta Kappa, International.

Curry, L. (1990). A critique of research on learning styles. *Educational Leadership, 48*(2), 50–52, 54–56.

Davies, D. (1991). Schools reaching out: Family, school, and community partnerships for student success. *Phi Delta Kappan, 72*(5), 376–382.

Dembo, M. (1994). *Applying educational psychology in the classroom* (5th ed.). New York: Longman (see chapter 9).

Discussion. (1985). What's the funniest thing that's happened in your class this year. *English Journal, 74*(8), 43–36.

Edwards, R. A., & Jones Young, L. S. (1992). Beyond parents, family, and school involvement. *Phi Delta Kappan, 74*(1), 72–81.

Good, T., & Brophy, J. (1990). *Educational psychology: A realistic approach* (4th ed.). New York: Longman (see chapter 12).

Harrison, C. J. (1990). Concepts, operational definitions, and case studies in instruction. *Education, 110*(4), 502–505.

Henson, K. T. (1986). Inquiry learning: A new look. *Contemporary Education, 62*(4), 181–183.

Henson, K. T. (1993). *Methods and strategies for teaching in secondary and middle schools* (2nd ed.). New York: Longman (see chapters 5, 6).

Hittleman, D. R., & Simon, A. J. (1992). *Interpreting educational research: An introduction for consumers of research.* New York: Merrill.

Joyce, B., Weil, M., & Showers, B. (1992). *Models of teaching* (4th ed.). Needham Heights, MA: Allyn and Bacon.

Kagan, S. (1989–1990). The structural approach to cooperative learning. *Educational Leadership, 47*(4), 12–15.

Katz, L. G., & McClellan, D. (1991). *The teacher's role in social development.* Urbana, IL: ERIC Clearinghouse on Elementary and Early Childhood Education.

King, A. (1990). Reciprocal questioning: A strategy for teaching students how to learn from lectures. *The Clearing House, 64*(2), 131–135.

Knapp, M. S., & Shields, P. M. (Eds.) (1991). *Better schooling for the children of poverty: Alternatives to conventional wisdom.* Berkeley, CA: McCutchan.

Kohn, A. (1991). Caring kids: The role of the schools. *Phi Delta Kappan, 72*(7), 496–506.

Lee, J., & Pruitt, K. W. (1978). Homework assignments: Classroom games or teaching tools? *The Clearing House, 53*(1), 31–35.

Otten, N. (1986). Punchlines as paradigms. *English Journals, 75*(4), 51–53.

Phelps, P. H. (1990). Helping teachers excel as classroom managers. *The Clearing House, 64*(3), 241–242.

Ramsey, I., Gabbard, C., Clawson, K., Lee, L., & Henson, K. T. (1990). Questioning: An effective teaching method. *The Clearing House, 63*(9), 420–422.

Schaps, E. & Solomon, D. (1990). Schools and classrooms as caring communities. *Educational Leadership, 48*(3), 38–40.

Schomoker, M. (1990). Sentimentalizing self-esteem. *The Education Digest, 60*(7), 55–56.

Schunk, D. H., & Meece, J. L. (Eds.). (1992). *Student perceptions in the classrooms.* Hillsdale, NJ: Erlbaum.

Slesnick, T. (1986). That's funny? *Classroom Computer Learning, 6*(5), 70–71.

Smith, L. J., & Smith, D. L. (1986). Experimental learning: Teaching teachers to transfer their knowledge. *Journal of Reading, 29*(4), 342–345.

Solomon, S. (1989). Homework: The great reinforcer. *The Clearing House, 63*(2), 63.

Winton, J. J. (1991). You can win without competing. *Middle School Journal, 22*(3), 40.

Zeigler, V., Boardman, G., & Thomas, M. D. (1985). Humor, leadership, and school climate. *The Clearing House, 58*(8), 346–348.

How Personal Should Instruction Be?

PREPARING TO USE THE CASE

Background Information

The increased demands on teachers in recent years keeps teachers running. Many teachers are now being assigned to new roles. Research studies have found that teachers should be involved in conducting action research studies in their classrooms. Of course, this takes time. Many teachers are being elected to serve on site-based school councils; this takes an enormous amount of time. The results of a combination of these new responsibilities given to teachers can lead to stress and tension.

When under pressure to get tasks completed and when facing tension and stress, individuals often lose their ability to focus on the needs of others. Yet, time after time when asked to what they attribute the high levels of success in their classrooms, teachers of the year have repeatedly responded by saying that it is their relationship with each student.

But beginning teachers often find it difficult to determine just how personal they should be with their students. There is a thin line that when crossed teachers become very vulnerable.

The following case concerns a young teacher who wants badly to maintain a close, friendly rapport with his students, yet this perceptive teacher knows that he must not go too far in personalizing his teaching.

As you read this case, think about the strategies you can use to establish a close, working relationship with your students and how you can develop strategies that will communicate your intentions on a professional basis.

Topics for Reflection
1. Teachers' contacts with students outside the classroom
2. The role of humor in teaching
3. Teachers' needs to support their students
4. The need to personalize teaching
5. Teachers' needs to encourage and support their students

THE CASE

Cedar City is a small southern town of about 13,000 residents. A city it's not. One flashing caution light and its "City Limits" signs are the only visible evidence that it has to support its name. The reaction of most visitors is that Cedar City is a good place to be *from*. Others are even less kind, pointing out that the only thing that prevents Cedar City from being a hick town is that it isn't even a town.

But the residents of Cedar City are not bothered by outsiders' comments. They have a satisfied feeling about their town. Their open, trusting nature is often completely misunderstood by visitors. For example, the town's one real estate office has a sitting area for guests. Each day, during the noon hour, the town's only realtor, Mr. John Grimes, leaves the outside door open. In the waiting area, Mr. Grimes places a sign on his desk that reads, "I have gone home for lunch. Please pour yourself a cup of coffee and make yourself at home. If you are in a hurry, you can use my phone to call me at 304-8626. Otherwise, I'll be back at about 1:30."

There is a rumor that until recently, the mayor of Cedar City took a daily stroll from one end of main street to the other looking for strangers. When he saw one, he introduced himself and offered to buy the visitor a cup of coffee. Whenever a stranger accepted his offer, the mayor provided not only a cup of coffee but also a very persuasive sales pitch on the qualities of Cedar City.

The School District

Both the size and the casual appearance of Cedar City are in many ways deceptive. While visitors might imagine that the inhabitants sit on their porches and watch the grass grow, the fact is that the residents of Cedar City are very active. Cedar City is the home of Cedar Mills, which makes some of the nation's highest-quality linens and bedding. The founders of Cedar Mills have lived in the town for several generations. They love their community, and display this love by supporting their schools. Cedar City Junior High may be the first junior high school in the country to have separate gymnasiums for boys and girls, two completely furnished exercise rooms, an indoor Olympic-size swimming pool, and a 20-lane bowling alley.

The well-equipped gyms and exercise rooms lead one to conclude that the resident philanthropists are sports enthusiasts, but the support given for athletics is actually small compared to that given to the academic programs of Cedar City schools. Especially impressive is the direct financial support that the owners of Cedar Mills give annually to elevate the salaries of all teachers in the Cedar City schools.

The School

Cedar City Junior High is a one-story 1960s building that still looks open and inviting. The open design with windows that extend from the ceiling to the floor gives the rooms plenty of lighting. The furniture is exceptionally good as compared to most furniture in junior high schools. The teaching methods at the school are different from class to class because the open-minded administration not only tolerates, but actually encourages, all teachers to experiment with new innovations. Teachers here are especially encouraged to conduct action research in their classes.

Ms. Jackie Lane who serves as principal at the school is forward thinking on such issues as teachers as professionals. As she has expressed in several faculty meetings, Ms. Lane believes that teachers can be professionals only if they engage in some research.

The Faculty

The faculty at Cedar City Junior High are congenial and dedicated. Almost every year one or more of the faculty members receive statewide recognition. Within the past five years, the State Art Teacher of the Year Award and the State Foreign Language Teacher Award have been received by Cedar City Junior High faculty members. Last year, one of the social studies teachers received one of 20 National Institute of the Humanities awards.

Almost all of the teachers at this school give presentations at statewide professional conferences. Several of the teachers write textbooks for major publishers. At this time none of them has begun conducting classroom research. Ms. Lane is perplexed with their reluctance to become involved with research, but she is not discouraged. She says that she just has to find the right incentive; then they will get involved on their own volition.

The reason that these teachers give for not conducting research is that they are too busy meeting the needs of their students. Ms. Lane knows how busy these teachers are, but she wonders whether this is the major deterrent that keeps them from conducting any research.

The Teacher

Paul Stinson was impressed with Ms. Lane when he interviewed for a position at Cedar City. Although his education program had not prepared him to conduct high-powered research, he was confident that he could develop these skills as he taught, perhaps through a combination of course work, in-service workshops, and private reading. He felt good knowing that his new principal believed enough in him and the other teachers to ask them to experiment and to conduct action research in their classrooms.

The positive impression Ms. Lane made, the school district's attractive salary schedule, and the well-equipped science laboratory are the main features that attracted Mr. Paul Stinson to teach eighth-grade science at Cedar City Junior High. The wit and charm of 23-year-old Mr. Stinson are two of the qualities that attracted his employers to him. Whatever the reasons for hiring Mr. Stinson, the eighth-graders, and the rest of the residents, are glad that he chose the system and that it chose him.

Mr. Stinson is a thorough planner, and all of his plans have a unique element. Into each lesson he plans humor. Last Monday was the first day of study for his gifted section of eighth-grade science in a unit on geology. Before Mr. Stinson began introducing the unit, a thin, freckle-faced, red-haired boy named Everett Barnes shouted from the doorway as he entered the room, "Mr. Stinson, why do we have to study this stuff?" Mr. Stinson acted stunned and hurt. As their teacher quietly pouted, the students began to laugh. When all the students had taken their seats, Mr. Stinson slowly and carefully moved to the front of the class and sat down on a tall stool.

To begin the lesson, Mr. Stinson held up three rocks. "There are three types of rocks: sedimentary, metamorphic, and ignorant—I mean igneous." He paused for a moment and continued. "Actually," he explained, "all rocks are ignorant." "But some are nice," he continued as he held up a piece of gneiss. He then told the class a story about rocks. The students sat entranced. (Incidentally, in his biological-science class he uses the same approach when he introduces a unit on reptiles. "There are three deadly, poisonous snakes in this state, but you don't have to worry about them because I killed three poisonous snakes last year." Then he introduces the three types of local poisonous snakes. Although his humor is perhaps a little corny, his caring attitude causes his jokes to succeed with students of all ability levels.)

Next Mr. Stinson introduced the scientific method. He explained that Sir Francis Bacon was the first to develop the scientific method. "You remember Bacon; he's the one who discovered the process of preserving pork by freezing it in snow." Again the students laughed. On a serious note, he then told them that refrigeration was one of Sir Francis Bacon's many discoveries. By the end of the period, Mr. Stinson carefully tied the major concepts introduced during the hour into a tightly structured lesson.

During most of the lessons, the students were willing to sit back and enjoy their teacher's witty comments, and Mr. Stinson usually enjoyed most of the wit of his bright students. But occasionally a few students seemed to want to take over the class, or would turn to each other and make insulting comments. Whenever Mr. Stinson noticed this behavior developing, he would slowly climb down from his stool and walk over to the overactive students and stand nearby, continuing the lesson without commenting on the misbehavior. The infractions usually ceased. If not, he often placed his hand on a misbehaving student's shoulder without saying anything to the student. No words were needed; the students got the message. Sometimes when the chattering got too loud Mr. Stinson lowered his voice. Those students who were interested in hearing him shushed their noisy classmates.

Mr. Stinson frequently spent his planning periods watching the students practice basketball or cheerleading. Each spring he planned field trips for all of his students. Each winter he planned a science fair. This endeavor alone required him to give up several weekends, as he always helped students from his lower-ability sections identify project topics, and he always offered to help students plan and develop their projects.

When students volunteered to develop projects for the fair, Mr. Stinson was careful to find something good to say about the projects. This is the same way he related to students in class when they turned in projects or test papers; he always wrote positive comments on each student's paper.

It was clear to everyone that Mr. Stinson enjoyed teaching and believed that every student in his classes was capable of learning whatever topic was being studied. In fact, he used his humor to motivate his students; while they enjoyed his entertaining dialogue, they also learned the central concepts of each lesson before they realized what had happened.

The Incident

Mr. Stinson's students frequently reciprocated his warmth and enthusiasm by challenging him to participate in a variety of activities at school including tennis matches, billiards, and basketball. It was the first day of spring and a party was planned around the outdoor city pool. A group of students asked him to attend the social function. Their level of enthusiasm was very convincing, but Mr. Stinson wondered whether he should maintain some distance between himself and his students. To accept the invitation might be going too far; yet to refuse might upset his students. He wondered if he had caused a problem by being too close to his students. Perhaps he should remove the humor from his future lessons.

The Challenge

If you were in Mr. Stinson's place, what changes, if any, would you make in your instruction?

ISSUES FOR FURTHER REFLECTION

1. Mr. Stinson was prepared for the one perpetual question that all teachers hear: "Why do we have to study this stuff?" In answering this question, Mr. Stinson used his strong rapport with students. Is this wise, or is a teacher obligated to use logic to answer students' questions?

2. How much do you believe that Mr. Stinson's wide acceptance by his students resulted from his interactions with them outside the classroom? On what evidence do you base your answer?

3. Cedar City has a friendly, small-town atmosphere. To what extent should teachers' out-of-school contacts with students be affected by the nature of the community?

4. Mr. Stinson effectively used humor when teaching his lessons, but he did this at the expense of getting off the subject. For example, he directed the students' attention

away from biology long enough to give some personal information about Sir Francis Bacon's life. In light of the current emphasis on achievement, do you believe that a teacher is justified in taking this liberty? Why? Why not?

5. A much simpler and faster answer to the question about the subject's importance is that the students will be held accountable for it on their next test or they will need to understand this content in order to pursue the more advanced concepts next year. What are your reactions to these two explanations?

6. The question "Why do we have to study this stuff?" implies a certain amount of apathy for the subject. To what degree, if any, do you believe teachers are responsible for motivating their students?

7. Mr. Stinson frequently used nonverbal communications as part of his classroom management strategies. Specifically, he used this method to control student disrespect for their classmates. Do you think this is necessary? Explain your answer.

8. What evidence is there in this case that Mr. Stinson uses reinforcement in his classes? Do you think this affects the students' perception of Mr. Stinson? If so, how?

9. Recent research shows that teachers' levels of confidence in their students' abilities affect student achievement levels. What can you say about Mr. Stinson's level of confidence in the ability of his students? Can you give specific evidence to support this statement?

10. The upcoming event for which Mr. Stinson received the invitation from his students is described as a social event, and it is being held at a city pool rather than on school grounds. Should this affect his decision to accept or reject the invitation? Why or why not?

11. How do you believe this teacher's use of praise affected his relationship with them? What determines whether the use of praise will be effective?

12. How did Mr. Stinson's focus on central concepts in the lesson affect his rapport with students?

13. How might this school's administration affect Mr. Stinson's instruction?

SUGGESTED READINGS

Armstrong, D. G., Henson, K. T., & Savage, T. V. (1993). *Education: An introduction* (4th ed.). New York: Macmillan (see chapter 11).

Bellon, C. B., Bellon, J. J., & Blank, M. A. (1986). *What really works: Research-based instruction.* Knoxville, TN: Bellon and Associates.

Berliner, D. C. (1991). Creating the right environment for learning. *Instructor, 99*(5), 16–17.

Berliner, D. C. (1989). Effective schools: Teachers make the difference. *Instructor, 99*(3), 14–15.

Bracey, G. W. (1991). Teachers as researchers. *Phi Delta Kappan, 72*(5), 115–117.

Brown, D. S. (1990). Middle level teachers' perceptions of active research. *Middle School Journal, 22*(2), 30–32.

Buckner, J. H., & Bickel, F. (1991). If you want to know about effective teaching, why not ask your middle school kids? *Middle School Journal, 22*(3), 26–29.

Bugler, K., & Fraser, B. (1990). *Window into science classrooms: Problems with higher-level cognitive thinking.* New York: Falmer.

Cooper, L. R. (1991). Teachers as researchers. *Kappa Delta Pi Record, 27*(4), 115–117.

Cornett, C. E. (1986). *Learning through laughter: Humor in the classroom* (Phi Delta Kappa Fastback, No. 241.) Bloomington, IN: Phi Delta Kappa Foundation.

Curry, L. (1990). A critique of research on learning styles. *Educational Leadership, 48*(2), 50–52, 54–56.

Davies, D. (1991). Schools reaching out: Family, school, and community partnerships for student success. *Phi Delta Kappan, 72*(5), 376–382.

Dembo, M. (1994). *Applying educational psychology in the classroom* (5th ed.). New York: Longman (see chapter 9).

Discussion. (1985). What's the funniest thing that's happened in your class this year? *English Journal, 74*(8), 43–46.

Edwards, R. A., & Jones Young, L. S. (1992). Beyond parents, family, and school involvement. *Phi Delta Kappan, 74*(1), 72–81.

Good, T., & Brophy, J. (1990). *Educational psychology: A realistic approach* (4th ed.). New York: Longman (see chapter 12).

Harrison, C. J. (1990). Concepts, operational definitions, and case studies in instruction. *Education, 110*(4), 502–505.

Henson, K. T. (1986). Inquiry learning: A new look. *Contemporary Education, 62*(4), 181–183.

Henson, K. T. (1993). *Methods and strategies for teaching in secondary and middle schools* (2nd ed.). New York: Longman (see chapters 5, 6).

Hittleman, D. R., & Simon, A. J. (1992). *Interpreting educational research: An introduction for consumers of research.* New York: Merrill.

Joyce, B., Weil, M., & Showers, B. (1992). *Models of teaching* (4th ed.). Needham Heights, MA: Allyn & Bacon.

Kagan, S. (1990). The structural approach to cooperative learning. *Educational Leadership, 47*(4), 12–15.

Katz, L. G., & McClellan, D. (1991). *The teacher's role in social development.* Urbana, IL: ERIC Clearinghouse on Elementary and Early Childhood Education.

King, A. (1990). Reciprocal questioning: A strategy for teaching students how to learn from lectures. *The Clearing House, 64*(2), 131–135.

Knapp, M. S., & Shields, P. M. (Eds.) (1991). *Better schooling for the children of poverty: Alternatives to conventional wisdom.* Berkeley, CA: McCutchan.

Kohn, A. (1991). Caring kids: The role of the schools. *Phi Delta Kappan, 72*(7), 496–506.

Otten, N. (1986). Punchlines as paradigms. *English Journal, 75*(4), 51–53.

Phelps, P. H. (1990). Helping teachers excel as classroom managers. *The Clearing House, 64*(3), 241–242.

Porter, A., & Brophy, J. (1988). Synthesis of research on good teaching. *Educational Leadership, 45*(8), 74–85.

Ramsey, I., Gabbard, C., Clawson, K., Lee, L., & Henson, K. T. (1990). Questioning: An effective teaching method. *The Clearing House, 63*(9), 420–422.

Schaps, E., & Solomon, D. (1990). Schools and classrooms as caring communities. *Educational Leadership, 48*(3), 38–40.

Schomoker, M. (1990). Sentimentalizing self-esteem. *The Education Digest, 60*(7), 55–56.

Schunk, D. H., & Meece, J. L. (Eds.) (1992). *Student perceptions in the classrooms.* Hillsdale, NJ: Erlbaum.

Smith, L. J., & Smith, D. L. (1986). Experimental learning: Teaching teachers to transfer their knowledge. *Journal of Reading, 29*(4), 342–345.

Snapp, J. C., & Glover, J. A. (1990). Advance organizers and study questions. *The Journal of Educational Research, 8*(5), 266–271.

Winton, J. J. (1991). You can win without competing. *Middle School Journal, 22*(3), 40.

Zeigler, V., Boardman, G., & Thomas, M. D. (1985). Humor, leadership, and school climate. *The Clearing House, 58*(8), 346–348.

Read It Again?

PREPARING TO USE THE CASE

Background Information

Students become actively engaged in instructional activities for a variety of reasons. One view holds that there is a relationship between the personal interest that students take in a subject and the amount of effort made. When students are excited by the subject, see meaning and relevance in it, they tend to be more highly motivated.

A second view suggests that the organizational structure—the way a subject is presented—influences the level of student involvement. Students prefer certain presentation modes to others. Some students are more attuned to working in groups, while others prefer working independently. Some students learn better when material is presented through print, while others find greater success when material is shown visually. Some students prefer studying carefully sequenced material, while others enjoy discovering ideas from a less organized presentation.

A third view argues that the fear of failure may affect the amount of effort students make. Afraid to fail, some students will take few risks. On the other hand, other students thrive on the tension and anxiety that may accompany material that appears impossible to master, at least at the outset.

Another view suggests that the relationship students have with the teacher will influence their engagement in a subject. For some students, the inspiration provided by the teacher will help them achieve in almost any setting. In such cases, material perceived to be boring or too difficult may be mastered by virtue of students' desire to please the teacher.

This case is about a social studies teacher who must find a way to motivate his students when he discovers that many of them in his sociology class have already read a book that is required reading in the class. Faced with the choice of either making several students reread the book, or allowing students to make individual choices about the reading assignment, the teacher gives each student the freedom to choose. In the process of making the decision and carrying it out, he experiences two confrontations with his peers. In the end, he must defend the decision he has made.

Topics for Reflection
1. Motivation
2. Instructional planning
3. Multicultural education
4. Meeting individual student interests and needs
5. Teacher decision making
6. Conflict resolution
7. Teacher collaboration
8. Teacher evaluation

THE CASE

Basil Herman looked forward to the second semester. His first semester had been successful. The three government classes and two history classes—one American history and one world history—had gone well. His first year at Claybourn High School, a larger urban school in a southeastern city, was off to a good start.

He believed the fact that he was black was an advantage, as two-thirds of the students in his class shared his culture. He also felt that attending Madison State—a historically black college—better prepared him for working with minority students. After a semester, he was equally convinced of his ability to communicate with the small percentage of white students.

He was buoyed by a recent evaluation conducted by Erving Clements, social studies department chairperson at Claybourn. For the last week he had pulled a copy of the evaluation from his file every day to boost his ego (see Figure 1). He even slept with it by his side the day he received it. He pulled it from the file again and stared at it with pride.

"This is one of the finest evaluations I've given a beginning teacher," Mr. Clements had told him.

There were only two areas in which Mr. Clements had marked him as "average": confidence and creativity.

"You have tremendous potential," Mr. Clements said. "But you need to start being more decisive. Become more independent. Take more risks."

As he planned for the second semester, Basil had kept Mr. Clements's remarks in mind. With a new preparation—a sociology class—and three more government classes he wondered how he might be more decisive or risk-taking.

The opportunity came during the first day in his sociology classes. Following the curriculum guide, he had dusted off 57 copies of Richard Wright's *Black Boy* housed in the social studies storage room and had organized them for distribution

Teacher: _____Basil Herman_____   Evaluated by: _____Clements_____

Time: ____2nd period____   Class: _____History_____   Date: _____12/15_____

5 = superior, 4 = excellent, 3 = average, 2 = poor, 1 = very poor

	5	**4**	**3**	**2**	**1**
Dress (appearance)	×				
Promptness	×				
Dependability	×				
Communication	×				
Cooperation	×				
Friendliness	×				
Confidence			×		
Creativity			×		
Judgment		×			
Organization		×			
Knowledge	×				
Adherence to curriculum guide	×				
Use of varied teaching methods		×			
Student interest generated	×				
Classroom control	×				
Grading techniques	×				

Comments:
One of the finest first-year teachers I have observed. Needs to be more independent, creative, thought-provoking, and risk-taking. Should become an outstanding teacher.

FIGURE 1 Claybourn high school teacher evaluation form

in his classroom. After taking attendance in his second-period sociology class, he lectured on the early life of the author, Richard Wright, in Natchez, Mississippi, and his move to Memphis and to Chicago. He talked about *Native Son,* how it had marked a high point in black fiction, had been adapted to the Broadway stage by Orson Welles, and had been made into a movie by Wright himself. Throughout the lecture he focused on Wright's use of characters to describe society.

"For the first two weeks of this class," he concluded, "we will look at society through the eyes of Richard Wright in his autobiography, *Black Boy.*"

At this point he began distributing the book, handing a stack of the paperbacks to the first person in each row to pass down the row.

"For tomorrow, I would like for you to read the first 36 pages," Mr. Herman said. "In the time remaining you can begin the assignment."

Three hands shot in the air.

"Mr. Herman," one student said.

"Yes?" the teacher responded.

"Some of us have already read *Black Boy*," the student said.

"How many of you have already read the book?" Mr. Herman asked.

Nearly one-fourth of the students said they had.

"When did all of you read the book?" Mr. Herman inquired.

"In Mrs. Knoll's English class last semester," a second student said.

"I read it on my own last summer," another student offered.

Confused as to what to do next, Mr. Herman said, "For those of you who have already read *Black Boy,* please reread the assigned pages for tomorrow with the rest of the class. We will discuss the assignment further tomorrow."

He tried to contact Mrs. Knoll before his fifth-period sociology class, but without success. After taking roll, Mr. Herman asked how many students had already read *Black Boy.* Six students said they had read it in Mrs. Knoll's class during the first semester.

"Bear with me today," Mr. Herman said. "Toward the end of the period I'll talk with each of you who has read the book."

Using the same lecture notes from second period, he taught the class. After giving the assignment, Mr. Herman asked the six students who said they had read the book to visit with him at his desk in the front of the room.

"How was the book used in your English class?" Mr. Herman asked.

"Mrs. Knoll divided the class into five groups. Each group could choose an American writer to read," one student said.

"We chose Richard Wright," another said.

"And you read *Black Boy*?" Mr. Herman asked.

The six students nodded.

"We'll discuss this more tomorrow," Mr. Herman said. "For now, please read the pages assigned."

After school, Mr. Herman rushed to Mrs. Knoll's classroom. As he entered, Mrs. Knoll was erasing the chalkboard.

"Mrs. Knoll, can we talk for a minute?" Mr. Herman asked.

"If you don't mind my tidying the room," she said. "I have a forensics club meeting in here in about 20 minutes."

"I'm Basil Herman," he began.

"The new social studies teacher," Mrs. Knoll interrupted. "How may I help?

"I'm not sure there is anything you can do now," Mr. Herman responded. "But maybe we can avoid a problem in the future."

"What is the problem?" Mrs. Knoll asked.

"The book *Black Boy* is required reading in the sociology class. It's outlined in the school district's social studies curriculum guide."

"So what does this have to do with me?" Mrs. Knoll asked.

"Several students in my sociology classes read the book in your class," he continued.

"So what's your point?" Mrs. Knoll challenged.

"I'm in an awkward position. I don't know whether to make all my students read *Black Boy* or come up with another assignment for those who have read it. It would be much easier to have all the students reading the same book at the same time," he retorted.

"Mr. Herman, one of my purposes in English is to encourage young people to read. When I give my students a chance to choose what they want to read,

I don't get in their way. I want them to enjoy the experience. If that inconveniences you or any other teacher in this school, it's unfortunate. My job's to inspire my students, not make life easier for other teachers," she concluded.

"I don't think you understand," Mr. Herman said. "The curriculum guide . . . ."

"Don't tell me about the curriculum guide," Mrs. Knoll interrupted. "I helped write it a decade ago. Please excuse yourself, Mr. Herman. I must finish preparing for the forensics club."

"Perhaps we could talk about this some other time," Mr. Herman said. "I really don't think it is fair to the students to be placed in this kind of a situation."

"I don't see this as their problem. It's your problem," Mrs. Knoll stressed. As she turned away from him, she coldly retorted: "Good day, Mr. Herman."

Mr. Herman returned to his room. On the way back he wondered if he should stop to discuss the matter with Mr. Clements. Remembering the department chairperson's urging to be more self-reliant, he decided not to bother Mr. Clements. "I've relied too much on him already," he thought.

At home that night Mr. Herman developed a list of books written by black authors. It included:

- Richard Wright, *Native Son*
- Jean Toomer, *Cane*
- Ralph Ellison, *Invisible Man*
- James Baldwin, *Go Tell It on the Mountain*
- Ann Petry, *Country Place*
- Nella Larson, *Quicksand*
- Maya Angelou, *I Know Why the Caged Bird Sings*

When he finished, he had a list of 32 authors and a book title for each.

The next day he typed the list, made copies of it, and distributed it to his sociology students. He reminded the students that the overriding goal of reading *Black Boy* was to gain insights on American society from Richard Wright's perspective. He went on to point out that other authors' views are as worthy. Accordingly, he told them that they could continue reading *Black Boy* or could purchase or get a library copy of one of the other books on the list he handed out. For half of the period, Mr. Herman introduced sociological concepts that would be covered as they read *Black Boy* or another book of choice. For the remainder of the class, he released students, two at a time, to go to the library to check out a book from the list.

By the end of the week, every student in his sociology class had obtained a book. While most had kept the school copy of *Black Boy,* nearly one-third of the students in both classes selected a book from the list. Mr. Herman was pleased with the resulting interest and discussion. He felt that students' providing examples from a variety of books to illustrate the sociological concepts broadened their knowledge and enriched the quality of discussion.

On Monday morning when he checked his mail before the start of school, he was struck by a note from Mr. Clements. It said simply: "See me immediately!"

He put the note and other mail in his briefcase and walked to Mr. Clements's room. When he entered, Mr. Clements was seated at his desk.

"You wanted to see me?" Mr. Herman asked.

"Yes, come here and sit down."

Mr. Herman walked to the front of the room and took a seat.

"What is the chaos in your sociology classes?" Mr. Clements asked.

"Chaos?" Mr. Herman countered. "I don't see it that way."

"Let me put it another way," Mr. Clements said. "What book is *required* reading of *all* students in sociology?"

"But . . . "

"But what?" Mr. Clements interrupted angrily. "*Black Boy* is specified in the district's curriculum guide. How can you defend what you are doing?"

The Challenge

You are Mr. Herman. How will you defend your decision to use texts other than the one specified in the curriculum guide?

FURTHER ISSUES FOR REFLECTION

1. What reasons would you give for allowing students to choose what they want to read in the sociology classes?
2. What evidence in the case led you to give these reasons?
3. Which of the reasons is the most compelling? Why?
4. Defend your response to question 1 by describing motivation theory in support of your position.
5. Defend your response to question 1 by describing learning theory in support of your position.
6. What relationships do you see between allowing for student choices and classroom control?
7. What strategies would you recommend for addressing the fact that in any class some of the students will be highly motivated, while many others will not?
8. How independent can a teacher afford to be in making assignments? To what extent might the length of time a teacher has been teaching affect your answer to this question? Explain.
9. How would you interpret the contradiction between Mr. Herman's being encouraged to be more creative and confident and the criticism he receives from Mr. Clements when he does show creativity and confidence?
10. If Mr. Clements insists that you comply literally with the curriculum guide, how will you proceed?
11. What are possible consequences of returning to the original assignment, requiring all students to read the same book, once you have allowed them to choose a book to read?
12. What are possible consequences of disregarding Mr. Clements?
13. Of the consequences you listed in response to the preceding two questions, which are the most serious? Explain your answer.

SUGGESTED READINGS

Ball, D., & Feiman-Nemser, S. (1988). Using textbooks and teachers' guides: A dilemma for beginning teachers and teacher educators. *Curriculum Inquiry, 18*(4), 401–423.

Blumenfeld, P. (1992). Classroom learning and motivation. *Journal of Educational Psychology, 84*(3), 272–281.

Conn, S. (1988). Textbooks: Defining the new critieria. *Media and Methods, 24*(4), 30–31, 64.

Dembo, M. (1994). *Applying educational psychology in the classroom* (5th ed.). New York: Longman (see chapter 4).

Driscoll, M. P. (1986). The relationship between grading standards and achievement: A new perspective. *Journal of Research and Development in Education, 19*(3), 13–17.

Duke, L. R. (1986). Teaching the accepted methods of your profession: The teacher as risk taker. *English Journal, 75*(5), 53–55.

Glenn, C. (1987). Textbook controversies: A disaster for public schools? *Phi Delta Kappan, 68*(6), 451–455.

Good, T., & Brophy, J. (1990). *Educational psychology: A realistic approach* (4th ed.). New York: Longman (see chapters 11, 12, 16).

Harris, I. B. (1986). Communicating the character of deliberation. *Journal of Curriculum Studies, 18*(2), 15–32.

Henson, K. (1993). *Methods and strategies for teaching in secondary and middle schools* (2nd ed.). New York: Longman (see chapter 7).

Mathews, K. (1992). Helping teachers motivate students: Five case studies. *ERS Spectrum, 10*(3), 23–28.

Neeper, A. (1991). Teaching for transfer: A simple method to upgrade lesson plans. *Social Studies Texan, 7*(3), 58–60.

Newby, T. (1991). Classroom motivation: Strategies of first-year teachers. *Journal of Educational Psychology, 83*(2), 195–200.

Pratton, J., & Hales, L. W. (1986). The effects of active participation on student learning. *Journal of Educational Research, 79*(4), 210–215.

Snelbecker, G. (1988). Instructional design skills for classroom teachers. *Journal of Instructional Development, 10*(4), 33–40.

Who Can Motivate Michael?

PREPARING TO USE THE CASE

Background Information

Being well-prepared, offering an interesting lesson, but having students show little response is one of the most frustrating experiences for teachers. Students may not show interest in a lesson for a variety of reasons. They may not enjoy the subject being taught. They may not like the teacher or the method of teaching that the teacher uses. They may not get support from home to do well in school. Emotional, social, physical, and/or intellectual problems may affect their level of interest in class.

Whatever the reason for disinterest, teachers are faced with the ongoing challenge of educating every student. As a result, teachers are responsible for exploring ways to enable students to achieve.

In recent years, greater attention has been placed on working more closely with parents through a parent-education program as one way to address the problem of student disinterest. Showing parents how to organize and supervise study time at home, to create and use enrichment activities in the community (e.g., visits to museums), to provide reinforcement for learning, and to communicate regularly with teachers are some of the elements of a parent-education program.

Teacher collaboration offers another way that student motivation problems can be explored. Working together, teachers can develop a broader understanding of a student's needs and wants and can share insights as to how strategies they have tried with a particular student might result in improved learning. Bringing teachers together to plan, develop, and evaluate curricula; exploring students problems; and considering other issues have become an integral part of the teacher empowerment movement.

This case is about a middle school student who is much more successful in agriculture, a subject that greatly interests him, than he is in other subjects. In order to try to help him be as successful in other subjects, a group of teachers meet with the student and his mother. How to motivate the student to be more successful in all his academic work is of primary concern.

Topics for Reflection
1. Motivation
2. Type of parent involvement and responsibility for children's learning
3. Instructional planning
4. Teacher collaboration
5. Meeting individual student interests and needs

THE CASE

Martha and Kurt Grey were finishing a typically late dinner during harvest season when the phone rang. Mrs. Grey looked at her husband. "Who would that be so late?"

"Don't know," he answered.

Mrs. Grey walked to the phone in the living room, picked it up, and answered it to hear, "This is Virginia DeValle, Michael's English teacher. I'm sorry to call so late, but . . . ."

"Is Michael in trouble?" Mrs. Grey interrupted, her voice quavering. She dreaded these calls, knowing how angry her husband got whenever there was trouble with Michael at school. He was a firm disciplinarian who always warned Michael that "the paddling you get at home will be twice as bad as the one you get at school." And he enforced his warning.

"No," the voice on the line continued, "but I thought we might meet to talk about Michael's progress in some of his classes before he gets too far behind. He is having some difficulty with English and math, but is doing good work in other subjects. And he excels in Mr. Graham's agribusiness class.

"Ms. Martin, Michael's math teacher, Mr. Graham, and I would like to meet with you and Mr. Grey and Michael tomorrow after school, if that would be convenient."

"Well," Mrs. Grey hesitated. "I suppose I could come in. But there's no way my husband can leave the field unless it rains bad. The weather's supposed to be good, so it'd just be me."

"We would really like to be able to meet with both of you and Michael, if that would be possible some other time," Mrs. DeValle replied.

"Not during harvesting," Mrs. Grey insisted. "I can meet with you, but Michael has to get right home to help his father. They can't be there." Mrs. Grey knew that even if a thunderstorm flooded the fields, making them untillable, getting Kurt to school for any reason was nearly as improbable as getting him to church on Sunday. She had been successful at that only once in the 27 years of their marriage. That was to attend her sister's wedding, and not without some struggle.

"I do believe it is important that we talk about Michael's progress as soon as possible," Mrs. DeValle stressed. "Let's go ahead and meet at 3:15 tomorrow. I'll be in the lobby in the front entrance to the school. See you there?"

"Yes, I'll be there," Mrs. Grey responded reluctantly. Having attended similar meetings in the past, she doubted that one more meeting would have any effect on Michael's school performance.

"Goodbye, Mrs. Grey. I'll see you tomorrow," Mrs. DeValle said.

"Goodbye, Mrs. DeValle," Mrs. Grey responded, slowly lowering the receiver.

By this time, Mr. Grey was standing in the doorway between the kitchen and the living room. Having overheard part of the conversation, he remarked: "Michael's in trouble again. Right?"

"No, Kurt, he's not," Mrs. Grey interjected. "Michael's doing really well in agribusiness. He needs some help in English and math, but he's *not* in trouble."

"Michael's going to be a good farmer someday. If crops keep bringing in good money in the next few years, maybe we can buy a couple hundred more acres so he'd have some land of his own, besides helping me," Kurt dreamed aloud. "It's in the genes. My dad and me was never much good in school, especially in English and math," he said, as he walked toward the porch. "I'm going to read the sports."

Mrs. Grey walked up the stairs to Michael's room and knocked on the door.

"Come in," Michael called out.

"Michael, Mrs. DeValle called."

"Oh yeah, what did she want?"

"Don't you know?" Mrs. Grey retorted impatiently.

"No."

"She wants to meet tomorrow to talk about your progress in English and math. She said you're not doing very well in those subjects."

"I'm doing okay."

"Then why do I have to meet with your teachers tomorrow after school?" Mrs. Grey challenged.

"I don't know," he shrugged.

"Michael, I just want to help. Tell me what's wrong. Why are you having trouble in English and math?"

"Mrs. DeValle and Ms. Martin don't like me," Michael explained.

"Michael, you always use that excuse," Mrs. Grey responded angrily. "Anytime you have a problem in school it's someone else's problem. Not yours."

Mrs. Grey left the room, frustrated.

The next afternoon at three, Mrs. Grey arrived at Chester Junior/Senior High School. The Chester school serves the town of Chester (population 5,300) and several small "blinker light" communities—Shire (327), Mulligan (673), Isle City (876), and Avon (464). The small communities are located nearly equidistant from Chester and as a result, have not operated as independent school districts for more than a half century. Farming and agribusinesses provide most of the work for members of the communities. A small number of retail stores, service industries, and professional offices, primarily located in Chester, serve the farming communities.

"Good afternoon, Mrs. Grey," Mrs. DeValle greeted, as Mrs. Grey entered the lobby of the school.

"Hello."

"We're going to go to the guidance counselors' conference room. Ms. Martin and Mr. Graham are waiting for us," Mrs. DeValle instructed.

Mrs. DeValle, a 16-year veteran at the Chester school, is a mainstay in both the school and the community. Born in Mulligan, her only years away from the community were the four she spent in a small liberal arts college 43 miles south of her birthplace. Childless, she had "adopted" all her students, carefully charting their progress once they left Chester and "mothering" them while they were there.

She had taken a special interest in Michael, for she felt he had much more potential than he showed. Challenges, such as Michael, spark Mrs. DeValle's interest in teaching. "There have been many other Michaels in 16 years," she had thought. She had reviewed his grades, talked to elementary teachers, and had initiated the meeting. To some parents and faculty her "mothering" was interpreted as meddling.

As Mrs. DeValle led Mrs. Grey down the front corridor of the building, she engaged Mrs. Grey in conversation. "The Greys have been in Farmingham County for some time, haven't they?"

"Nearly a century. Both Kurt's father and his father owned land in the county," Mrs. Grey remarked warmly, "We moved into the original farmhouse when we were married 27 years ago."

"Must be a lot of pride in your home," Mrs. DeValle added.

"Yes, the Greys have worked hard to improve the land, make it more productive. And we've expanded the old farmhouse. Remodeled the old porch. Enclosed it with glass and put in a woodburning stove so we can use it in the winter. Also redid the kitchen and built on a family room."

"Here we are," Mrs. DeValle interrupted, as she opened the door to the guidance counselors' conference room.

As the two entered, Mr. Graham and Ms. Martin stood. Mr. Graham extended his arm to shake hands, saying: "Hello, Mrs. Grey, I'm Mr. Graham, Michael's agribusiness teacher."

Mr. Graham had come to Chester Junior/Senior High School a year ago, having taught three years in a high school in a neighboring state. At 31 years of age he was comparatively old for having taught for only four years. After graduating from a major agricultural university, he had tried to make a living as a farmer. He turned to teaching the next year, seeing that he could not support his wife and two daughters from farming alone. With the income earned as a teacher he was able to continue farming on a small scale.

Mr. Graham shares his knowledge and love of farming in his classroom and laboratory. He thinks of himself as a "hands-on" teacher, inspiring his students to apply what they learn through projects. He is viewed by students as a popular teacher. To Mr. Graham, Michael is one of the best students in his class. He sees himself in Michael—a farm boy who yearns to spend the rest of his life on the family farm. He sees nothing wrong with such a dream and is committed to preparing his students to attain it.

As Mrs. Grey shook hands with Mr. Graham, Ms. Martin introduced herself as Michael's math teacher. As a first-year teacher, Ms. Martin was pleased to be hired in the state where she had spent her entire life. Being close to family had been a motivating force in her choice of a teaching position. She recognized that majoring in mathematics had expanded the choice of schools. As a math major, she had excelled in mathematics throughout her education. She had trouble understanding why her students were not as excited or interested in math.

Michael is a special frustration. "If he didn't understand the problem," she had thought, "I would not be so upset." Not turning in homework or showing disinterest especially angered her. She had discussed Michael with other teachers and had tried, unsuccessfully, to influence his behavior in more positive ways.

"Please sit down," Mrs. DeValle requested. Then she came to the business at hand.

"Mrs. Grey, what we would like to do is to share some of our concerns about Michael's work in school, beginning with Ms. Martin and then me. Then we'd like to discuss some things that we can all do to help Michael. I've asked Mr. Graham to be here, mainly because Michael does extremely well in the agriculture course. He might be able to share some ideas to help us. Is that all right as an agenda?"

"That's fine," Mrs. Grey acknowledged.

Ms. Martin began. "Mrs. Grey, I've checked Michael's prior work in math. He has remained at grade level or better on standardized math tests over the years. As I grade his papers, I believe he understands most of the basic concepts and operations on the surface. But he gets careless when he applies a concept or operation to solving a problem.

"For example," she went on, pulling a paper from a stack in front of her, "here are four problems on the first page of this test that are wrong. In all four problems he followed the process correctly, but the answers are wrong. And here are several similar homework papers. It's not that Michael does not understand. He doesn't seem to concentrate as much as he should when he does work in class."

"Is there anything you could share with us, Mrs. Grey, that would help Ms. Martin better understand why Michael has trouble concentrating on his math work?" Mrs. DeValle asked.

"No, not really. At home he gets done what he sets out to do. If he likes doing something and wants to finish it, he gets it done fast and does a good job," Mrs. Grey responded.

"Michael has similar problems in my English class," said Mrs. DeValle. "And about once a week he misses a homework assignment. Ms. Martin says she has the same problem. Does Michael do homework at home?"

"Not very often, I don't think. My husband and I have told him he has to get his work done in study hall. He's got so many chores. And now with harvesting, it's worse. He has to work on the farm from the time he gets home from school until dark, and sometimes till about two or three in the morning," Mrs. Grey noted.

"What about weekends?" Ms. Martin queried.

"Michael and I go to church on Sunday morning. When we get home, we have a big dinner. Then most times, this time of year, Michael helps his father mend fences, tend to cattle, or work in the fields. There's always something to do on the farm, even on weekends,'' Mrs. Grey explained.

"Michael's performance is above average in my class,'' Mr. Graham offered. "In fact, he's one of the best students I've had in a couple of years. What surprises me is that when I give assignments where he must deal with math or English, he has no difficulty.''

"Yesterday, the class computed crop yields for corn, oats, and soybeans, based on different weather factors—days of sunshine, amount of rain, level of humidity, daily temperatures, and so forth,'' Mr. Graham continued. "Each student had his own set of factors and a formula to use. Michael breezed through the assignment.''

"I told you he can do what he sets his mind to do and enjoys doing,'' Mrs. Grey interrupted.

"Last week, students handed in 500-word reports on tracking farm produce from planting to the table. Again, Michael turned in an excellent paper. He submitted a paper on the coffee bean, and traced its route from Latin America and other parts of the world to coffee cups in American homes,'' Mr. Graham expounded.

"Was the paper grammatically sound?'' Mrs. DeValle asked.

"The paper was well organized. Spelling and punctuation were good,'' Mr. Graham replied. "I'd be happy to share the paper with you,'' he concluded, staring at Mrs. DeValle. This was not the first time Mr. Graham felt that Mrs. DeValle was questioning the rigor of his course. Because his course was an elective, most often taken by students on a noncollege-preparation track, the class and the students enrolled had often been the object of jokes made by teachers who teach required subjects. He had suspected that Mrs. DeValle had been an instigator of the joking on several occasions.

"I told you Michael can do it. He can do it when he wants to, and if his schoolwork is made interesting,'' Mrs. Grey added, more assuredly than before.

"Well, we need to work together to help Michael be as successful in all his schoolwork as he is in Mr. Graham's class. I think we share in the responsibility,'' Mrs. DeValle said.

"We're all in this together,'' Mr. Graham replied approvingly.

The Challenge

What can be done to help Michael be more successful?

ISSUES FOR FURTHER REFLECTION

1. Describe theories of motivation. In what ways do you see each as useful in helping teachers approach problems of student motivation?
2. Which theory of motivation do you believe is most important in addressing Michael's lack of performance in some subjects in comparison to agriculture? Defend your answer.
3. If you were Mr. Graham, what immediate steps would you take in your class with Michael to provide motivation for him to improve in math and English?

4. What are the possible consequences of your response to question 3?

5. Explain the motivation theory that supports your response to question 3.

6. If you were Ms. Martin, what might you plan to do in math to help Michael improve in that subject?

7. What are the possible consequences of your response to question 6?

8. Explain the motivation theory that supports your response to question 6.

9. If you were Mrs. DeValle, what would you do to motivate Michael to be more successful in English?

10. What are the possible consequences of your response to question 9?

11. Explain the motivation theory that supports your response to question 9.

12. If you were any one of the teachers, what might you recommend that Mr. and Mrs. Grey do to increase your role in motivating Michael to do better in all of his school subjects?

13. What are the possible consequences of your response to question 12?

14. Explain the motivation theory that supports your response to question 12.

15. Describe additional information that you would like to have before making recommendations for helping Michael improve in school.

16. What ethical issues might arise from the application of motivation theory to trying to change Michael's behavior?

SUGGESTED READINGS

Alderman, M. (1990). Motivation for at-risk students. *Educational Leadership, 48*(1), 27–30.

Barth, R. (1979). Home-based reinforcement of school behavior: A review and analysis. *Review of Educational Research, 49*(3), 436–458.

Bates, J. (1979). Extrinsic reward and intrinsic motivation: A review with implications for the classroom. *Review of Educational Research, 49*(4), 557–576.

Bergin, D. (1992). Leisure activity, motivation, and academic achievement in high school students. *Journal of Leisure Research, 24*(3), 225–239.

Blumenfeld, P. (1992). Classroom learning and motivation. *Journal of Educational Psychology, 84*(3), 272–281.

Chrispeels, J. (1991). District leadership in parent involvement. *Phi Delta Kappan, 72*(5), 367–371.

Cole, B. (1988). Teaching in a time machine: The "make-do" mentality in small-town schools. *Phi Delta Kappan, 70*(2), 139–144.

Coleman, J. (1987). Families and schools. *Educational Researcher, 16*(6), 32–38.

Corno, L. (1992). Encouraging students to take responsibility for learning and performance. *Elementary School Journal, 93*(1), 69–83.

Davies, D. (1991). Schools reaching out: Family, school, and community partnerships for student success. *Phi Delta Kappan, 72*(5), 376–380, 382.

Deer, J. (1988). Assessment of children's motives, attitudes, and perceptions. *Moral Education Forum, 13*(4), 18–34, 37.

Dembo, M. (1994). *Applying educational psychology in the classroom* (5th ed.). New York: Longman (see chapters 4, 7).

Fairchild, T. (1987). The daily report card. *Teaching Exceptional Children, 19*(2), 72–73.

Good, T., & Brophy, J. (1990). *Educational psychology: A realistic approach* (4th ed.). New York: Longman (see Part Five).

Henderson, A. (1988). Parents are a school's best friends. *Phi Delta Kappan, 70*(2), 148–153.

Henniger, M. (1987). Parental rights and responsibilities in the educational process. *Clearing House, 60*(5), 226–229.

Henson, K. (1993). *Methods and strategies for teaching in secondary and middle schools* (2nd ed.). New York: Longman (see chapters 7, 12).

Lewis, A. (1992). Student motivation and learning: The role of the school counselor. *School Counselor, 39*(5), 333–337.

Mathews, K. (1992). Helping teachers motivate students: Five case studies. *ERS Spectrum, 10*(3), 23–28.

Moore, B. (1987). Effective planning and motivation play key roles in higher achievement. *Reading Improvement, 24*(4), 256–261.

Newby, T. (1991). Classroom motivation: Strategies of first-year teachers. *Journal of Educational Psychology, 83*(2), 195–200.

Okey, J. (1991). Integrating instruction and motivational design. *Performance Improvement Quarterly, 4*(2), 11–21.

Pasch, M., Sparks-Langer, G., Gardner, T., Starko, A., & Moody, C. (1991). *Teaching as decision making: Instructional practices for the successful teacher.* New York: Longman (see chapters 4, 7, 10).

Porter, A. (1987). Teacher collaboration: New partnerships to attack old problems. *Phi Delta Kappan, 69*(2), 147–152.

Stage, F. (1989). Motivation, academic and social integration, and the early dropout. *American Educational Research Journal, 26*(3), 385–402.

Tomlenson, T. (1992). *Hard work and high expectations.* Washington, DC: U.S. Department of Education.

Walde, A., & Baker, K. (1990). How teachers view the parents' role in education. *Phi Delta Kappan, 72*(4), 319–321.

CASE 24

Setting Low Expectations

PREPARING TO USE THE CASE

Background Information

In recent years, critics of education have charged that many students lack a desire to succeed academically, and that many schools fail to set high expectations for students. They argue that their claims are evident in a process they have labeled, *dumbing down,* that is, lowering standards for all students so that more can graduate from high school. Such criticisms have illuminated questions about individual student differences and the role of motivation in academic success.

Like many topics that confront teachers, motivation is complex. There is no universal law that provides an errorless explanation of why students behave in certain ways. A number of theories, nevertheless, have been developed to provide insights as to how factors such as personality and experience affect behavior. Each theory attempts to provide a segment of reality by concentrating on certain factors such as parental relationships, self-perception, teacher expectations, previous academic performance, and past experiences.

Motivation is highly dependent on an individual's self-assessment of worth. If certain students believe that they are doomed to failure, they will likely have little desire to put forth effort. Attribution theory, for example, helps to explain how the feedback of parents and teachers helps to mold an individual's self-perception. Because of the relationships among self-concept, aspirations, and education, motivation plays a pivotal role in teaching. Teachers are expected to understand motivational theory and apply this information skillfully in structuring learning experiences for their students.

Problems associated with low achievement and low self-esteem in students have received considerable attention in the professional literature. Far less information

has focused on students who set unrealistic expectations for their academic performance or career aspirations. In this case, you will read about an eighth-grade
student in an impoverished community who sees himself as extremely talented.
He possesses an extroverted personality, and he freely shares his lofty goals with
others. Partly for these reasons, he is viewed by his parents, teachers, and peer
students as a very able individual. Yet his performance on examinations in mathematics class indicates that he is not mastering the content of the course. The
student and his parents argue that the problem rests with a first-year teacher.

The teacher, after consulting with an experienced colleague, decides that
honesty is the best policy. He believes that this student's potential has been over-
estimated, and accordingly concludes that the student will increasingly encounter
failure in academic work. Among the critical questions confronting the teacher
are the following two:

1. Is he correct in his assessment of this student?
2. Should a student's aspirations be lowered in order to expose him to
   more realistic learning opportunities?

Topics for Reflection
1. Self-perceptions of ability
2. Teacher expectations
3. Parental influence on student self-perceptions
4. Test anxiety
5. Structuring learning experiences for students with inflated
   perceptions of ability
6. Attribution theory

THE CASE

The Community

Steel Town was once a booming industrial city of more than 200,000 residents.
Steel mills, a major auto factory, and dozens of smaller manufacturing operations
located here during and after the Industrial Revolution to take advantage of natural
resources, especially an abundance of water supplied by one of the Great Lakes.
Today the main street of Steel Town looks like it was the scene of a small war.
Most buildings have either been demolished or are standing empty in various states
of disrepair. Except for an occasional liquor store, drugstore, or pool hall, the
once busy street is deserted.

Now there are less than 85,000 residents in Steel Town—92% are either
African Americans or Hispanics. Primary industries shut down or moved elsewhere
more than two decades ago. Left behind were a number of environmental scars,
reminders of how little concern there was for protecting water, land, and air
quality. Families that could afford to escape did so long ago. Crime is pervasive,
and the per capita murder rate is one of the highest in the United States.

The School District

Local government is the largest employer in Steel Town and the public school system is the largest single governmental employer. Fifty years ago, the school district had eight high schools—two of which were considered lighthouse schools. Because of declining enrollments, only three remain—and none is considered to be a model school. The dropout rate for the district is nearly 40%; and only about 15% of those who graduate from high school enroll at four-year institutions of higher education.

Statewide achievement tests exhibit that most schools in Steel Town have scores well below the state average. In recent years, the state department of education has provided direct assistance, human and financial, in an effort to aid the district. One of the programs that has been developed is a recruitment effort to attract outstanding young teachers to work in the school system. Included are financial incentives for new employees. Teachers and administrators sarcastically refer to them as "signing bonuses." Since being initiated, the recruitment program has had modest success.

The School

The building that houses McKinley Junior High School is nearly 50 years old. The drab yellow brick building sits on a single city block. Containing grades 7 and 8, McKinley has approximately 600 students.

The principal, Dallas Bacon, has worked in the Steel Town school district for more than 20 years. He has been principal at the school for nearly seven of those years. Because of enrollment declines and a corresponding reduction in the number of teachers, only a handful of faculty at McKinley has less than 10 years of professional experience. In the past three years, only two new teachers have joined the staff. The faculty jokingly refer to them as the "bonus babies," a label associated with the fact that each received the financial incentive to work in Steel Town. The newest teacher at the school is Ray Morris.

The Teacher

Ray Morris grew up on a grain farm in South Dakota. He attended a small liberal arts college where he majored in mathematics. In his sophomore year, he decided to become a teacher at the urging of one of his professors. It was during the last semester of his senior year when he first learned of Steel Town. A recruiter was visiting the campus, and at the urging of the placement office director, Ray met with her. Four months later, he moved to Steel Town to teach at McKinley Junior High.

With the exception of a few vacations and college, Ray had spent very little time away from the family farm in South Dakota. His adjustment to Steel Town was difficult. He decided to live in an adjoining city—one that had far fewer social and economic problems. Each day he drove 17 miles to his school—but it was like driving into a different country. He could tell precisely when he had entered

Steel Town by seeing the deteriorated houses and feeling the jolts he received when he failed to avoid the numerous potholes in the streets.

At first, Ray had told himself that he made a big mistake by coming to work in Steel Town. But by late October, his self-doubts started to subside as he adjusted to his new environment. He now had several good friends on the faculty, and he found working with the students to be intrinsically rewarding. Winston Gray, a science teacher in his mid-50s, had become his best friend at McKinley. The two had their preparation periods scheduled at the same time, and this allowed them to interact almost every day. Gray was willing to answer questions and to provide advice—but he did neither unless he was requested to do so.

The Problem

Although administrators at McKinley went to great lengths to avoid the use of the term *tracking,* they nevertheless paid attention to student achievement and ability in scheduling students into classes in language arts, science, social studies, and mathematics. Hence, Ray's eighth-grade math class was composed of students who had done well in the subject in the past. It was a small class with only 13 students.

Toward the end of the first semester, Ray had become concerned about the performance of one his students—Malcolm Daily. Although the student had received virtually all As in previous math classes, Ray found him to be a marginal student—especially in this class composed of the school's most able students. In class, Malcolm exuded confidence. He was almost always the first to volunteer to answer questions, and his overt behavior indicated that he thought he was the smartest student in the group. Even his classmates seemed convinced, and many treated him as if his self-perceptions were accurate. Yet his scores on quizzes and examinations did not substantiate his self-imposed status. His scores on written tests were usually the lowest, or near the lowest, in the class. It seemed that the more structured a task, the less able he was to complete it successfully.

Confused by Malcolm's performance, Ray decided to keep a log detailing the student's actions in class. After six weeks, several recurring behaviors became evident:

1. Frequently when Malcolm failed to answer a question or solve a problem for which he had volunteered in class, he would have a criticism of the problem or the way in which it was posed. For example, Ray gave students data about a fictional company manufacturing light bulbs. Included were figures about all investments made by the company in the last year. He posed the question, "What percent of the company's investments in the last year were in marketing and advertising?" The answer required that the students add the figures for these two functions and then divide the sum by the total for annual investments. Malcolm immediately raised his hand, indicating he knew the answer, but once at the chalkboard, he struggled. He made a division error in the second

stage of the problem. When this was pointed out to him, he argued with the teacher that he was confused by the question.

2. When Malcolm did not do well on tests or quizzes, he had two or three standard rationalizations. A common response was that he was expecting a much more difficult test. Accordingly, he would contend that he studied the wrong material. Another excuse he used was that he was not feeling well at the time of the test. But his favorite explanation was that many bright people simply did not do well on written tests.

3. Once every two weeks, Ray had a math contest that was similar to a spelling bee. Students were asked to select a problem from three categories, "average," "difficult," and "very difficult." If a student successfully answered, he or she would earn 1, 2, or 3 points respectively for his or her team (the students were divided into two teams). After several months, students were reluctant to have Malcolm on their team because he always selected questions from the "very difficult" category—and he rarely was able to answer them correctly. By contrast, other students rarely selected the most difficult problems.

4. When Malcolm encountered failure, he tended to remind the teacher and his classmates of his performance in previous classes and his high goals in life. He often told his peers and teachers that he was still trying to decide whether to become a physician or a scientist.

During parent conferences held midway through the first semester, Malcolm's mother attended, but his father did not. At the time of the conference, Ray was still unsure about Malcolm's performance in his class, but he did point out to Mrs. Daily that her son was having difficulty with tests. He asked if Malcolm usually had problems with tests.

His mother responded, "My son is a very bright boy. He doesn't like to take tests, and maybe that is why he doesn't do well. His father thinks that too much emphasis is placed on tests anyway."

Shortly following the parent conference, students were given a quiz. Again Malcolm did not do well. He stayed after class to talk to his teacher.

"Mr. Morris, I just wasn't feeling too well yesterday. I had a headache, and I know I could do better. Can you give me a project to do outside of class so I can make up the points I lost on the quiz?"

Ray decided not to grant the request. He gave the student two reasons. First, he had not done this for other students; thus he was not sure it would be the fair thing to do. Second, he indicated that he was concerned whether Malcolm really knew how to do the math problems covered by the quiz.

Over the next month, Malcolm's performance did not improve, and Ray decided to examine the student's permanent file. This was an act Ray tried to avoid because he felt that the contents of student files might prejudice decisions he made as a teacher. But given his concerns for Malcolm, he made an exception. Data in the file revealed that Malcolm scored in the average range on group ability tests and slightly above average on achievement tests. Yet his grades were mostly A's. There were several documents in the file that supported his academic performance. They were written by former teachers who praised Malcolm's high motivation and aspirations. For example, his mathematics teacher in the seventh grade wrote the following note on his final grade report:

> It was a pleasure to have Malcolm in my class. He is bright and highly motivated. He does best when he is able to structure his own learning experiences. I don't think he likes to take tests. He performs at a higher level when he can express himself verbally. His effort was outstanding.

After reviewing the file, Ray made an appointment with Mr. Bacon, the principal, to discuss Malcolm. During that meeting, the principal indicated that no other teacher had expressed concern regarding this student. The principal added that he was not unduly concerned that a student with modest ability test scores had high grades.

"I put more stock in his grades than I do those test scores," he told Ray.

After his meeting with Mr. Bacon, Ray met with two colleagues who also had Malcolm in class, Miss Prichard and Mrs. Best. Miss Prichard had him in language arts and Mrs. Best was his science teacher. Miss Prichard said that Malcolm was creative, and his assignments done outside of class were always quite good. Mrs. Best said that Malcolm had not done especially well on two tests, but he was given an opportunity to do extra assignments to boost his grade. The assignments were always well done. When asked about test performance, Miss Prichard said that she did not give tests; rather grades in her class were based on student assignments and projects.

On numerous occasions, Ray also discussed Malcolm with his friend and colleague, Winston Gray. He told him about his log and the contents of Malcolm's file. Winston had never had Malcolm as a student, but he knew the boy. His advice to Ray was to be honest with the parents and the student. He said that it would be better for the student to adjust his self-perception than to go on believing he could accomplish tasks beyond his reach. He further concluded that Malcolm was benefiting from the fact that he was in an environment where his high aspirations were atypical. Hence, others admired him without really considering whether his expectations were realistic. Students at McKinley rarely talked about going to college. Discussions of whether there was any merit in finishing high school were far more common.

With the semester examination just one week away, Ray called Malcolm's parents and asked that they have a conference with them. This time, Mr. Daily accompanied his wife. After sharing his concerns about Malcolm's performance, Mr. Daily, a supervisor in the city's sanitation program, launched into a verbal blast of the young teacher.

"My boy is an excellent student. He's done well in math in all his previous grades. You want to know why he's having trouble? Maybe you ought to look in the mirror. Maybe it's your tests! Maybe you don't know how to handle really smart kids! For you to stand there and tell me Malcolm has a problem is an insult."

Ray tried to retain his confidence. He took a deep breath and said, "I could be part of the problem, but I didn't ask you to see me to place blame. I want to help Malcolm. I want to find ways to improve his achievement in mathematics."

Mr. Daily interrupted, "All this talk about improving education. The governor says we don't expect enough from our kids. Here's a boy who has big plans, high hopes. And we get someone like you to come here and tell him he can't make it. Well, I'm not going to stand for that."

"I'm not trying to tell your son or you that he can't make it. I'm simply trying to convey the message that he is not mastering much of the material in this math class. This problem will become increasingly serious as he encounters advanced math classes. I want to have him tested by our school psychologist so that we can get a clearer picture of his academic ability."

"Nobody's testing my son," the father shouted. "He's not crazy. He's not troubled. I'm getting him out of your class. You don't seem to understand these kids. And you surely don't understand the folks in Steel Town. I'm wasting my time with you, I'm going to see the principal."

The Challenge

Analyze Ray's decisions in this case. Would you have done anything differently?

ISSUES FOR FURTHER REFLECTION

1. Is it common for parents to set academic and career expectations for their children?
2. In what ways do parents reinforce their children's self-perceptions?
3. What is test anxiety? What leads you to believe or not believe Malcolm's contention that most really intelligent persons do not do well on written tests?
4. Do you believe that teachers are influenced by the past performance of students, that is, how they did in previous academic work?
5. To what extent do you believe that cultural differences are an issue in this case?
6. In general, should teachers be candid with students about their academic ability?
7. What activities could you suggest that might have been more effective in motivating Malcolm in a positive manner?
8. Is it possible for one to have excessive motivation?
9. If Malcolm was attending school in an affluent suburban district, do you think he would have been treated differently by his teachers? Why or why not?
10. Assess the advice that Winston Gray gave to Ray. Do you think it was good advice?
11. What do you think of Ray's suggestion that Malcolm be examined by the school psychologist?
12. Should a student with average ability be discouraged from setting lofty goals such as becoming a physician? Why or why not?
13. Why would students continue to see Malcolm as a bright student even though he repeatedly fails in certain tasks?
14. Explain Malcolm's tendency to opt for very difficult tasks when given the opportunity.

15. In the case, there are several indications that Malcolm performs better when he is able to have control over his learning experiences. Is this information relevant? Why or why not?

16. Do you believe that the school's practice of placing the most able students in one class of mathematics is relevant to this case? Why or why not?

17. What is your opinion of Ray's practice of not looking at student files unless there is a serious problem?

SUGGESTED READINGS

Bardwell, R. (1984). The learning of expectations and attributions. *Education and Treatment of Children, 7*(3), 237–245.

Dembo, M. (1994). *Applying educational psychology in the classroom* (5th ed.). New York: Longman (see chapter 4).

Good, T., & Brophy, J. (1990). *Educational psychology: A realistic approach* (4th ed.). New York: Longman (see pp. 356–487).

Harrington-Lueker, D. (1989). Are today's fast-track parents pushing their children too hard? *American School Board Journal, 176*(4), 27–29.

Henson, K. (1993). *Methods and strategies for teaching in secondary and middle schools* (2nd ed.). New York: Longman (see chapter 12).

Marsh, H. (1983). Relations among dimensions of self-attribution, dimensions of self-concept, and academic achievement. *Journal of Educational Psychology, 76*(6), 1291–1308.

Marsh, H. (1986). Self-serving effect (bias?) in academic attributions: Its relation to academic achievement and self-concept. *Journal of Educational Psychology, 78*(3), 190–200.

Seginer, R. (1983). Parents' educational expectations and children's academic achievement: A literature review. *Merrill-Palmer Quarterly, 29*(1), 1–23.

Serna, L. (1989). Implications of student motivation on study skills instruction. *Academic Therapy, 24*(4), 503–514.

Tierno, M. (1991). Responding to the socially motivated behaviors of early adolescents: Recommendations for classroom management. *Adolescence, 26*(103), 569–577.

Wagner, J. (1983). Self concept: Research and educational implications. *Studies in Educational Evaluation, 9*(2), 239–251.

Wigfield, A. (1988). Children's attributions for success and failure: Effects of age and attentional focus. *Journal of Educational Psychology, 80*(1), 76–81.

Yee, D., & Eccles, J. (1988). Parent perceptions and attributions for children's math achievement. *Sex Roles: A Journal of Research, 19*(5–6), 317–333.

CASE 25

Getting Children to Achieve

PREPARING TO USE THE CASE

Background Information

Children who come to school for the first time present a myriad of challenges for the teacher. At the outset, helping children learn and obey rules is an overriding concern. Getting children to learn to care for themselves—from tying their shoes to combing their hair—may consume a substantial amount of time for some children. Given the short attention span of children at this age, time must be carefully organized so that interest in activities is maintained. Helping children adjust from the home environment to the school environment stands as a major task.

Taking into account the widely differing characteristics of children provides another important challenge for the teacher. Intellectual ability, physical and social development, and cultural and economic background may vary greatly among students in the class.

While the concepts and skills to be taught at this age are basic and cover some introductory content from all the traditional disciplines, the way to organize how they are taught presents a critical challenge to the teacher. Numerous questions must be answered, including:

1. When is it most appropriate to model the expected instructional outcome?
2. When should visual material be chosen over text?
3. When should children be utilized to teach their peers?
4. How can play be used to instruct? How much time should be devoted to memorization?

5. How much time should be provided for observation?

6. How much time should be scheduled for practice?

In orchestrating instruction, the teacher must determine how each instructional decision affects each child's learning. Adjustments must be made to improve each child's learning over time. Finding a way to motivate each child to succeed occupies the greatest part of the teacher's planning time. An understanding of motivation theory can assist the teacher in getting children to achieve. Knowing how to apply behavioral, need, and cognitive theories can enhance the teacher's ability to get children to achieve.

In this case a kindergarten teacher must find a way to motivate children in her two half-day classes. Both classes are highly heterogeneous. Several cultural groups are represented in each class. The economic background of the children is diverse. There is a great range in abilities among the children. How to address the diversity she faces in the class and how to motivate the children to achieve are the challenges the teacher faces.

Topics for Reflection
1. Achievement
2. Individual differences
3. Instructional planning
4. Instructional strategies
5. Motivation
6. Multicultural education
7. Teacher intervention
8. Teacher values and beliefs

THE CASE

The Community

Los Altos is a large urban center with a highly diverse population of approximately 700,000 people. Tourism, banking, and finance are the primary employers in this year-round, warm-weather port city. Nearly 65 percent of the city's employed population work in service-related occupations. Because of its location on the West Coast, in recent years the city has received a large influx of refugees from Southeast Asia.

Twelve percent of the population of Los Altos are Asian, 3 percent are Arab, 27 percent are African-American, 48 percent are Hispanic, and 10 percent are white. Twenty-seven different languages, including dialects, are spoken in this metropolitan area. Most of the neighborhoods in Los Altos are racially and ethnically segregated. There is little integrated housing. Within the last 17 years the racial breakdown of the city has gone from 73 percent white and 27 percent minority population to 10 percent white and 90 percent minority.

The School District

Los Altos Unified School District is a K–12 district and has the state's fourth largest enrollment. As the community has changed, the schools have been affected by "white flight" to private schools and to suburban school districts. At the same time, among minority groups many residents with high socioeconomic status have also chosen to send their children to private schools or have moved to the suburbs. In response, a federal court judge has placed the district in a court-mandated, countywide desegregation plan, which is a "tri-ethnic" plan that lumps both Asians and whites into a "majority" classification. All other groups are considered minorities. The Hispanic and African-American populations comprise the other segments of the "tri-ethnic" plan. The judge has ruled that every effort must be made to provide racial balance in the schools. A balance of 60 percent to 40 percent minority/majority or 60 percent to 40 percent majority/minority is required.

The school district is divided into three geographic areas. Area A, the northern part of the district, is populated mostly by white and Asian residents, with a sprinkling of minority inhabitants of high socioeconomic status. People who live in this area are employed primarily in professional positions. Area B is the east-central and southeast part of the district. For the past decade, it has been largely populated by Hispanics. More recently, emigrants from Southeast Asia have tilted the racial and ethnic balance. Most of the citizens are factory workers and service employees. Area C is the western third of Los Altos Unified School District. African-Americans, largely employed in blue-collar jobs, occupy this region of the city.

Each of the three areas has a superintendent, a curriculum specialist, a personnel and a financial-affairs officer, and a health, safety, and transportation officer. The district superintendent, Larry Brock, has served in this position for 14 years. When he became superintendent, he surrounded himself with loyal administrators hired from the "outside." Each subordinate administrator in the district has autonomy in making decisions. Dr. Brock prides himself on being an effective delegator.

The School

Los Altos Central Elementary School, a K–6 school, was erected in 1928. It is the oldest school building left in the city. At least 12 percent of the students who begin the year at Central Elementary leave before the end of the school year. About 3 percent of these departing students return the following year, because their parents are seasonal farm workers who come back to the neighborhood when their work is done. There are 360 students and 23 faculty and staff members. Two sections of classes are usually offered at each grade level, except kindergarten, which has one section only. Nearly 25 percent of the students speak a primary language other than English.

Mr. Frederick Alvarez, the principal, has a bachelor's degree in elementary education and a master's degree in educational administration. He was born and has lived all of his life in Los Altos. He is known as a strict disciplinarian and a hard-line follower of school policies and procedures. He is extremely loyal to the Area B superintendent, who is also Hispanic and a lifetime resident of Los Altos. Most of the teachers at Central Elementary are African-American and Hispanic. Four of the 23 faculty and staff members are white, and five are Asian-American.

The Teacher

Donna Liu is one of the Asian-American teachers on the staff. For all but the first six years of her life she has resided with her parents and two brothers in an integrated neighborhood in Los Altos. Her parents own and operate a restaurant in Echo Park, the Los Altos neighborhood in which they live. Both of her brothers are older. One works in the family business; the other is an accountant with a computer company.

Ms. Liu is a new graduate of Los Altos State University. For most of her life she intended to work in the family business. While she completed a precollege curriculum in high school, she matriculated at Los Altos University, declaring a major in economics and a minor in marketing in the school of business. After one semester, she became disenchanted with business. Because not all of her course work would transfer to the elementary school teaching credential, she took courses during two summers "to catch up."

Donna Liu takes pride in her creative ability. As a college student, she participated in a folk-dance group, exhibited a showing of watercolors, and performed in the university orchestra. She also ran cross-country on the track team. She approached her first year of teaching with confidence and excitement.

Her position at Central Elementary serves as a fifth or internship year in which she is being supervised by Naydean Todd, her mentor teacher. The internship year is a relatively new requirement passed recently by the state legislature. Every prospective teacher must undergo this probationary year. The salary is the same as formerly paid to beginning teachers. At the end of the year, her principal—Fred Alvarez—must make a recommendation to the department of education concerning certification for Ms. Liu. His options are to recommend for immediate certification, for a second year of internship work, or for dismissal from the school.

Mr. Alvarez has taken the position that he will make a recommendation, but will rely heavily on input from experienced teachers who serve as mentors in his school. Mrs. Naydean Todd has been at Central Elementary for 23 years. She came to the school as one of the first African-American teachers in a group of four hired as a part of the district's aggressive affirmative-action plan. Like Ms. Liu, she has resided in Los Altos most of her life. She moved to the city from Birmingham, Alabama, when she was three years old. She also attended Los Altos State, when the institution was still a college. For her mentoring work, Mrs. Todd receives 50 minutes of released time one day each week. This schedule is designed to allow her to observe Ms. Liu.

Mrs. Todd is considered a "pillar" of the school. Not only has she taught longer than any other teacher there, but she has also twice been named Teacher of the Year in the school district. She is known as a straightforward, no-nonsense, demanding teacher. She is impatient, expecting other teachers to be as hardworking and as skilled as she.

Ms. Liu has two sections of kindergarten—one in the morning and one in the afternoon. She has 26 children in the morning and 23 in the afternoon. The morning class consists of 7 white, 10 African-American, 6 Hispanic, and 3 Asian children. Nearly one-third of the youngsters come from single-family homes and live in low-income, government-subsidized housing. Another third come from blue-collar families. The remainder have parents who hold professional positions. A wide range of social maturity and academic abilities is reflected in the class. The afternoon class is much less balanced, with 2 white, 18 African-American, 2 Hispanic, and 1 Asian child enrolled. More than half of the children come from welfare homes. Only three of the students come from homes where the parents occupy white-collar jobs. Most of the children are of low ability.

The Incident

The first few weeks have been hectic for Ms. Liu. Organization of the classroom has not been a problem. Two days after commencement she was at Central Elementary developing learning centers, making colorful bulletin boards, and preparing daily schedules for activities. With pride she created hats of different shapes and colors, each with one child's name on it, to be used as name tags the first few days of school. She organized the closet space in the classroom, identifying each child's space with a picture of a zoo animal. Although the janitors had cleaned her room before she arrived, Ms. Liu had coaxed her brothers to help polish the floors, scrub the walls and windows, and clean the desks and chalkboards on a weekend before the start of school.

She prepared two general areas in the classroom: one for small-group reading and one for "quiet time."

Each of her five learning centers has a focus. One is stocked with various plastic and wooden manipulatives (puzzles, building blocks, figures). A second center serves as a science area. Jars with insects and small animals, plants, and rocks adorn the table. A third center contains art materials—paper of different sizes, shapes, colors, and textures. Crayons of every conceivable color occupy two shoe boxes. Word cards, large letters of the alphabet, lined paper, and pencils are stacked on a fourth table. A record player, records, and "dress-up" clothes are neatly organized on a fifth table.

The "quiet time" area has an old, worn couch, an oversized stuffed chair, several colorful beanbag pillows, and a fluffy throw rug. Adjacent to this area is the small-group reading area where another throw rug was fitted in the midst of several bookshelves jammed tightly with simple readers and picture books.

Ms. Liu has been provided with a paid aide for both sections of her class. Mrs. Valerie Munoz, the mother of two children enrolled in the upper grades at Central Elementary, is assigned to the morning class. Martha Spinnel, a 62-year-old widow and grandmother, is assigned to the afternoon class. Ms. Liu had visited briefly with both aides before the start of school, but because they were not required to work before the first day of classes, she was not sure how she would work with them. Nonetheless, she was pleased to have their assistance.

The first day of school had been trying. In the first section of kindergarten 15 children came to class. Ms. Liu could not account for the other 11 on her roster.

Of the 15 children who arrived, 2 of the children spoke no English. Several cried when their mother or father left. A few of the children wore dirty, worn clothes and appeared hungry. This suspicion was verified during the snack period, when several children kept asking for more food or tried to take food from other children's desks. A couple of shouting matches and a scuffle with fists had resulted. Through the morning Ms. Liu felt as if she were riding a high-speed, nonstop Ferris wheel. Several children constantly vied for her attention. She found that the ability level of the children varied immensely, from youngsters who could not recognize shapes and colors, tie their shoes, zip their pants, or put on their jackets to others who not only knew shapes and colors but also could print their names, phone numbers, and a few words. Three of the children could even read some of the simple materials she had prepared for later in the year.

The afternoon went in the similar way, although it was not as tense. A greater number of students listed on her roster arrived, but she faced the same problems with highly varied ability levels. Unlike the morning, when no one had become ill, during the afternoon two children vomited. At the end of the day Ms. Liu was exhausted. She had assumed that getting through the first day was the test and that the coming days would get better.

They did not. Each day seemed to mirror the first. Attendance during each session was spotty. She spent time each night trying to contact parents, with mixed success. Several children had no phone in their homes. In most instances when she did reach a parent, relative, or sibling on the phone, there was an excuse for the student's absence: The child had been ill; the parents had overslept; the car had broken down. Because she could not reach each child's parent, she decided to visit the homes of children who were absent. This effort had similar results. In some cases the address she was given was incorrect. In one instance there was an empty lot at the address to which she had driven. In several cases the parents appeared embarrassed when she arrived. In only a few instances did she appear to be welcome.

The aides had not been as helpful as she had hoped. Mrs. Munoz had trouble following directions. Although she was expected to spend most of her time in clerical work, Mrs. Munoz preferred interacting with the children. Ms. Liu spent an inordinate amount of time each day redirecting Mrs. Munoz. In contrast, Martha Spinnel did precisely what she was asked to do. However, she was slow and careless. Ms. Liu found herself correcting Mrs. Spinnel's mistakes. In some ways having an aide in the class was like having an additional child in the room.

On Friday morning of the first week, Mrs. Todd was scheduled to visit Ms. Liu in her classroom. Midway through the morning, Mrs. Todd arrived. Immediately, as Mrs. Todd entered, several of the children scrambled around her and tugged at her dress. Ms. Liu, with some struggle, managed to get the children back to their learning centers. Mrs. Todd took a seat in the corner in the back of the room. With a notepad and pen in hand she recorded the following notes:

- Lacks confidence, seems unsure of self.
- Variety of centers provides interest (at some centers children do not seem to have a purpose).

- Focuses mostly on management.
- Children spend little time on skill building and achievement.
- Aide appears to jump from activity to activity. Doesn't stay with or follow through with an activity.
- Children appear to like Ms. Liu. They are friendly toward her, vie for her attention (some by acting out in negative ways).
- Has difficulty maintaining overall order.
- Room is neat, tidy, and colorful.

After 50 minutes of observing, Mrs. Todd got up to leave. On her way out she stopped and said to Ms. Liu, "Let's have lunch together as planned. I'll meet you back here in your room at noon. We'll go over my notes at that time."

"Okay," Ms. Liu said, "See you then."

From the time Mrs. Todd left until the morning class was dismissed, troubled thoughts flashed across Ms. Liu's mind. All of them pointed to the fact that she didn't think the class went well during the observation. As she had packed a lunch that day, she waited for Mrs. Todd to arrive from the cafeteria and prepared the classroom for the afternoon session. At two minutes past noon Mrs. Todd, carrying a tray of food, tapped at the door. Ms. Liu hurried to the door and opened it.

"Thank you for taking time from your lunch hour to visit with me," Ms. Liu greeted.

"No problem. I think it's probably the best time for both of us," Mrs. Todd observed.

After pushing stacks of children's books aside, they sat down together at one of the tables used for an open reading center. "Let's go over my notes," Mrs. Todd began.

Over the weekend Ms. Liu thought about the kindergarten classes.

The Challenge

You are Ms. Liu. What steps would you take to motivate the children in your classes?

ISSUES FOR FURTHER REFLECTION

1. What motivational strategy appears most necessary to help Ms. Liu get the children to achieve?
2. What behaviors are exhibited by the children that contribute to her inability to motivate them to achieve?
3. In what ways might Ms. Liu's behavior be a contributing factor?
4. In what ways might Ms. Liu's inexperience be a contributing factor?
5. What is known about the attitudes of the children that might explain some of the difficulty Ms. Liu faces?
6. What is known about the work habits of the children that might explain some of the difficulty?

7. What relationship exists between the organization of content and the children's level of motivation?

8. What role do the children's parents play in motivating them to achieve?

9. What might Ms. Liu do to strengthen the parents' role in motivating their children to achieve?

10. Has the behavior of the aides contributed to classroom difficulties? Explain.

11. What additional information would be helpful in analyzing the difficulty Ms. Liu is having in motivating the children?

SUGGESTED READINGS

Ames, C. (1992). Classrooms: Goals, structures, and student motivation. *Journal of Educational Psychology, 84*(3), 261–271.

Blumenfeld, P. (1992). Classroom learning and motivation: Clarifying and expanding goal theory. *Journal of Educational Psychology, 84*(3), 272–281.

Bredekamp, S. (Ed.). (1986). *Developmentally appropriate practice.* Washington, DC: National Association for the Education of Young Children.

Chance, P. (1992). The rewards of learning. *Phi Delta Kappan, 74*(3), 200–207.

Corno, L. (1992). Encouraging students to take responsibility for learning and performance. *Elementary School Journal, 93*(1), 69–83.

Curtis, S. (1987). New views on movement development and implications for curriculum in early childhood education. In C. Seefeldt (Ed.), *Early childhood curriculum: A review of current research* (pp. 257–270). New York: Teachers College Press.

Deci, E. (1992). Autonomy and competence as motivational factors in students with learning disabilities and emotional handicaps. *Journal of Learning Disabilities, 25*(7), 457–471.

Dembo, M. (1994). *Applying educational psychology in the classroom* (5th ed.). New York: Longman (see chapters 4, 6, 7).

Elkind, D. (1986). Formal education and early childhood education: An essential difference. *Phi Delta Kappan, 67*(9), 631–636.

Genishi, C. (1987). Acquiring oral language and communicative competence. In C. Seefeldt (Ed.). *Early childhood curriculum: A review of current research* (pp. 75–106). New York: Teachers College Press.

Good, T., & Brophy, J. (1990). *Educational psychology: A realistic approach* (4th ed.). New York: Longman (see chapters 14, 15, 16, 17).

Henson, K. (1993). *Methods and strategies for teaching in secondary and middle schools* (2nd ed.). New York: Longman (see chapters 3, 5, 7, 8, 9).

Kuykendall, J. (1992). Creating classroom cooperation. *Contemporary Education, 63*(3), 221–224.

Pasch, M., Sparks-Langer, G., Gardner, T., Starko, A., & Moody, C. (1991). *Teaching as decision making: Instructional practices for the successful teacher.* New York: Longman (see chapters 8, 9).

Zahn, G. (1986). Cooperative learning and classroom climate. *Journal of School Psychology, 24*(4), 351–362.

CASE 26

Teacher Effectiveness: Unrealistic Expectations Produce Anxiety

PREPARING TO USE THE CASE

Background Information

During the 1990s *teacher empowerment* has become a household term to most teachers. It is more than a term; it is a promise to involve teachers in school decisions that reach far beyond the teachers' own classrooms. Attempts to significantly increase students' levels of achievement have shown that increasing the achievement levels for an entire school population requires changing the structure of the school. Such attempts have shown that the only way to improve a school's structure is by involving teachers with decisions about how the school is operated; teachers must be involved in all types of decisions, ranging from practices in curriculum development to decisions about what the school wants to accomplish and how best to spend its funds to achieve these goals.

Parents, too, are being involved more than ever before in major decision making in schools throughout the nation. Some interesting things happen when people are involved in decision making. For example, they are willing to give more of their time and energy to the work. They also begin to identify with the mission. Repeatedly, parents who serve on site-based school councils develop a keen determination to assure that the school achieves its goals.

The increased attention the media have given to education in recent years has also raised the level of overall awareness of the importance of education to the welfare of the individual and the nation. Do not be surprised if you discover that the community where you teach is dominated by such determined individuals. Couple the high priority that people are now assigning to education with the increasing belief of most parents that their children are above average, and the results are high parental expectations on the teacher to assure that children reach their academic capacities.

The following case involves a teacher who tries hard, maybe too hard, to take his students to their potential. As you read it, think about the significance of students' self-concepts and the effect of this teacher's behaviors on the self-concepts of his students.

Topics for Reflection
1. The relationships between self-concept, motivation, and achievement
2. The relationship between teachers' expectations and their students' achievement levels
3. The effects of objectives on motivation and anxiety
4. The effects of anxiety on academic performance

THE CASE

Madisonville, a city of 100,000, is the home of one of the nation's space-flight centers. Great emphasis is placed on education. When the space industry first moved to the area some 30 years ago, Madisonville was a sleepy little town of less than 10,000 people. But the city planners were aware that attracting scientists, engineers, and mathematicians to the area would require first-rate schools. The rapid growth in population was paralleled by a rapid growth in size and quality of the schools. Salaries were increased significantly for several years until they were far above the rest of the state. Madisonville residents are justified in taking great pride in their school system.

The Schools

Madisonville Senior High, which once housed grades 7–12, expanded so much that the lower three grades were removed, leaving only grades 10–12. A new junior high, Madisonville Junior High School, was built on a campus adjacent to the high school. All of the new elementary schools that sprang up in the county over the past 30 years have been established as first-rate schools equipped with the best faculty and facilities available anywhere. Almost all of the teachers in the area hold master's degrees, and several have doctorates in education or in their teaching fields.

Deerfield Junior High is a rural school located about ten miles from Madisonville. When the students graduate from Deerfield, they are bused to Madisonville Senior High for grades 10–12. Most Madisonville High graduates go on to one of the state's two major research universities. In recent years, an increasing number of Madisonville graduates have received scholarships at such institutions as Stanford, Harvard, and M.I.T. This is not surprising for a school whose students win top national recognition every year.

The Teachers

Lyle King and Clay Rutledge grew up in the Deerfield community. Both attended one of the state's major research universities. Their high school friendship continued as they roomed together throughout their college years. Because both of them chose to major in mathematics, they were classmates in the majority of their courses. Both were excellent students and were always among the top performers in their classes. Neither had given much thought to the type of job he wanted; they just enjoyed math.

During their senior year, both Lyle and Clay decided they wanted to teach high school math. It seemed too late to change colleges, so they finished their degrees and immediately entered a new fifth-year program. Although called the fifth-year program, nobody completed the program in just one academic year, but by going to school full-time during each summer preceding and following the academic year, both Lyle and Clay completed the program in 16 months.

As they approached the end of their program, Lyle and Clay both applied for teaching positions at Madisonville Senior High, but they were told that unlike most schools in the state, which seemed always to have a shortage of math teachers, for years, Madisonville had maintained a standing list of experienced applicants waiting for an opening. They were advised to submit their applications and get their names added to the waiting list.

They followed this advice, while continuing their search for local teaching positions. Lyle was offered the only vacancy at Madisonville Junior High. Clay was less fortunate but was offered a one-year position at Deerfield Junior High, which he gladly accepted. During this year, he would replace Mrs. Gail Wright, who had taken a pregnancy leave of absence.

The Incident

Although Clay had to settle for teaching at what he knew was a far less prestigious school than Madisonville, he was not worried. After all, by the end of the year a position would probably open up at Madisonville. But Clay was concerned with the fact that he would be teaching at the junior high level. His fifth-year program had provided rather extensive field experiences, but all of them—including his student teaching—had been at the senior high level.

Clay found another aspect of Deerfield to be a significant asset—the privilege of teaching with a highly competent, professional faculty. Because Deerfield Junior High was one of six feeder schools for Madisonville Senior High, he reasoned that there would be little difference between the two schools. After all, over time, the two schools had essentially the same students and the same parents. In fact, the success of Madisonville Senior High depended on the quality of teaching and learning that occurred in Deerfield Junior High and the other feeder schools.

Having met the Deerfield faculty, Clay was sure that he would fit in well with such a professional group of teachers. Although he didn't tell them, he made a silent resolution to pull his share of the weight at Deerfield by making sure that students learned as much or more in his classes than they learned in their other classes.

After only a couple of weeks into the term, Clay found the job much more challenging than he had anticipated. In fact, the job of teaching math to the students at Deerfield Junior High proved to be a nearly impossible challenge. When they were together, the age group was noisy, but as individuals, most students were likeable. Clay wondered why he was no longer elated over this new assignment. As he pondered the situation, he concluded that it was the paradoxical nature of this job that made it both frustrating yet, at the same time, somewhat satisfying. Some of his students were very serious-minded (the college-bound group); others were completely apathetic. On one day the group would be serious, displaying mature behavior, but on the next day even the more serious students would behave like immature, irresponsible children. During some lessons, they accepted responsibility with little prodding, but for other lessons they had to be coddled and "spoonfed." Clay remembered reading about the paradoxical nature of adolescence. His methods text explained it as a perpetual dilemma. Adolescents strive to be accepted as adults, yet they are pressured by their peers to behave immaturely.

Throughout the first grading period, Clay made a special effort to discuss each student's daily progress. He was a little surprised and worried to see that many of these students had rather low expectations for themselves. David Steel was a fairly bright student and a well-mannered youngster. During one of Clay's one-on-one discussions with him, David openly expressed his level of expectations for himself. "Mr. Rutledge, I'm just no good at math. I'll try to earn a C or a D, but I've got to be honest with myself. I just wasn't cut out for math."

At first Clay wondered why David's remarks worried him so much. Then he realized that David's view of himself was fairly typical of most of his classmates who held equally low expectations of themselves. Clay knew that as long as students aimed for making C's or D's there was little chance that they would exceed these expectations.

As the first six-week grading period ended, Clay saw that his previous concerns had been justified. Several students in his class did not do well at all. Some of the parents, unhappy with their children's grades, requested a meeting with him to discuss the situation. Following the meeting, they concluded that Clay was not as effective as Ms. Wright, and they expressed concern to the principal, Ms. Cole, who summoned Clay for a discussion. Ms. Cole has served as principal for five years. Prior to this position, she was assistant principal, and before that she taught for seven years. Through the years, Ms. Cole had kept up with the latest innovations. She had continued taking courses at the university and she also read professional journals and attended noncredit workshops. Incidentally, she was responsible for bringing several in-service workshops right to her faculty. The Deerfield teachers had a good role model in Ms. Cole. Clay wondered if he would ever be as self-assured and competent as she was.

Clay entered the office feeling certain that some of the parents had expressed their concern to Ms. Cole. "Good morning, Mr. Rutledge. Thanks for coming. I think you know there's been some concern among some parents about the rate of progress of their children. I hope you understand that it's not unusual for these parents to express concern over academic matters. They know that competition is keen at Madisonville High, and they want to be sure that their children are well prepared. Math is the one subject of greatest concern, since for many of our students it's a stumbling block for admission to and success in college.''

"Ms. Cole, I understand, and I am equally concerned about this problem. I explain each lesson thoroughly. Sometimes these students absorb the new content like sponges, and the next day they seem completely resistant and determined to learn nothing. I teach all lessons the same way. I lecture for the first half of the period, then I assign problems. I may grade papers while they're busy working on their seat assignments, but I always welcome questions. Oh yes, and I always give homework assignments.''

"How about objectives? Do you have objectives identified for each lesson? And do you share these objectives with the students?''

"I usually tell them that they'll need to master this lesson in order to go on to the next one. This year, for the first time, during the first week, I held an orientation session with each class, and at that time I told them how each lesson builds on the previous one, and each year on the previous year. I also told them that if they get behind in this class they probably will never catch up. They need to know this so they'll understand how important it is to get all of their work done.''

"I see," Ms. Cole nodded. "Some of the parents said that their major concern is that their children are developing attitudes of hopelessness. Have you done anything that might cause them to feel inadequate in your class?''

"I just try to be realistic with them. Some kids simply don't have the ability to do math. I think I have to be honest with them, so I tell them that some of them won't make it. To do otherwise would just cause more pain later on," Clay explained.

"I know that it's hard to please everyone, especially when you're temporarily filling in for someone. I don't expect you to be another Mrs. Wright. Just try to relieve some of the anxiety among your students, and I'm sure everything will be fine. Please let me know if I can assist you. Thanks for coming in.''

As Clay left the office he wondered how he should begin correcting this problem. He thought, "I need a plan to achieve this goal.''

Over the next few days, Clay could think of nothing but his conversation with Ms. Cole. He knew that the parents were right. He wondered if he might solicit their help, but he was afraid to ask for it, for fear that his asking for help might be interpreted as a weakness. The parents already had enough reservations about him and his ability to teach.

Clay also considered going to some of the senior faculty members. They seemed nice and they also seemed to have it all together. He doubted that they had to worry so much about their students' success. But what if Ms. Cole learned that he was consulting with his colleagues? Might this be a dead giveaway that he was uncertain about how he should teach his classes? On the other hand, these experienced teachers might remember a time when they were struggling with their own expectations.

Finally, Clay thought about Ms. Cole, but his main concern was how to do the best for his students. His problem was that he didn't know what was best.

The Challenge

Suppose you were Clay. What would you do?

ISSUES FOR FURTHER REFLECTION

1. Clay has no stated objectives for each lesson. To what degree do you believe the absence of written objectives influences these students' feelings of inadequacy?
2. All of Clay's field experiences involved high school students, yet these students are junior high students. How might this affect his present students' feelings of inadequacy?
3. These concerned parents have high expectations for their children. Knowing this, should Clay hold above-average expectations?
4. Clay thinks he needs a plan to achieve the goal of getting these students to feel more capable. What steps might such a plan have?
5. Clay is being told by the principal that she does not expect him to be like Mrs. Wright, yet he is being compared to her by the parents. How should he respond to this?
6. Each section of Clay's classes contains some serious, college-bound students and some apathetic students. What can he do to respond to these diverse groups?
7. Clay's position at Deerfield is a temporary, one-year assignment. Should this affect his reaction to his session with Ms. Cole? If so, how? If not, why not?
8. Clay has said that he lectures for half the period and then gives the students an assignment to do in the second half of the period. Could his teaching methods be contributing to the existing problem?
9. What could Clay do to relieve some of the tension?
10. How should Clay's knowledge of Ms. Cole affect his decision?
11. How can Clay set his objectives at the right level when the students vary so much in ability?
12. Clay has a systematic approach to each lesson. How might this affect the students' motivation levels?
13. What special techniques can teachers use to inspire especially reluctant learners?
14. What can Clay do to bolster his own self-image?
15. Clay informed his students that if they get behind they probably will never catch up. How might this differently affect the high performers and the low performers?
16. How might Clay use these parents' high expectations to help resolve or reduce this problem?
17. Clay's attempts to motivate have resulted in increased student anxiety. What are some motivational strategies that never produce anxiety?

SUGGESTED READINGS

Campbell, L. P. (1990). Philosophy = methodology = motivation = learning. *The Clearing House, 64*(1), 21–22.

Chance, P. (1993). The hidden treasures of extrinsic rewards. *The Clearing House, 74*(3), 200–207.

Dembo, M. (1994). *Applying educational psychology in the classroom* (5th ed.). New York: Longman (see chapter 4).

Farris, R. A. (1990). Meeting their needs: Motivating middle level learners. *Middle School Journal, 22,* 22–26.

Good, T., & Brophy, J. (1990). *Educational psychology: A realistic approach* (4th ed.). New York: Longman (see chapter 14).

Henson, K. T. (1993). *Methods and strategies for teaching in secondary and middle schools* (2nd ed.). New York: Longman (see chapter 12).

King, A. (1990). Reciprocal questioning: A strategy for teaching students how to learn from lectures. *The Clearing House, 64*(2), 131–135.

MacDonald, R. (1991). Tutoring: An effective teaching tool. *Kappa Delta Pi Record, 28*(1), 25–28.

Magney, J. (1990). Game-based teaching. *Education Digest, 60*(5), 54–57.

Markle, G., Johnson, J. H., Geer, C., & Meichtry, Y. (1990). Teaching for understanding. *Middle School Journal, 22*(2), 53–57.

Manning, M. L., & Lucking, R. (1991). The what, why, and how of cooperative learning. *The Clearing House, 64*(3), 152–156.

Marshall, C. (1991). Teachers' learning styles: How they affect student learning. *The Clearing House, 64*(4), 225–227.

Phelps, P.H. (1991). Helping teachers excel as classroom teachers. *The Clearing House, 64*(4), 241–242.

Snapp, J. C., & Glover, J. A. (1990). Advance organizers and study questions. *The Journal of Educational Research, 83*(5), 266–271.

CASE 27

Out of Bounds

PREPARING TO USE THE CASE

Background Information

Classroom management and discipline are consistently ranked by first-year teachers as the most challenging demands of their job. How to motivate students to learn and how to respond to negative student behavior are keys to teacher success.

Potential behavior problems range from passive resistance to violence. Media reports abound with stories of students assaulting other students, teachers, and administrators. Few reports share the quiet, unresponsive attitude of uncooperative students. Teachers must find ways to respond quickly and decisively to any behavior problem that arises.

Creating and maintaining a productive learning environment for all students is the fundamental challenge. Organizing the classroom for positive social interaction, providing instructional activities that are interesting and highly motivating, offering reinforcement for student achievement, creating a caring and supportive environment, and modeling the kinds of behavior expected of students are important aspects of classroom management. Establishing clear and just guidelines for behavior and enforcing them consistently are key ingredients of effective discipline.

The range of disciplinary options to teachers is broad. At one end of the continuum, a behavior-modification view holds that through positive and negative reinforcement, students can be shaped to respond in particular ways to cues that teachers give. At the other end of the continuum, a humanistic view holds that students are capable of self-discipline, when given appropriate conditions to take responsibility for their own behavior. Through their personal beliefs about human behavior; the study of theories, research, and practice; and classroom experiences, teachers arrive at a personal view of discipline that falls somewhere on this continuum.

It is insufficient for teachers to simply be knowledgeable about, and committed to, a self-determined approach to discipline. Other factors, such as school policies and legal requirements related to corporal punishment, due process, and other issues, will also affect how teachers are able to manage classrooms and provide discipline.

Behavior problems are not limited to students. Confrontations with other adults may affect how teachers teach or how they interact with their students. Of particular difficulty are situations in which fellow teachers behave in indefensible ways.

This case is about a first-year teacher who encounters behavior problems with both a fellow teacher and a student in her class. This student, a popular athlete who behaves in ways to get attention from peers, disrupts the class. The conflict escalates when the student accuses the teacher of racial prejudice. How to defuse the situation and get the student to participate constructively in classroom activities are central issues.

Topics for Reflection
1. Classroom management and discipline
2. Intercultural communications
3. Peer pressure
4. Conflict resolution
5. Motivation
6. Teacher decision-making
7. Sexual harrassment

THE CASE

Alice Roberts, age 27, is an English, speech, and drama teacher at Oak Bloom High School. This is her first teaching position. She was born and has lived most of her life in Philadelphia, and is a graduate of the University of Pennsylvania. Between college graduation and employment, she spent four years abroad, traveling and holding down odd jobs so that she could see as much of Europe as possible.

Alice was a B + student in college and used much of her free time as an advocate for a variety of causes. She served in student government, was a member of a voluntary service group that worked with community social agencies, held office in a countywide nuclear-freeze group, and participated in civic theater performances.

The Community

Mansfield, Stacey, and Boonville are three small rural communities that make up the Oak Bloom School District. Mansfield, the smallest of the communities, has 723 people, Stacey has 987, and Boonville is the largest with 2,300 inhabitants. The primary economic base in these towns is farming. Approximately 70 percent of the working adults are engaged in agricultural occupations. Most of the remaining working adults are employed by a nearby General Motors plant located in Townsend, a city of 58,000 people. A few black and Hispanic families, most of whom are employed in the automobile manufacturing plant, have moved into the area. Residents in these three small communities are known traditionally as hard-working, conservative, religious people.

Alice took the job at Oak Bloom to "slow down the pace of life." She was tired of many aspects of big-city living—congested traffic, crime, and high housing and food costs. She had decided that a move to rural America would be good for her.

When she arrived in the community, she rented a turn-of-the- century wood frame house in Stacey. She found the people in Stacey to be warm and friendly. On weekends she attended community gatherings—pancake breakfasts, fish frys, and ice cream socials—went to as many rummage sales as possible, and did volunteer work at the local hospital. In a short time she became an active, welcomed member in the community.

After a few weeks following this routine, Alice grew restless. Compared to her earlier commitment to social and political issues, her hospital work seemed superficial and shallow. She began to yearn for museums, art galleries, a variety of ethnic foods, the symphony, plays and musicals, and voluminous libraries. Gradually, she began to regret her decision to move to the country.

The School District

Oak Bloom School District is a consolidation of the three towns. Until five years ago, each town had its own elementary, junior high, and high school. Historically, Mansfield was noted for its home economics and agriculture programs. Few of its graduating seniors went on to postsecondary training. Most stayed and worked in the community. Stacey had a similar history; however, its reputation was built upon outstanding basketball and track teams. In its division Stacey won two state basketball championships and was ranked consistently in state polls. While its track teams never won a state title, the school sent athletes to compete in the state track competition nearly every year. Boonville had a larger number of students attending postsecondary institutions, about 17 percent. Boonville enjoyed a reputation for fine mathematics and music programs. Each of the towns was known for strong support for its programs, high attendance at school events, and a competitive spirit.

The consolidation of the towns into Oak Bloom School District was painful. Each of the towns wanted to maintain its respective identity. During the merger, it was decided to develop a new identity; hence, all of the former mascots and team names were discarded. Given the southern location of the communities in this midwestern state, the new district adopted the nickname of "The Rebels." A Confederate flag now flies alongside both the state and American flags outside the administration building. A junior/senior high school building has been constructed two miles east of Boonville. Each of the existing elementary schools continues to operate in the towns.

Frank Zeitz has been the only superintendent in the school district. He was born and raised in the area and is a graduate of Stacey. Upon graduation from college, he returned to teach elementary school for six years at Boonville Elementary. During this time he completed his administrator's credentials and was named principal of the school, where he served for four years. When the consolidation occurred, Zeitz was a logical choice for the superintendent's job. He has since surrounded himself with loyal administrators, most of whom also grew up in the area. Each building principal has autonomy in making decisions. Dr. Zeitz prides himself on being an effective delegator.

Rollin Glenn has been principal of Oak Bloom High for five years. He is known as an administrator with great confidence in his teachers. Accordingly, he allows a high level of teacher participation in decision making. At the same time, he is a team player, loyal to the central administration. Prior to becoming an administrator, he had been a basketball coach and athletic director at one of the competing high schools in a neighboring county; hence, he continues to maintain close contact and support for athletic programs. Having been a successful coach, he is respected in the community.

One of Glenn's first goals was to build a small-school, "powerhouse" football team. He had hired Leon Weeks, a former all-American defensive lineman at State University, and a highly successful coach at a large, urban, parochial high school to accomplish this goal. During his first year at Oak Bloom, Weeks had managed to coach the team into its first winning record in over a decade. Quickly, the tall, handsome, and imposing 250-pounder had become a celebrity in the community. Mr. Glenn sought every advantage to use Weeks's success for public relations purposes.

Alice had enjoyed her interview with Rollin Glenn and particiularly appreciated his support for teacher involvement in decision making. Similarly, she had valued an interview with Frank Zeitz, who had stressed a goal of hiring a more diverse faculty. In contrast, she felt less positive about her relationship with the faculty at the high school.

Nearly all the faculty at Oak Bloom had spent their entire lives in rural communities. They were suspicious of anyone who appeared to be different. Clearly her urban upbringing and travels set her distinctly apart from them. Frank Zeitz had noticed this difference in the initial interview and saw hiring her as a way to begin to build a more balanced faculty. What this difference meant to Alice was that she was largely ignored by the faculty. As time progressed, she became more lonely. She is truly a loner in the school. This fact bothers her, but Alice does not dwell on it. In a way, she feels that being left alone works to her advantage. "I can do what I want to do without having someone watch over me," she thought. As a result, she believes she is better able to give her full attention to teaching.

The Incident

Alice felt even more uneasy about her relationship with Coach Weeks. Her initial meeting with him had left her suspicious and angry. It was after the first faculty meeting of the year. As teachers walked to the parking lot to get into their cars, Coach Weeks had approached her:

"Hey, welcome to Oak Bloom," he greeted, holding his hand out to shake hers.

"Thanks," she returned, putting her hand in his.

As she did, he grabbed her hand tightly, grabbed her in a bear hug, lifting her in the air and holding her there.

"Put me down," she yelled. "Put me down."

He slowly lowered her to the ground, but did not release his tight hold on her.

"Let go of me," she yelled, pounding on his chest.

As he slowly released his hold on her, he whispered in her ear, "You really enjoyed that, didn't you? We're going to have to get to know one another better."

Embarrassed by the scene, she cried as she hurried to her car. Once in the car, she sobbed harder. "I can't believe this happened," she thought to herself. The incident worried her for several days. She did not know what to do. Being relatively new to the community, she finally decided to keep the incident to herself.

Her second encounter with Coach Weeks occurred a few weeks later, as she experienced difficulty with a student in her first-period speech class. Alice took pride in this class, spending countless hours preparing interesting activities for students. She approached each day with enthusiasm, knowing how important it was to get off to a good start. How her first period went affected her for the rest of the day. Not all students viewed Alice's first-period speech class with the same enthusiasm.

Rodney McCallum, a black sophomore star football player at the school, has shown the least interest in the class. He missed the first two days of class, but had an excuse from the football coach. He had been soaking an injured ankle in the whirlpool in the athletic training room in the school. He was late to class by two or three minutes on three other occasions during the first three weeks of school. However, in each instance he presented a written excuse from the coach.

On days when students in the speech class gave short oral presentations, Rodney led a group of four other males in the class in heckling the students. These five students made faces at students giving speeches. The heckling was done in such a way that Alice, who sat in the back of the room when students made presentations, was unaware of the students' behavior. After the class, two students reported the heckling behavior to Alice. The next morning, before class, she confronted Rodney.

"I understand you and your friends were making faces at students giving speeches yesterday," she began.

"Who said that?" Rodney asked.

"That is not important. Did you or didn't you make faces?" Alice demanded, her voice increasing in intensity.

"No, I didn't," Rodney responded. "Why are you always giving me a hard time?"

"I'm not giving you a hard time. I want you to pay attention, participate in class, and learn. I care about you," she concluded. Rodney turned, walked back to his seat, and sat down. As he did, he muttered loudly enough so that Alice could hear: "You're prejudiced." Until class began, he placed his face down against his folded arms pressed against the desk top.

At the end of the school day, Alice decided she would try to talk with Coach Weeks. She went to the athletic department office to look for him, hoping to find him before he had left for football practice. She arrived at his office, just as he was leaving.

"Hi," he said, "I knew you'd finally come around to see me. But you're too late to watch me change clothes," he bellowed.

"Don't kid yourself," she retorted. "I'm not interested in you. But I am interested in one of your players, Rodney McCallum."

"Like 'em young, eh?" he said, chuckling.

"You're impossible," Alice shrieked, as she stormed out of the office.

She walked directly to Mr. Glenn's office. She described both incidents to him and asked him to talk to Coach Weeks. Glenn agreed to do so, but he also told her that similar allegations had been made by other teachers. He concluded the conversation, saying: "I know Coach Weeks was just joking with you. It's just his way. Don't make too much out of this. Social grace is not a strength of his. Besides, he's just lonely. Wants companionship. You understand what it's like to be single, don't you, Ms. Roberts?"   *Principal*

"Right," Alice responded briskly. Mr. Glenn's remarks infuriated her. However, she knew she should not share her feelings with him. Accordingly, she shook his hand and said: "Thank you for listening." As she left his office, Mr. Glenn remarked: "Feel free to come talk anytime you want."

On a Thursday during the third week of classes Rodney began mumbling barely audible statements that a few students around him could hear. He said, "This class stinks. Ms. Roberts is ugly." These and other negative comments continued to the point that Alice finally overheard Rodney and his friends chuckling in response to a comment.

She stopped her lecture and asked: "What did you say, Rodney?"

Rodney replied, "I didn't say anything."

"What is so funny?" she asked, again directing her inquiry at Rodney.

"Nothing," Rodney responded.

Alice gave him a stern look, then continued lecturing. After class she expressed her concern about his behavior. She indicated that he had better be more attentive or she would have to take some form of disciplinary action.

At the beginning of Monday's class during the fourth week of school, Alice divided the students into groups of three. She went around the room counting off: "One-two-three, one-two-three, one- two-three." As she did, students were buzzing with anticipation of a small-group activity. When she got to Rodney, he was one of two students left who did not have a group. She pointed to the first student and said, "You're a one." She pointed to Rodney and said, "Rodney, you're a two. And I'll be a three," she concluded. "We can work together."

"No way I'm gonna be in a group with no damn teacher!" Rodney blurted out loudly. The class became silent.

The Challenge

You are Alice Roberts. How will you respond to Rodney McCallum's behavior, to Leon Week's advances?

ISSUES FOR FURTHER REFLECTION

1. What would you do immediately in response to Rodney's remark?
2. What are possible negative consequences of your response? What are possible positive consequences?
3. What are the possible causes of Rodney's behavior?
4. What has Alice done that may contribute to Rodney's negative behavior?
5. What are some possible long-term solutions for dealing with Rodney's behavior?
6. What are some actions that Alice might have taken earlier to shape Rodney's behavior?
7. What beliefs about classroom management and discpline appear to emerge from Alice's approach to dealing with Rodney?
8. What do you know about adolescent development that might be useful in resolving the conflict between Alice and Rodney?
9. In what ways might cultural differences affect how Alice interacts with Rodney?
10. To what extent do you believe that her interaction with Coach Weeks may affect how she relates to Rodney?
11. How should she respond to Coach Weeks's advances? What are the potential consequences of any actions you propose?
12. What legal issues arise? How can these issues be addressed?

SUGGESTED READINGS

Allen, J. D. (1986). Classroom management: Students, perspectives, goals, and strategies. *American Education Research Journal, 23*(3), 437–459.

Batesky, J. A. (1986). Twelve tips for better discipline, *Contemporary Education, 57*(2), 98–99.

Clapp, B. (1989). The discipline challenge. *Instructor, 99*(2), 32–34.

Covaleskie, J. (1992). Discipline and morality: Beyond rules and consequences. *Educational Forum, 56*(2), 173–183.

Dembo, M. (1994). *Applying educational psychology in the classroom* (5th ed.). New York: Longman (see chapters 7, 10).

Good, T., & Brophy, J. (1990). *Educational psychology: A realistic approach* (4th ed.). New York: Longman (see Part 6).

Henson, K. (1993). *Methods and strategies for teaching in secondary and middle schools* (2nd ed.). New York: Longman (see chapters 9, 13).

Lunenburg, F., & Schmidt, L. (1989). Pupil control ideology, pupil control behavior and the quality of school life. *Journal of Research and Development in Education, 22*(4), 36–44.

McDaniel, T. R. (1986). A primer on classroom discipline: Principles old and new. *Phi Delta Kappan, 68*(1), 63–67.

McFadden, A. (1992). A study of race gender bias in the punishment of school children. *Education and Treatment of Children, 15*(2), 140–146.

Pasch, M., Sparks-Langer, G., Gardner, T., Starko, A., & Moody, C. (1991). *Teaching as decision making: Instructional practices for the successful teacher.* New York: Longman (see chapters 8, 9).

Petty, R. (1987). A common sense approach to behavior problems. *Principal, 67*(1), 29–31.

Render, G. (1989). Assertive discipline: A critical review and analysis. *Teachers College Record, 90*(4), 607–630.

Robinson, K. (1992). Classroom discipline: Power, resistance, and gender. *Gender and Education, 4*(3), 273–287.

Schmidt, F., & Friedman, A. (1987). Strategies for resolving classroom conflicts. *Learning, 15*(6), 40–42.

Schockley, R., & Sevier, L. (1991). Behavior management in the classroom: Guidelines for maintaining control. *Schools in the Middle, 1*(12), 14–18.

Schonberger, V. L. (1986). Effective discipline: A positive approach to self-direction and personal growth. *Contemporary Education, 58*(1), 30–34.

Shenkle, A. (1989). Discipline: Redirecting responsiblity. *Learning, 17*(8), 30–33.

Short, R., & Short, P. (1989). Teacher briefs, perceptions of behavior problems, and intervention preferences. *Journal of Social Studies Research, 13*(12), 28–33.

Shrigley, R. L. (1986). Teacher authority in the classroom: A plan for action. *NASSP Bulletin, 70*(490), 65–71.

Walsh, K. (1986). Classroom rights and discipline: A simple and effective system. *Learning, 14*(7), 66–67.

CASE 28

Spare the Rod and Spoil the Teacher?

PREPARING TO USE THE CASE

Background Information

Because teachers often have little time to interact with each other, a number of writers have described their work life as "isolated." But such characterizations should not lead you to conclude that teachers are unaffected by those around them. Schools are organizations composed of individuals and groups; and collectively, people within any institution, and especially professional staff within a school, tend to embrace values and beliefs that give each school a unique identity.

When beginning teachers join a school's faculty, they become integral parts of that institution. Schools, just like General Motors or I.B.M., are organizations composed of individuals and groups who function in an environment where there is a multitude of formal and informal rules and regulations. Novice teachers soon realize that others in the organization are attempting to "socialize" them. The ease or difficulty of this process will depend on two primary factors: (1) the degree to which the professional staff adheres to a common set of values and beliefs, and (2) the degree to which the individual teacher's personal and professional values and beliefs are congruent with those of the school. In schools where there are strong cultures, that is, where most teachers adhere to a common philosophy, a new faculty member can expect that his or her peers will demand conformity. By contrast, schools with weak cultures place fewer socialization demands on new teachers.

In this case, you will read about the experiences of a beginning teacher who is employed in a school with a rather strong culture. This teacher is confronted with a difficult discipline-related problem that tests whether she will adhere to an established norm. The novice teacher must interface her own values and beliefs, her professional knowledge and ethical standards, and expectations of her peers. The problem revolves around the use of physical punishment, and the teacher must weigh her own interests against those of her students.

The following factors are especially critical to the decision the teacher must make: (1) the teacher's knowledge relative to the effects of punishment on student behavior, (2) the teacher's knowledge of the legal and ethical dimensions of using corporal punishment, (3) the teacher's knowledge of the socialization process in the school, and (4) the teacher's ability to separate personal values and beliefs from professional knowledge when professional decisions must be made. The situation for this teacher is made more difficult by the fact that she finds herself in an environment where she is the only inexperienced teacher.

Topics for Reflection
1. Classroom management and discipline
2. The effect of teacher values and beliefs on the learning environment
3. Punishment as a means of changing student behavior
4. Interfacing personal values and beliefs with professional knowledge
5. The socialization of new teachers

THE CASE

The Community

Johnson Falls is a relatively small city that has had remarkable growth in the past decade. Recently, a major Japanese manufacturing company decided to build a new electronics plant there. It was the third new industry to locate in Johnson Falls since an industrial park was first developed on the edge of the city six years ago. The current population of 17,300 is nearly double what it was just 20 years ago.

Mayor Jane Anderson is fond of saying that her city has become a model for the state and the entire Southwest. In making this boast, she points to population increases, relatively low housing and land costs, the presence of a state university in the community, bountiful natural resources, and a good local school system. Just four months ago, the mayor was featured on a segment produced by one of the major television networks entitled, "American Cities on the Move." Most residents were extremely proud of the publicity.

But growth has also produced concerns. Taxes, especially for schools and city services, increased 35% in the last five years. Virtually all new residents in Johnson Falls came not from the Southwest, but from northeastern and midwestern states. This fact is noteworthy, because their assimilation into the community tended to be more difficult than for persons who already lived in the Southwest. Not infrequently, lifelong residents referred to their new neighbors who came from other regions of the United States as *outsiders*.

Johnson Falls State University, a regional state institution primarily serving nine contiguous counties, has also experienced rapid growth. Fifteen years ago, there were only 2,300 students enrolled; today there are over 7,000 full- and part-time students taking courses. Teacher education had always been a major mission of the institution.

New residents in Johnson Falls were recently described by a demographer from the university as "a mix of professional, managerial, semiskilled workers employed in both public service positions and in private industry." In a study completed for the city, he noted that industrial development has not only produced its own jobs, it also has had the secondary effect of producing more jobs in the public sector—most notably in city government, the school system, and the state university.

For many natives of Johnson Falls, growth has been bittersweet. For example, some landowners profited from escalating property values as subdivisions and businesses were built on land that previously was used for farming. And local businesses profited from increased sales. But growth also spawned increasing levels of conflict. For example, there were divergent views about operating local government (e.g., taxes for more recreational areas) and the desirability of Johnson Falls becoming a larger city. There also was an increase in social problems such as drug abuse and crime, and the expanding population necessitated the construction of several new schools.

The Public Schools in Johnson Falls

Meeting the needs of a rapidly growing community often places stress on public elementary and secondary schools. This certainly was true in Johnson Falls. Just seven years ago, the school district consisted of a junior/senior high school and two elementary schools. Now, there was a new high school, a middle school (located in the former junior/senior high school), and five elementary schools.

The employment of a new superintendent of schools two years ago provides an excellent example of how differing values in the community can become a source of conflict. The school board, consisting of seven members elected at large, recently experienced significant change. A slate of three candidates, all of whom had lived in the community less than four years, won the last election. Upon being seated on the board, the three aligned themselves with one of four veteran board members who had been an outspoken critic of the superintendent. Collectively they decided to dismiss Mr. Roland Sparks who had served as superintendent of the district for 18 years. This was done just one month after the new board members took office. The vote was four to three, with the three board members who voted against dismissal all being lifelong residents of Johnson Falls. The new majority on the board cited a need for new leadership ideas and vision as the reason for their action.

Tensions in the community over the dismissal of Mr. Sparks were intensified some two months later when the board announced the employment of Dr. Thad Burdlow as the new superintendent. He was a New Yorker who had never set foot in the Southwest, and despite the fact that the board showed unity in employing him, many residents believed that one of the two current administrators who applied for the position should have been selected for this job. For the lifelong residents, this decision was another indication that their town was being taken away from them.

Superintendent Burdlow took office just months after Mayor Anderson assumed her post. And even though they were viewed as representing different elements of the community, they developed a close and productive working relationship. They shared two beliefs: (1) a good city needs a good public school system, and (2) that improvements in the school system had not kept pace with growth and improvements in the city.

The School

Northside Elementary School is the oldest of the five elementary schools in the district. Located in an established part of town, it has an enrollment of approximately 300 students. Because of its geographic location, it has not been affected by population growth as have the other elementary schools.

There has been little change in the staff at Northside in the past 15 years. Even the principal, Nancy Turkel, has spent her entire professional career at this school. She was a teacher for 11 years and is now in her 10th year as principal. Personnel records show that the school has the most experienced teaching staff of any of the schools in the district. Of the 13 teachers assigned to Northside, 10 are graduates of Johnson Falls High School and Johnson Falls State University.

Parents, students, and staff have a great deal of pride in Northside Elementary School. Many of the prominent residents of the community went to this school, and they continue to identify with it. Each year the school receives about 40 transfer requests from parents of students who reside in other elementary school areas in the district. In large measure, these requests are generated by Northside's reputation as "a traditional school where the basics are still stressed." It is viewed as a "no nonsense" type of school. Neither Principal Turkel nor the teachers do much to discourage this perception.

The Teacher

Carol Deangelo is truly in a unique position at Northside Elementary School. She is the only first-year teacher at the school; in fact, she is the first new teacher hired at the school in the past seven years. She moved to Johnson Falls two years ago when her husband, Tom, accepted a job with one of the local businesses.

Carol graduated from a liberal arts college in Pennsylvania just one month before she and Tom had to relocate. Arriving in Johnson Falls in late June, there were no teaching positions available with the public schools, so she decided to enroll at the state university to pursue her master's degree. While attending graduate school, she worked occasionally as a substitute teacher in several of the elementary schools. She hoped that this exposure would enhance her chances of eventually getting a full-time position.

At the end of the school year, a vacancy became available at Northside, but Carol thought she would have no chance of getting the position. A number of experienced teachers in other elementary schools in the district quickly applied for the post, and most everyone assumed that one of them would be transferred. That probably would have been the case had not the superintendent taken a personal interest in the matter. He was well aware of Northside's reputation, and he believed that the school would benefit if a younger, more recently educated teacher were selected. Through his assistant superintendent, his position on this matter was made abundantly clear to Nancy Turkel.

Although Carol had worked as a substitute in three of the elementary schools, Northside was not one of them. She knew only one teacher at the school, whom she had met in a night class at the university. In her interview with the principal and two representatives of the teaching staff, Carol was judged to be reserved, confident, and capable. She was seen as more mature than the other candidates. Of the four beginning teachers selected for interviews, she was viewed as the most likely to "fit in." Knowing that they had to satisfy the superintendent, the principal and two teachers decided to offer Carol the position.

Her assignment is teaching one of the two fourth-grade classes. There are 26 students in her class, a little more than average for the school. There were times when Carol wondered if she would ever survive until Thanksgiving. Especially during the first two months of the school year, it seemed that each of the 26 pupils was intent on challenging her authority. But gradually she gained confidence, and her students became comfortable with her.

Despite the fact that the teachers at Northside are a rather close-knit group, Carol kept pretty much to herself. She really didn't have time to socialize with the others. Occasionally she would talk to other teachers in the lunchroom or on the playground, but much of that conversation was casual. She spent two to three hours every evening preparing lessons and grading papers; and because she was trying to finish her master's degree, she was enrolled in a Tuesday night class at the university. Considering all of her commitments, she had a very busy schedule.

Carol did not think much about her relationships with the other teachers. She had expected that the more experienced teachers would be looking over her shoulder and constantly offering advice; and overall, she was happy that this was not the case. She also feared that she would be treated as an outsider, and there was little evidence that this was occurring. Carol felt she was doing a good job, and her perception was reinforced periodically by comments made by her principal.

The Incident

There are two fourth-grade classes at Northside, but rarely were the students brought together for group activities. On this day, however, both were in the library to view a videotape related to science. Carol was off to one side of the room where she was operating the VCR. The other fourth-grade teacher, Marge Stowe, decided that she would assume the responsibility of controlling pupil behavior. She walked slowly around the room while the tape was playing, trying to determine if the students were paying attention.

Mrs. Stowe has been teaching at the school for 29 years. She is respected by her peers, and it was obvious to Carol that she had a great deal of influence with the principal. As far as their personal relationship was concerned, Carol found her to be helpful and courteous, but also cautious. It was as if Mrs. Stowe was still trying to decide whether Carol really belonged at Northside.

About midway through the 40-minute videotape, Carol heard Mrs. Stowe yell, "Stop the VCR!" Pointing at two boys, she said, "You two, out in the hall right now!" Carol saw immediately that the two were students from her class. What luck! Her heart started to beat a little faster.

"What's wrong?" Carol asked.

"Those two have been jabbing each other and laughing ever since we started watching the tape. It just kept getting worse. They need to be disciplined," Mrs. Stowe proclaimed.

Then she turned to the students and said, "Mrs. Deangelo and I have to deal with these two boys who obviously have not learned to behave at school. We are going to be just outside the door in the hall, so you sit quietly while we are gone. I don't want to hear a peep out of any of you. We will be back in a minute and finish watching the tape."

With that she turned and headed for the hallway, motioning Carol to follow. As they reached the door, she whispered to Carol, "Go to your room and get your paddle. We have to teach these two a lesson. If you don't react immediately, students learn that they can get away with things. Even worse, the other students start to believe that they do not have to control their behavior. If there is one thing I can tell you based on all of my years of teaching, it is that you have to be a strong disciplinarian to be a good teacher."

Not wanting to continue the discussion in the doorway, Carol walked into the hall with Mrs. Stowe. The two boys were standing there looking frightened. They knew about Mrs. Stowe from students in her class, and they had a pretty good idea of what was in store for them. Carol walked away from the boys and waved to Mrs. Stowe to follow.

When they were a sufficient distance from the boys so that their conversation could not be overheard, Carol said, "But, I don't have a paddle."

"I do. You can use mine," Mrs. Stowe responded.

"Well, I'm not sure that I want to use it," Carol said. "I've never hit a student, and besides, I don't think it is the best way to deal with the problem."

Mrs. Stowe placed her arm on Carol's shoulder, looked her in the eye and said, "I know how difficult it is to be a new teacher—but listen, I know how these things should be handled."

Seeing that she needed a more convincing argument, Carol pointed out, "I believe that corporal punishment is against school board policy. Am I right?"

"It wouldn't surprise me," Mrs. Stowe answered. "But it is legal in this state, and with this school board who knows? They are changing rules so quickly who can keep up. All I can tell you is that all teachers in this school refuse to put up with rowdy behavior. Why do you think Northside has such a good reputation?"

Carol was truly surprised that this veteran teacher showed so little concern for school district policy. "What about Mrs. Turkel? Doesn't she restrict the types of punishment we use—especially if hitting students is against policy?"

Mrs. Stowe smiled slightly and said, "Nancy doesn't like to talk about discipline procedures. She's more than happy that we handle almost all the problems. The parents also support how we handle discipline here. I have never had a single parent tell me not to use stern discipline. Why, several of my students' parents were in my class 25 years ago. They now see why discipline was so important."

There was a pause. Carol stood in the hall. She was having a difficult time finding her next words.

Mrs. Stowe broke the silence, "Carol, I don't want my students to see these two boys getting away with their rude behavior. Now are you going to paddle these students or am I going to have to do it myself?"

The Challenge

Put yourself in Carol's position. Think about your values and beliefs. Think about what you have learned about children and discipline. What decision would you make?

ISSUES FOR FURTHER REFLECTION

1. Often physical punishment, especially with elementary school-age students, is defended on the grounds that it generates fear. That is, acts such as paddling serve as a deterrent because children are frightened by it. Do you agree?

2. Do you believe that it is best to discipline students in front of their peers? Why or why not?

3. To what extent does punishment alienate students?

4. What is the difference between eliminating behavior and suppressing it? Which is more likely to occur as a result of physical punishment?

5. What alternative forms of punishment could be used in this case?

6. Forget for a moment your personal decision in this case. What do you think most first-year teachers would do? Give a rationale for your response.

7. As a student, do you remember a teacher or administrator who paddled students? What is your current perception of that individual?

8. If state law permits corporal punishment, can a school board have a policy prohibiting it?

9. What do you believe will be the consequences for Carol if she refuses to paddle the students?

10. Would you want to teach in this school? Why or why not?

11. What is your impression of the principal in this case?

12. To what extent are community and organizational (school) conditions a factor in the way Northside operates as a school?

13. One option Carol has is to refuse to paddle the children and report this incident directly to Dr. Burdlow. Would you do that? Why or why not?

14. Suppose that Carol talks Mrs. Stowe out of paddling the students by assuring her that she will require the two boys to do a special science project. Would you be supportive of this decision?

15. Do you agree with the judgment that you have to be a stern disciplinarian to be a good teacher? Why or why not?

SUGGESTED READINGS

Agne, K. (1992). Caring: The expert teacher's edge. *Educational Horizons, 70*(3), 120–124.

Ball, J. (1989). Corporal punishment. *PTA Today, 14*(4), 15–17.

Barbour, N. (1991). Ban the hickory stick: Issues in education. *Childhood Education, 68*(2), 69–70.

Bauer, G. (1990). Corporal punishment and the schools. *Education and Urban Society, 22*(3), 285–299.

Cole, A. (1991). Relationships in the workplace: Doing what comes naturally? *Teaching and Teacher Education, 7*(5), 415–426.

Curwin, R., & Mendler, A. (1988). *Discipline with dignity.* Alexandria, VA: Association for Supervision and Curriculum Development.

Dembo, M. (1994). *Applying educational psychology in the classroom* (5th ed.). New York: Longman (see chapter 7).

Etheridge, C. (1989). Strategic adjustment: How teachers move from university learnings to school-based practices. *Action in Teacher Education, 11*(1), 31–37.

Good, T., & Brophy, J. (1990). *Educational psychology: A realistic approach* (4th ed.). New York: Longman (see chapter 21).

Gursky, D. (1992). Spare the child? *Teacher Magazine, 3*(5), 16–19.

Henson, K. (1993). *Methods and strategies for teaching in secondary and middle schools* (2nd ed.). New York: Longman (see chapter 13).

Hoy, W. (1990). Socialization of student teachers. *American Educational Research Journal, 27*(2), 279–300.

Kaplan, C. (1992). Teachers' punishment histories and their selection of disciplinary strategies. *Contemporary Educational Psychology, 17*(3), 258–265.

McEvoy, A. (1990). Child abuse law and school policy. *Education and Urban Society, 22*(3), 247–257.

Nolte, M. (1985). Before you take a paddling in court, read this corporal punishment advice. *American School Board Journal, 173*(7), 27, 35.

Quaglia, R. (1989). Socialization of the beginning teacher: A theoretical model from the empirical literature. *Research in Rural Education, 5*(3), 1–7.

Staton, A. (1992). Teacher socialization: Review and conceptualization. *Communication Education, 41*(2), 109–137.

Su, Z. (1990). The function of the peer group in teacher socialization. *Phi Delta Kappan, 71*(9), 723–727.

Wynne, E. (1990). Discipline in a good school. *Society, 27*(4), 98–101.

Preventing and Controlling Discipline Problems

PREPARING TO USE THE CASE

Background Information

Since the Gallup Poll of the Public's Attitude Toward the Public Schools began, almost a quarter century ago, the public has rated discipline the No. 1 problem of the schools more frequently than all other problems combined. Several related trends corroborate this public perception. As Wynne and Ryan (1993) report, the number of out-of-wedlock births has soared (650% for white, 15–19-year-old females since 1940), and the suicide rate for 15–24-year-old white males has increased 277% (p. 10). The public's perception of a significant deterioration in student behavior is further evidenced in the increase in youth arrests. Since 1950, the annual number of arrests of 25–34-year-olds has increased by almost 500 percent, and the annual number of arrests for 18–24-year-olds has increased by about 1,300 percent. The increase in number of arrests per year of 14–17-year-olds is even larger (about 2,000%).

As you read the following case, think about these trends and how they may be related. Consider other factors that may be influencing all of these negative trends.

Finally, as you read this case, remember the following behaviors which Brophy and Evertson (see Dembo, 1994) say characterize teachers in high-achievement classes:

- They prevent most potential problems from occurring.
- They move activities along at a good pace without confusion or loss of focus.

- They provide seatwork that is at the right level of difficulty for most students and is interesting enough to hold the attention of most students.

- They monitor the entire class continuously and can do two or more things simultaneously without having to break the flow of classroom events (Dembo, 1994, p. 360).

Topics for Reflection
1. The school as a microcosm of society
2. Students' self-concepts
3. Classroom-management strategies
4. Effective teaching strategies

THE CASE

Greenwood Elementary was the first school to offer a position to Josephina. The state's low salary base has driven most of the education majors to accept positions in neighboring states. But Josephina felt very lucky because Greenwood, in her words, is "an ideal community." Many would agree that regardless of the pay scale, the small town of Greenwood has much to offer its teachers. Its population of 50,000 is large enough to support its one excellent hospital and its nice shopping mall. Education is valued by Greenwood's residents, and in this community all teachers are considered important community leaders. The town is virtually free of traffic problems. A major city located only twenty miles away is an easy half-hour drive on the interstate. In the mid-1980s Greenwood Elementary was selected as a school of excellence. Its location and reputation attracted students from the upper-middle and lower-upper economic strata.

Greenwood Elementary School is one of four elementary schools in a district that also has three middle schools and two high schools. Greenwood Elementary serves about 600 students. The staff and faculty consist of a principal, an assistant principal, a counselor, a special educator, and 28 teachers. The pupil-teacher ratio is approximately 21 to 1.

Greenwood Elementary is the newest school in the district. The building is well lighted with plenty of natural light. The walls are painted light, earthy colors and are decorated with good artwork. The local district has a special system for introducing a number of famous masterpieces to the students. A large collection of framed prints decorates the walls throughout Greenwood Elementary as well as the walls in other schools throughout the district. Monthly, all prints are rotated from room to room throughout the school. At the end of the year, all of the prints in each school are exchanged for an entirely different set of prints from another school.

Josephina was impressed with the counseling services at Greenwood. The school counselor, Mr. Jim Wiggins, arranges for a speech therapist and an audiologist to administer diagnostic exams to identify any disabilities. Students with disabilities are given special help. Josephina is proud that her school serves all students.

But what impresses her most about Greenwood is the parents. Although the school year has been in session for only a few days, she can already tell that these parents care intensely about their children's education. This exemplifies the current wave of parent interest in education, she thought. But the exciting part was the recent articles she had read in some of her professional journals saying that intensive parent involvement is essential for maximum achievement at any school.

An article by Walde and Baker (1990) explained that some parents—not just low-income parents—simply don't care about their children's education. And many of those parents who do care are not able to contribute significantly to their children's education. Joyce Epstein (1991), co-director of the Center on Families, Communities, Schools, and Children's Learning, a principal research scientist at the Center for Research on Effective Schooling for Disadvantaged Students, and a professor of sociology at Johns Hopkins University, says that this is no excuse for parents not to be involved, since there are many programs that can help teachers learn how to help families work with their children at home.

Warren Chapman (1991) says that in Illinois, Urban Education Partnership Grants have funded demonstration projects that effectively serve the dual goals of school improvement and parent involvement. Evaluators interviewed people in 20 schools that received such grants and found that 87% of the participating schools accomplished over 90% of their goals.

After reading these articles, Josephina mused, it is good to know that such grants are possible in the event that I should need one, but I am thankful that the parents of Greenville seem able and more than willing to support their children's education.

The Teacher

Josephina Gomez was one of the brightest students in her graduating class. Throughout her program she applied her abilities well, earning a 3.5 overall grade point average and a 3.7 grade point average in her teacher-education courses. But Josephina's talents were shaded by her introverted personality. Her reluctance to speak out was often interpreted as a weakness; her peers often concluded that her unwillingness to express herself resulted from a weak knowledge base or from a general lack of ability.

Adjectives used by her peers to describe Josephina include "shy," "introverted," "shallow," and "weak."

Realizing that her shyness placed her in a vulnerable position in the classroom,

Josephina began searching for ways to compensate for this liability. Her first step was to make a trip to the nearby college library. In the education curriculum skills section she found several commercial curricula aimed at social skills development. Clearly, some of these programs were better than others and some would better meet the needs of particular schools. Josephina wondered how she could choose the best for her future needs. She found the following guidelines for selecting a social skills curriculum:

- **The cost of the curriculum** (many are available for less than $50).
- **The age of the students** who will receive instruction based on the chosen curriculum (curricula are available for preschoolers through high school-age children).
- **The level of training needed** to teach social skills using a selected curriculum. Several curricula (e.g., *Accepts* or *Skillstreaming*) are formatted in a way that is easy to understand simply by reading the material and observing someone using the materials. Other curricula require specific training (e.g., *Boy's Town*).
- **The evaluation system** that is built into the social skills curriculum. Those curricula that have assessment techniques and recording devices provided in the materials will require less teacher preparation time than those curricula that do not supply these materials.
- **The skills taught** based on those offered in the curriculum need to be social skills that are critical to the needs of the children who will be taught lessons based on the curriculum (Zirpoli & Malloy, 1993, p. 278).

Josephina noticed that these programs are designed for use with children and adolescents. They work best when used with small groups of 10 or less. Because of her love for classroom activities, she was further pleased to learn that role playing is frequently used to reduce misbehavior. But right now she wonders if the role playing itself wouldn't be a risk. Maybe she should first get some experience.

Josephina further discovered that another source that teachers can use to influence student behavior is their (teachers') powers. She was intrigued to learn that several books group teachers' powers into distinct types including: expert power, referent power, legitimate power, reward power, and coercive power.

Expert power results from others recognizing that a person has expertise. Some students respect teachers because of their mastery of their discipline. Remembering a couple of her more aggressive students, Josephina chuckled to herself, "Expert power won't go far with them. I'd better read on."

Referent power is enjoyed by teachers who maintain good relationships with their students. **Legitimate power** is that power which a teacher has by virtue of being a teacher. This type of power is usually more significant for elementary teachers than for high school teachers. Josephina continued mumbling to herself. "For several of these students, being a teacher offers no power, maybe a liability."

All teachers have **reward power,** or the ability to provide something that others need. With some students, the ability to give praise is a strong force; with others, the ability to issue grades is more influential. Finally, **coercive power** or the authority to use punishment is used by some teachers. Josephina wasn't too surprised to read that teachers who rely on coercive power seldom have classroom climates that permit students to grow socially.

Josephina returned feeling that her trip to the college library had been well worth the time. After all, she planned to be in this profession for the rest of her life. But she still wasn't satisfied. She felt that she needed more insurance, more strategy, more knowledge. The following week she visited with Mrs. Arnold, one of the senior faculty members at Greenwood.

Mrs. Arnold shared a contingency grading contract that she found helpful in some classes. She also said that she used a self-progress reporting system which made students focus on their own behavior. Each of her students is required to keep a record of progress portfolio that contains examples of the student's work. She lets each student select the work that the student particularly likes.

Josephina was equally pleased with her visit with Mrs. Arnold. Together, these two trips had given her some good ideas. She felt that at least it was a beginning.

The Incident

The first few days at Greenwood had gone as uneventfully as Josephina had hoped they would. She was excited over the opportunity to teach her favorite subject, language arts. But things could have gone a little more smoothly. For example, from the first day, as each lesson began, a few students ignored Josephina's request for silence. She decided to ignore their continuous chattering, hoping these few students would become interested in the lesson once they reached the writing activities; then all students would give her their undivided attention, Josephina believed. But this did not occur. In fact, each day as she stood at the front of the room introducing the day's lesson and giving pertinent information, the noise from the class became increasingly louder. Most student comments were unrelated to the content in the day's lesson. Now, at the end of the second week, the students had gotten so loud that other teachers had begun complaining, saying that Ms. Gomez's classes were so noisy that they were disturbing the other classes nearby.

As the first-period class got underway one morning, the inevitable happened. Bo Carter, who had recently devoted his time and energy to aggravating his teachers and classmates, had rushed through his seatwork and was now diligently pursuing this new interest by christening his neighbors with new names. Keith Adams, a light-complexioned and light-haired 15-year-old, was the chosen target for today's verbal abuse. Keith did not appear to mind the comments; in fact, he seemed to be completely ignoring them as Bo referred to him as "white-out," "liquid paper," "chalk head," and "Casper, the Friendly Ghost." Even though Keith ignored it, the name calling worsened.

As Josephina moved throughout the room, she came close enough to see this heckling behavior. As soon as she saw that trouble was building, she slowly walked away pretending not to notice, hoping that her distance would lessen the problem. Anyhow, Josephina concluded that she could not let herself be distracted from the lesson since she thought she could do only one thing at a time and do it well. Suddenly, without warning, Keith stood up and punched Bo squarely in the face. A burst of blood sprayed from Bo's nose. Seeing the blood frightened Bo and provided him with a surge of energy. He grabbed Keith and lifted him up, throwing him across a couple of desks. The other students watched with glee and welcomed the diversion from the otherwise boring lesson. Josephina was stunned by the violence, and she was shocked by the reactions of the other students. This was a progressive community. What could she do? She temporarily froze, watching in horror as Keith came crashing to the floor with Bo squarely across him, pinning his shoulders to the floor.

Then Josephina found herself running across the room and pulling at Bo's collar, shouting, ''Stop it! Stop it!'' The swinging and kicking suddenly stopped and a pall of silence fell over the class. Now everyone in the room was eyeing the teacher, eager to see her next move.

The Challenge

A major factor distinguishing between experienced teachers and many novice teachers is the practice of reflecting on critical incidents. The research clearly shows that students can be taught to relate more effectively with their peers and others (Zirpoli & Malloy, 1993, p. 277). At some point in your career you may face a crisis such as the one Josephina is now facing. Suppose you were Josephina. What would you do? Perhaps more important, what can you do to prevent such occurrences?

ISSUES FOR FURTHER REFLECTION

1. Did the incident come without warning?
2. Josephina remained positioned in front of the room throughout the lesson. How does the teacher's location in the classroom affect discipline?
3. Although Josephina knew that some students were not paying attention, she chose to begin the lesson anyway. Is this wise?
4. This group had gotten so noisy that other teachers had started to complain. Should the teacher care what others think? Why or why not?
5. To what degree are these students' comments related to the content in the lesson?
6. Bo had been consciously disturbing classmates for several days. How should this affect Josephina's reaction to the situation?
7. Do you think this incident could have been avoided if Josephina had stayed at her desk? Why or why not?
8. What do you think about Josephina's decision to focus only on one event at a time in order to do it well?
9. Bo rushed through his assignment so that he could have some fun at his classmate's expense. What does this say about Josephina's management plan?

10. What preventative measures might Josephina have taken to avoid problems such as this? During what part of the year should these methods begin?

11. Bo rushed through his classroom assignment. Does this information suggest anything about the quality of his work? Can you suggest any references that address this issue?

12. What can you say about Josephina's eye contact?

13. Suppose Josephina decided to send both students to their seats and resume class as though nothing had happened. Do you believe that this would minimize the seriousness of student participation in dangerous and unacceptable behavior?

14. What chance is there that with experience, Josephina will eventually develop a management system that will work well with all of her students?

15. Was Josephina's reasoning regarding her decision to move away from the trouble valid? It didn't work for Josephina, but what evidence is there that it wouldn't work most of the time?

16. Might Josephina's determination to continue with the lesson communicate to everyone that the lesson was more important to Josephina than any student's attempt to disrupt it?

17. The teacher could discuss this incident with the entire class. Do you think that the students might appreciate the opportunity to be involved in the resolution of the problem since the lesson was disrupted and they may think they deserve an explanation?

18. Is there evidence that it is time for the teacher to clarify the expectations that she holds for this class?

19. What other, perhaps better, alternatives might Josephina pursue to handle this problem and minimize the probability of its recurrence?

20. What classroom management skills might Josephina have used to avoid this incident?

21. What evidence, if any, is there that Bo is a low achiever?

22. What evidence, if any, can you find to indicate that Josephina was partly to blame for this event? How could she reduce the probability of recurrence?

SUGGESTED READINGS

Armstrong, D. G., Henson, K. T., & Savage, T. V. (1993). *Education: An introduction* (4th ed.). New York: Macmillan (see chapter 12).

Bell, T. H. (1993). Reflections one decade after "A Nation at Risk," *Phi Delta Kappan, 74*(8), 592–597.

Blumenthal, C., Holmes, G. V., & Pound, L. (1991). Academic success for students at-risk. In R. C. Morris (Ed.), *Youth at-Risk,* Scranton, PA: Technomic.

Bonds, C. W., Bonds, L. G., & Peach, W. (1992). Metacognition: Developing dependence in learning. *The Clearing House, 66*(1), 56–59.

Boschee, F. (1992). Small-group learning in the information age. *The Clearing House, 65*(2), 89–92.

Brophy, J. (1991). Effective schooling for disadvantaged students. In M. S. Knapp and P. M. Shields (Eds.), *Better schooling for the children of poverty: Alternatives to conventional wisdom* (pp. 211–234). Berkeley, CA: McCutchan.

Brophy, J., & Alleman, J. (1990). *Activities as instructional tools: A framework for analysis and evaluation.* East Lansing, MI: Michigan State: Institute for Research on Teaching.

Brown, B. B. (1990). Peer groups and peer cultures. In S. S. Feldman and G. R. Elliott (Eds.), *At the threshold: The developing adolescent* (pp. 171–196). Cambridge, MA: Harvard University Press.

Caissy, G. A. (1992). Developing information processing skills in the middle school. *The Clearing House, 65*(3), 149–151.

Chance, P. (1993). The hidden treasures of extrinsic rewards. *Phi Delta Kappan, 74*(3), 200–207.

Chandler, T. A. (1990). Why discipline strategies are bound to fail. *The Clearing House, 64*(2), 124–126.

Chapman, A. D., Leonard, J. J., & Thomas J. C. (1992). Co-authoring: A natural form of cooperative learning. *The Clearing House, 65*(2), 44–46.

Chapman, W. (1991). The Illinois experience: State grants to improve schools through parent involvement. *Phi Delta Kappan, 72*(5), 355–358.

Charles, C. M. (1989). *Building classroom discipline: From models to practice* (3rd ed.). New York: Longman.

Cooper, H. (1989). *Homework.* White Plains, NY: Longman.

Cooper, H. (1990). Synthesis of research on homework. *Educational Leadership, 47*(3), 85–91.

Crosby, E. A. (1993). The at-risk decade. *Phi Delta Kappan, 74*(8), 598–604.

Curry, L. (1990, Oct.). A critique of the research on learning styles. *Educational Leadership, 48*(2), 50–56.

Dagley, D. L., & Orso, J. K. (1991, Sept.). Integrating summative and formative modes evaluation. *NASSP Bulletin, 75*(536) 75–82.

Dembo, M. (1994). *Applying educational psychology in the classroom* (5th ed.). New York: Longman (see chapters 8, 9, 10, 11).

Downs, W. R., & Rose, S. R. (1991). The relationship of adolescent peer groups to the incidence of psychosocial problems. *Adolescence, 26*(102), 473–492.

Doyle, W. (1991). Classroom tasks: The core of learning from teaching. In M. S. Knapp and P. M. Shields (Eds.), *Better schooling for the children of poverty: Alternatives to conventional wisdom.* Berkeley, CA: McCutchan.

Dunn, R., Beaudry, J. S. & Klavas, A. (1989). Survey of research on learning styles. *Educational Leadership, 48*(6), 50–58.

Dunn, R., Shea, T. C., Evans, W., & MacMurren, H. (1991). Learning style and equal protection: The next frontier. *The Clearing House, 65*(2), 93–95.

Edwards, C., & Stout, J. (1989–1990). Cooperative learning: The first year. *Educational Leadership, 47*(4), 38–41.

Elam, S. M., Rose, L. C., & Gallup, A. M. (1991). The 23rd Gallup poll of the public's attitude toward the schools. *Phi Delta Kappan, 73*(1), 41–56.

Elam, S. M., Rose, L. C., & Gallup, A. M. (1992). The 24th Gallup poll of the public's attitudes toward the public schools. *Phi Delta Kappan, 74*(1), 41–53.

Ellsworth, R. A., Donnell, P., & Duell, O. K. (1990). Multiple-choice test items: What are textbook authors telling teachers? *Journal of Educational Research, 83*(5), 290–293.

Epstein, J. L., & MacIver, D. J. (1990). National practices and trends in the middle grades. *Middle School Journal, 22*(2), 36–40.

Epstein, J. L. (1991). Paths to partnership: What we can learn from federal, state, and school initiatives. *Phi Delta Kappan, 72*(5), 350–354.

Etscheidt, S. (1991). Reducing aggressive behavior and improving self-control: A cognitive behavioral program for behaviorally disordered adolescents. *Behavioral Disorders, 16*(2), 107–115.

Fielding, G., & Shaughnessy, J. (1990). Improving student assessment: Overcoming the obstacles.'' *NASSP Bulletin, 74*(529), 90–98.

Friedman, R. S. (1991). Murray high school: A nontraditional approach to meeting the needs of an at-risk population. In R. C. Morris (Ed.), *Youth at Risk*. Lancaster, PA: Technomic.

Frisby, C. L. (1991). Thinking skills instruction. *Educational Forum, 56*(1), 21–36.

Gathercoal, F. (1990). Judicious discipline. *Education Digest, 60*(7), 20–24.

Geisert, G. & Dunn, R. (1991). Effective use of computers: Assignments based on individual learning style. *The Clearing House, 64*(4), 219–223.

Glickman, C. (1991). Pretending not to know what we know. *Educational Leadership, 48*(8), 4–9.

Goldstein, A. P., Reagles, K. W., & Amann, L. S. (1990). *Refusal skills, preventing drug abuse in adolescents.* Champaign, IL: Research Press.

Good, T., & Brophy, J. (1990). *Educational psychology: A realistic approach* (4th ed.). New York: Longman (part 6).

Griswold, P. A. (1990). Assessing relevance and reliability to improve the quality of teacher-made tests. *NASSP Bulletin, 74*(523), 18–23.

Gronlund, N. E. (1991). *How to write and use instructional objectives* (4th ed.). New York: Macmillan.

Harris, K. H., & Longstreet, W. S. (1990). Alternative testing and national agenda for control. *The Clearing House, 64*(2), 90–93.

Hawley, R. A. (1990). The bumpy road to drug free schools. *Phi Delta Kappan, 72*(4), 310–314.

Heger, H. K. (1992). Finding psychic rewards in today's schools: A possible task. *The Clearing House, 65*(6), 342, 344–346.

Henson, K. T. (1993). *Methods and strategies for teaching in secondary and middle schools* (2nd ed.). White Plains, NY: Longman (see chapter 13).

Hoerr, T. R. (1992). How our school applied multiple intelligence theory in our school. *Educational Leadership, 50*(2), 67–68.

Johns, F. A. & MacNaughton, R. H. (1990). Spare the rod: A continuing controversy. *The Clearing House, 63*(9), 338–392.

Johnson, J., Carlson, S., Kastl, J., & Kastl, R. (1992). Developing conceptual thinking: The concept attainment model. *The Clearing House, 66*(2), 117–121.

Jones, V. (1991). Responding to students' behavior problems. *Beyond Behavior, 2*(1), 17–21.

Joyce, R., Weil, M., & Showers, B. (1992). *Models of Teaching.* Needham Heights, MA: Allyn and Bacon.

Kagan, S. (1990). *Cooperative learning: Resources for teachers.* San Juan, CA: Resources for Teachers.

Kaplan, J. S. (1991). *Beyond behavior modification: A cognitive-behavioral approach to behavior management in the schools* (2nd ed.). Austin, TX: Pro-Ed.

Keating, D. P. (1990). Adolescent thinking. In S. S. Feldman & G. R. Elliott (Eds.), *At the threshold: The developing adolescent* (pp. 54–90). Cambridge, MA: Harvard University Press.

Kennedy, J. M., & Williams, P. (1993). Does it matter who makes the rules? *Kappa Delta Pi Record, 29*(2), 43–45.

Lewellen, J. R. (1990). Systematic and effective teaching. *The High School Journal, 63*(1), 57–63.

Magney, J. (1990). Game-based teaching. *The Education Digest, 60*(5), 54–57.

Marshall, C. (1991). Teachers' learning styles: How they affect student learning. *The Clearing House. 64*(4), 225–227.

Martin, J. E. (1992). Gifted behaviors—Excellence for all. *The Clearing House, 66*(1), 37–40.

McCullum, H. (1991). Instructional strategies and classroom management. In M. S. Knapp & P. M. Shields (Eds.), *Better schooling for the children of poverty: Alternatives to conventional wisdom* (pp. 273–310). Berkeley, CA: McCutchan.

Means, B., & Knapp, M. S. (1991). Cognitive approaches to teaching advanced skills to educationally disadvantaged students. *Phi Delta Kappan, 73*(4), 282–289.

Means, B., & Knapp, M. S. (1991). Introduction: Rethinking teaching for disadvantaged students. In B. Means, C. Chelemer, & M. S. Knapp (Eds.), *Teaching advanced skills to at-risk students* (pp. 1–26). San Francisco: Jossey-Bass.

Morris, R. C. (Ed.). (1991). *Youth at Risk.* Lancaster, PA: Technomic.

Muncey, D. E., & McQuillan, P. J. (1993). Preliminary findings from a five-year study of the coalition of essential schools. *Phi Delta Kappan, 74*(6), 486–489.

National Education Goals Panel (1991). *Goals report.* Washington, DC: U.S. Government Printing Office.

Neely, R. O. & Alm, D. (1992). Meeting individual needs: A learning styles success story. *The Clearing House, 66*(2), 109–113.

Neufeld, B. (1991). Classroom management and instructional strategies for the disadvantaged learner. In M. S. Knapp & P. M. Shields (Eds.), *Better schooling for the children of poverty: Alternatives to conventional wisdom* (pp. 257–272). Berkeley, CA: McCutchan.

Newstead, S. E. (1992). A study of two "quick and easy" methods of assessing individual differences in student learning. *British Journal of Educational Psychology, 62,* 299–312.

Nystrand, M., & Gamoran, F. (1991). Student engagement: When recitation becomes conversation. In H. C. Waxman & H. J. Walberg (Eds.), *Effective teaching: Current research* (pp. 257–276). San Francisco: McCutchan.

Parsons, J., & Jones, C. (1990). Not another test. *The Clearing House, 64*(1), 17–20.

Phelps, P. H. (1991). Helping teachers excel as classroom managers. *The Clearing House, 64*(4), 241–242.

Popham, W. J., & Hambleton, R. K. (1990). Can you pass the test on testing? *Principal, 69*(3), 38–39.

Powell, R. R., & Garcia, J. (1991). Classrooms under the influence: Adolescents and alcoholic parents. *The Clearing House, 64*(4), 277.

Prawat, R. S. (1992). From individual differences to learning communities—our changing focus. *Educational Leadership, 49*(7), 9–13.

Reyes, D. J. (1990). Models of instruction: Some light on the model muddle. *The Clearing House, 63*(1), 214–216.

Richardson, A. G., & Fergus, E. E. (1993). Learning style and ability grouping in the high school system: Some Caribbean findings. *Educational Research, 35*(1), 69–76.

Richardson, R. E., & Evans, E. D. (1993). Empowering teachers to halt corporal punishment. *Kappa Delta Pi Record, 29*(2), 39–42.

Rosenshine, B., & Meister, C. (1992). The use of scaffolds for teaching higher-level cognitive strategies. *Educational Leadership, 49*(7), 26–33.

Rowe, J. W. (1990). To develop thinking citizens. *Educational Leadership, 48*(3), 43–44.

Sapon-Shevin, M. (1993). Why even gifted children need cooperative learning. *Educational Leadership, 50*(6), 62–63.

Savage, T. V. (1991). *Discipline for self control.* Englewood Cliffs, NJ: Prentice-Hall.

Slavin, R. E. (1989–1990). Research on cooperative learning: Consensus and controversy, *Educational Leadership, 47*(4), 52–54.

Smith, M. W. (1991). Evaluation as instruction: Using analytic scales to increase composing ability. *Middle School Journal, 22*(3), 21–25.

Stefanich, G. P. (1990). Cycles of cognition. *Middle School Journal, 22*(2), 47–52.

Theilheimer, R. (1991). Involving children in their own learning. *The Clearing House, 65*(2), 123–125.

Thomas, J. (1992). Individualized teaching. *Oxford Review of Education, 18*(1), 59–74.

Torrance, E. P. (1992). Creatively gifted, learning disabled individuals. *Educational Forum, 56*(4), 399–404.

Vockell, E. L. (1991). Corporal punishment: The pros and cons. *The Clearing House, 64*(4), 279–283.

Walde, A. C. & Baker, K. (1990). How teachers view the parents' role in education. *Phi Delta Kappan, 72*(4), 319–322.

Wiggins, G. (1989). Teaching to the authentic test. *Educational Leadership, 46*(7), 41–47.

Winton, J. J. (1991). You can win without competing. *Middle School Journal, 22*(3), 40.

Wolfe, D. P. (1989). Portfolio assessment: Sampling student work. *Educational Leadership, 46*(7), 35–39.

Wynne, E. A. & Ryan, K. (1993). *Reclaiming our schools.* New York: Merrill. (see chapter 1).

Young, D. B. (1993). Developing thinking skills: What teachers can do. *National Association of Laboratory Schools Journal, 17*(3), 32–52.

Zirpoli, T. J., & Malloy, K. J. (1993). *Behavior management.* New York: Merrill.

When Students Decided Not To Be Fair

PREPARING TO USE THE CASE

Background Information

Evaluating student work and assigning grades is one of the most difficult tasks confronting a teacher. In your own experiences as a student you have probably been exposed to a variety of instructors—individuals who possessed different philosophies about education and teaching. As a result, it is not likely that your high school teachers used identical procedures to assess your academic work. Nor is it likely that they used identical standards to assign letter grades. Did you prefer some methods of grading and evaluation over others?

Evaluation is critical to both the teacher and the student. For the instructor, such data are critical for planning future lessons and instructional techniques. This information also helps the teacher determine if he or she is successfully reaching the objectives of a specific course. Evaluation provides the student with feedback indicating levels of performance. If learners are to improve and grow, they require accurate information about previous performance. In this regard, evaluation has two broad purposes: (1) to help teachers and students to improve performance, and (2) to allow teachers and students to determine if they are meeting expected standards of performance.

Often testing and evaluation are confused. The latter process is more comprehensive and includes a variety of inputs in addition to test results (e.g., classroom participation, completion of homework assignments). Unfortunately, it is not uncommon for testing to be conducted without an understanding of how the results will be precisely used in the evaluation process. When this occurs, the selection of an appropriate type of test and the construction of test questions usually are not tied to specific evaluation objectives. Accordingly, the probability of error in using test results is increased. For this reason, establishing purpose to a student evaluation process is a critical first step to grading.

First-year teachers encounter a number of unique circumstances as they begin their careers. The nature of the community, the climate of the school, and the quality of the faculty and administration are three of these conditions. For example, you may start your career in a school that has rigid policies regarding tests, evaluation, and the assignment of student grades. Or you may be employed in a school where you are expected to make all these decisions on your own. You may work in a school where you will be assigned a mentor, or where the principal works extensively with new faculty. On the other hand, you may end up in a school where everyone more or less leaves you alone. Because of the diversity of communities and schools, you cannot assume that the practices that you will face in your first position are identical, or even similar, to those that you experienced in clinical courses or student teaching.

This case focuses on a beginning teacher who encounters challenges from students and parents after the first-semester grades in a home economics class are distributed. She uses a grading system with prescribed point ranges, and many of the students in her class become angry when they receive low grades. This is especially true because most of the students did well on quizzes and the final examination, but they received low grades from peers on classroom projects. As you read this case, reflect on how you might have approached testing, evaluation, and grading differently.

Topics for Reflection
1. Test construction
2. Relationship of test data to evaluation
3. Prescribed ranges for student grades
4. Providing students with periodic feedback
5. Formative versus summative evaluation
6. Communicating expectations to students

THE CASE

Allison Schmitt decided to become a teacher when she was a senior in high school. In large measure, her career choice was influenced by Denise Norman, a home economics teacher whom she had come to admire. Being an average student in high school, Allison did not feel that her teachers showed much personal interest in her—that is, until she enrolled in Mrs. Norman's foods class in her junior year. For the first time in her high school experience, Allison felt important in a class; the teacher obviously liked her, and, she received an ''A'' in the course—something she had not previously accomplished. In her senior year, she enrolled in Mrs. Norman's clothing class and received another ''A.'' Mrs. Norman frequently talked to Allison about going to college and becoming a teacher. Prior to this encouragement, Allison had given little thought to her life after high school. In the spring of her senior year, Mrs. Norman took Allison to visit her alma mater, Southwestern State University. A week later, Allison applied for admission.

Academic work at Southwestern State University was not easy for Allison. Even some of the courses in her major, home economics, proved to be difficult for her. But she worked hard and attended summer school between her sophomore and junior years so that she would have to take fewer courses in the subsequent academic years. Her student teaching, completed in a high school approximately 20 miles from the university during the second semester of her senior year, proved to be a rewarding experience. Her critic teacher was a friendly person, but she rarely offered advice. Allison interpreted this as approval of her performance. She received an "A" in student teaching and graduated with a 2.56 grade point average (on a 4.0 system). In late June, she landed a teaching position at Uniondale High School.

Uniondale is a community undergoing substantial change. Although it remains essentially a farming community, its proximity to the state's largest city is responsible for its demographic transition. A combination of better highways and the growing desire to escape the inner city has made Uniondale an increasingly popular residential community. Three new subdivisions are currently under construction within one mile from the interstate highway. Many of these homes are expensive and attract upper-middle-class executive families.

When Allison interviewed to teach home economics at Uniondale High School, she was truly impressed with the new school facility. Built in the early 1990s in anticipation of continued growth in enrollment, the building cost over $35 million. The home economics facilities were the best she had ever seen. The foods laboratory, for example, included the latest equipment and technology. She even had her own office in the home economics complex. During her interview, she was especially impressed by the principal, Dr. Stan Waller. He was a relatively young administrator, perhaps in his early thirties, who told Allison that he wanted to build a quality faculty who were willing to assume professional responsibility.

In late July, about a month before school was to start, Allison called Dr. Waller and asked if Uniondale High had a policy on student grading. She told him she was working on materials for the school year, and she had not found anything in the student handbook mandating standards for grades. The principal told her that the school did not require a standard grading scale; however, that did not mean that the school did not have a policy concerning grading. Each teacher had to file a grading plan in the principal's office during the first week of school. Dr. Waller suggested that Allison might find it beneficial to talk to one or more of the experienced teachers about student evaluation. He even gave her the telephone numbers of two of them.

At this point Allison had not moved to Uniondale, and she was apprehensive about calling teachers she had not yet met. Because she would not be moving to her apartment in Uniondale until three days before the start of school, she decided to move forward with planning on her own. She thought about calling her friend, Mrs. Norman, who had retired and moved to Arizona, but she decided not to bother her either. Instead, she went into the attic of her parents' home and dug out a box of materials from high school. Among the various items were the grading systems Mrs. Norman had used in her classes. Allison decided that they would make a good guide for developing her evaluation criteria.

During the first two weeks of August, Allison prepared course outlines that would be distributed to students on the first day of class. One of the classes she was assigned to teach was Foods I, an introductory course in home economics. Students normally took the course for two semesters. In teaching foods, Mrs. Norman used peer evaluations to assess in-class cooking projects. She felt that students worked harder to gain approval from peers. This concept was infused into Allison's syllabus for Foods I, and under the section labeled, "Evaluation and Grading," the following information was provided:

In an effort to be fair to all students, a system of grading on the curve will not be used. Every student has an opportunity to make an "A" in this course. Semester grades shall be determined by a point system:

360 to 400 points = A
320 to 359 points = B
280 to 319 points = C
240 to 279 points = D
239 or less points = F

Points are distributed as follows:

4 quizzes (25 points each) = 100 points
4 projects (25 points each) = 200 points
class participation   = 50 points
final examination   = 50 points

Allison was a little unsure about how well peer evaluations would work; thus she decided not to use it in her other classes. Foods I would be an experiment.

Allison's Foods I class consisted of 242 students, 20 of whom were females. Most of the students were juniors, but there were three seniors in the group. When the course outline was distributed, Allison discussed its content. She made a special point of emphasizing the aspect of peer evaluation related to in-class cooking projects. None of the students raised questions or objections about peer evaluations or about the grading procedures in general.

Quizzes were given approximately every four weeks, and they were a combination of multiple-choice and true-false questions addressing subject matter covered since the previous quiz. Allison discussed the quizzes when she returned them to the students.

The in-class cooking projects were staggered so that six students did them in a given week. The students enjoyed these experiences, because they got to taste the different dishes that were prepared. Each student's project was rated by the other 23 students in the class. This was done by recording a numeric value from 1 to 50 on a form which was then given directly to the teacher. Students were not required to put their names on the rating forms. After collecting them, Allison calculated a mean score. This became the student's grade for that project.

The first in-class projects were completed during September. The mean scores received by the 24 students on their first in-class project ranged from 32 to 48. The 32 was given to Ralph Hogan, a senior football player who told everyone he was taking the class because he would be a lifelong bachelor. Ralph managed to burn pudding. In some instances Allison did not agree with the student assessments for the first projects, but the student reactions to the process were so positive that she did not want to change anything.

The second projects were completed during October. Having now experienced the process and learning how the peer evaluation system worked, several of the students decided they would "get even" with students they thought had given them low scores on the first project. Even though the scoring process was confidential, rumors had been started that suggested low scores were being given by some as a joke. Average points students received on the second projects dropped markedly to a range of 28 to 36. Several students in the class had not given any other student a score of more than 20 points. Now Allison was becoming concerned, and she spoke to the class about being fair in assigning points.

The third and fourth projects only got progressively worse. One student in class gave every other student a total of 12 points on each project. By November, virtually all of the students were convinced that low scores were being given regardless of the quality of work. Many decided that the only way to protect themselves was to give others low scores. The number of points awarded on the third projects ranged from 19 to 34; on the fourth project, the points ranged from 14 to 34.

Although Allison knew that many of the students were being unfair in grading their peers, she could not readily find a solution to the problem. Fortunately, most of the students had done very well on the quizzes. After considering some options, she decided to compensate for what had happened with the scoring of student projects by constructing a very easy final examination. She made it an essay test with the intention of being very liberal in awarding points. No student received less than 45 points.

After she calculated final grades for the course, her gradebook contained the data shown in Table 1. There were no "A's" and just three "B's." Allison knew this would create a problem. Several of the students in her class were honor students who had very good grades.

Allison made an appointment with Dr. Waller to discuss the grades in her Foods I class. She carefully explained the circumstances that led to the low grades. She emphasized that this was an experiment and that she tried to compensate for the project scores by making the final examination quite easy. The principal seemed reluctant to get involved.

TABLE 1 Foods I fall semester

Student	Quiz Total	Projects Total	Class Participation	Final Exam	Total Points	Course Grade
Anderson, Debra	93	125	48	48	314	C
Bell, Bob	90	103	45	47	285	C
Brown, Janice	87	105	45	46	283	C
Carber, Mary	96	130	48	49	323	B
Dillon, Leona	84	96	43	45	268	D
Eagan, Elaine	86	95	44	46	271	D
Hogan, Ralph	73	90	40	45	268	D
Jalepski, Rose Ann	94	120	48	49	311	C
Kizer, Delta	86	93	47	47	273	D
Lunamin, Marcia	84	104	46	47	279	D
Minelti, Tony	73	84	40	45	242	D
Munster, Tricia	96	135	49	50	330	B
O'Rourke, Nadine	85	101	46	46	278	D
Powers, Susan	86	95	48	47	276	D
Ranger, Janice	98	122	46	50	316	C
Stewart, Alice	86	99	47	46	278	D
Summers, Zelda	74	92	40	45	251	D
Talbot, Brett	80	100	45	45	270	D
Termechi, Andrea	97	130	50	50	327	B
Tupper, Rachel	90	105	40	45	290	C
Ultman, Elizabeth	93	98	48	49	288	C
Walker, Tricia	85	110	47	47	289	C
Willett, April	84	104	40	46	274	D
Yeoman, Deloris	85	106	45	45	281	C

"Allison, you made the decision to use the grading formula," he told her. "I don't know how you can change it at this point. You probably will get some complaints, and you should be prepared to handle them. But tell me, what do you see as the purpose of grades?"

Allison was caught off guard by the question. "Grades are required. All of us have to give them, don't we?"

"Sure," the principal responded, "but what purposes do you see in giving grades?"

Allison thought for a moment and then said, "They communicate the level of progress being made to the student and the student's parents."

Dr. Waller did not indicate whether he thought Allison had provided a good answer. Instead he concluded their brief meeting by saying, "Think about why you give students grades. Maybe that will help you decide what evaluation criteria you will use in the future."

Within days after the grades were distributed, it was evident that the principal had underestimated the number of complaints that would be forthcoming. Thirteen of the students or their parents called Allison to complain about grades in the class. The first came from John Ultman, Elizabeth's father, who called Allison at her apartment the very evening that grades were distributed. After telling her why he was calling, he made a point of letting her know that he was an elementary school principal in a neighboring district. Allison felt a little more intimidated after learning this fact.

The father outlined his concern, "What upsets me most is the fact that Elizabeth did extremely well on your tests. She only missed one point on the final and a total of seven points on four quizzes. How can you give someone with those scores a ''C''?

Allison explained what had happened in the class, but her comments seemed to increase Mr. Ultman's anger.

"This is even worse. You let students play games with grading. Do you realize how this will hurt our daughter? She is a very good student. In fact, this is the first ''C'' she has received since she came to Uniondale High School. I am requesting that you reconsider your grade for her. It is the fair and just thing to do."

Other complaints were similar. Most of the parents also called Dr. Waller to express their dissatisfaction with the grading policies in Foods I. The principal told parents and students that he would not force Miss Schmitt to change the grades, because under school policy, grading was a matter within the professional scope of teachers. He noted that Miss Schmitt had made known her grading format to all students during the first week of school and no student raised an objection to them.

The complaint that bothered Allison most was the one from Mary Carber. She was an excellent student who truly deserved an ''A'' in Foods I. In fact, Mary is at the very top of her class, and the ''B'' in this course hurt her chances of becoming class valedictorian next year.

"I only took this course because I thought it would be interesting," Mary told Allison. "I never thought that I would get a ''B''. Isn't there something you could do?"

Allison really regretted what had happened in Foods I. Since she did not include peer grading in her other courses, the problem was isolated to this one class. She was deeply troubled by what had occurred; and the fact that Dr. Waller had distanced himself from the problem added to her discomfort. During the weeklong semester break, she wrote to each of the students in her Foods I class explaining that grading policies would be changed for the second semester.

Dear Students:

As I told you at the beginning of the semester, using peer evaluations for in-class projects in Foods I was an experiment. Obviously, it did not work well. Thus peer grading will not be used in the second semester. Although each of us must accept some blame for what occurred, I am ultimately responsible. I have decided against changing grades, because I don't believe two "wrongs" make a "right." I hope we have all learned something from this experience. Most of all, I hope you will be back in my foods class during the second semester.

Sincerely,

Miss Schmitt

When the second semester started, only 13 of the 24 students were still enrolled in the foods class. Nine of the students were successful in finding some other class. Nearly half of those who were still enrolled had tried to do the same thing, but they were not successful.

The grading format for the second-semester foods class remained intact with the exception that Miss Schmitt would be grading the student projects. All 13 students said they felt more comfortable with that change.

The Challenge

Analyze Allison's policies on grading. If you were in her position, what might you have done differently?

ISSUES FOR FURTHER REFLECTION

1. In the case, Allison used a peer-assessment practice that was employed by one of her former teachers. Is it common for beginning teachers to emulate the practices of teachers they have admired?

2. Assume you had to teach this foods class. Develop your own grading policy and defend it.

3. What are the strengths and weaknesses of peer grading?

4. Why do you think Allison failed to change her grading policy when it became evident that the students were not being fair in grading each other's projects?

5. Assess the practice of establishing prescribed ranges (fixed standards) for grades. Is it a better system than grading on the curve?

6. To what extent was the evaluation process in Foods I formative and summative?

7. What is your opinion of the principal in this case? Would you like him to be your supervisor? Why or why not?

8. Assess the school's policy of allowing each teacher to develop his or her own grading practices. If teachers are true professionals, should they not have this latitude?

9. From time to time, questions have been raised about weighting grades in elective courses such as home economics, physical education, and industrial technology in calculating grade point averages and class ranks. What is your opinion on this matter?

10. The principal told parents and students that: (a) Allison's grading practices were made known during the first week of school, and (b) no one questioned or challenged them. If you were a parent of one of these students, how would you react to those statements?

11. What might have been done after the first two months of this class to avoid the grading problem that occurred?

12. One could look at this case from several perspectives. Analyze the decision not to change grades from three viewpoints: (a) moral/ethical, (b) professional, and (c) legal.

13. If you were Allison's friend and colleague, what would you advise her to do at this point?

14. Do you think that any of the following factors affected what happened in this case: (a) Allison's own ability as a student? (b) The changing demographic nature of the

community? (c) The principal's desire to increase enrollments in home economics? (d) The absence of a practice of assigning mentors to first-year teachers at Uniondale High School?

15. What is your assessment of Allison's decision to construct an easy final examination and to grade the tests liberally so that all students received high scores?

16. Why did the principal think that it was important to link purpose to Allison's criteria for assessing pupil progress?

17. Assess Allison's grading system for the second semester.

SUGGESTED READINGS

Agnew, J. (1985). *The grading policies and practices of high school teachers.* (ERIC Reproduction Service Document No. ED 259 022)

Canady, R., & Hotchkiss, P. (1989). It's a good score! Just a bad grade. *Phi Delta Kappan, 71*(1), 68–71.

Clark, C., & Nelson, M. (1991). Evaluation: Be more than a scorekeeper. *Arithmetic Teacher, 38*(9), 15–17.

Dembo, M. (1994). *Applying educational psychology in the classroom* (5th ed.). New York: Longman (see chapters 12, 13).

Gilman, D., & Swan, E. (1989). Solving G.P.A. and class rank problems. *NASSP Bulletin, 73*(515), 91–97.

Good, T., & Brophy, J. (1990). *Educational psychology: A realistic approach* (4th ed.). New York: Longman (see chapters 26, 29).

Henson, K. (1993). *Methods and strategies for teaching in secondary and middle schools* (2nd ed.). New York: Longman (see chapters 14, 15).

Madgic, R. (1988). The point system of grading: A critical appraisal. *NASSP Bulletin, 72*(507), 29–34.

Nottingham, M. (1988). Grading practices—Watching out for land mines. *NASSP Bulletin, 72*(507), 24–28.

Ornstein, A. (1989). The nature of grading. *Clearing House, 62*(8), 365–369.

Pasternack, S. (1981). Properly motivated, students become good peer graders. *Journalism Educator, 36*(3), 17–18.

Seigel, J. (1991). Considerations in calculating high school GPA and rank-in-class. *NASSP Bulletin, 75*(537), 96–109.

Terwilliger, J. (1989). Classroom standard setting and grading practices. *Educational Measurement: Issues and Practice, 8*(2), 15–19.

Thomas, W. (1986). Grading—Why are school policies necessary? What are the issues? *NASSP Bulletin, 70*(487), 23–26.

CASE 31

Testing: A Challenge for All

PREPARING TO USE THE CASE

Background Information

Testing and evaluating are as much a part of teaching as planning lessons or instructing. Every teacher, regardless of grade level or subjects, is responsible for developing and maintaining a successful testing and evaluation program, and most teachers find that this responsibility is their least favorite part of teaching. So don't be surprised if you hear teachers remark, "Teaching would be great if it weren't for the testing and grading."

For generations, objective tests primarily have been used in American schools. For several decades, the multiple-choice, true-false, matching, and fill-in-the-blank tests have predominated. In the most recent generations, machine scoring has become a staple in many schools. Even without this accommodation, such objective tests have attracted most teachers because they can be quickly scored and also because they have specific answers.

This extensive use of objective tests is unique to Americans in that it does not reflect the type of evaluation that characterizes British schools. On the contrary, British schools have relied on essays for tracking student progress. The essays require students to synthesize information from different sources and to internalize that information, telling why the content in their lessons is important to them. This synthesizing and internalizing gives added meaning, a deeper understanding of the content under study. Naturally, the practice of writing essays over 11 or 12 years makes the British high school graduate more articulate in writing and speaking.

Another questionable practice that characterizes testing and evaluation in America is the use to which it is directed. If asked why we test, most Americans might say that we have to determine how well students have done, as opposed to measuring how well students are doing, so that adjustments can be made to teaching and studying to improve student performance. A psychomotrist might express these ideas more succinctly by saying that we have overused summative evaluation and underused formative evaluation.

Within the past couple of decades, added emphasis has been given to the use of criterion-referenced evaluation and objectives. This shift has resulted from an accountability movement which began in the 1970s. The education reform programs throughout the nation are keeping the accountability movement alive, and are having some interesting effects on testing and evaluation in elementary and secondary schools. On the one hand, the reform is calling for increased scores on standardized achievement tests. On the other, many of the programs are calling for progress reports, requiring students to analyze their progress using qualitative methods. Students monitor their own achievement on an ongoing basis.

Although the reform programs require different types of testing, most share such characteristics as curriculum alignment (aligning what is taught with that which is tested), valued outcomes (general statements of what the schools want the students to be able to do, and how they wish future citizens to behave), and authentic testing (tests that measure behaviors that lead toward the school district's valued outcomes).

As you read the following case, be assured that the roles of testing and evaluation will continue to change and become more important. Think about your future responsibilities to your community and your students. You must develop and maintain testing and evaluation programs that will serve both.

Topics for Reflection
1. Formative evaluation vs. summative evaluation
2. Criterion-referenced evaluation vs. norm-referenced evaluation
3. The impact of education reform on testing and evaluation
4. The purposes of evaluation
5. The effect of evaluation on learning

THE CASE

The Public Schools in Paris County

Pine Grove is one of three schools in Paris County. The Paris County School Board is comprised mostly of farmers. These are hard-working, no-nonsense, community-minded people who want the best for their children and the community. There are no educators on the school board, yet on separate occasions different board members have visited effective schools in other districts. Since the reform efforts have been mounting in the state, a series of articles in the state's major newspapers has reported the generally poor performance of the state's schools. These articles have increased the level of concern of the Paris Board members for upgrading their schools.

Hans was especially proud of his evaluation program. Throughout his student-teaching semester, he had experimented with several strategies, hoping to increase the students' academic performance. One strategy that he made full use of was unannounced quizzes which were given to keep students on task at all times with their homework. Hans also made frequent references to the forthcoming exams. Both of these strategies were aimed at motivating students; the goal was to encourage them to put more effort into their schoolwork. Unfortunately, the students responded negatively to these quizzes and reminders. Several students became tense with the mention of either.

Another part of the evaluation system that Hans uses is a norm-referenced system for converting raw scores to letter grades. Numerical scores are recorded for each term project, homework assignment, and test. Later the numbers are rank ordered. All numbers in the top cluster are assigned "A"s, the second cluster "B"s, and so forth. Hans likes this system because he knows that no student is earning a higher letter grade than another student who has performed better.

Hans purposefully constructs each major test so that no student will be able to complete all problems. His rationale for using these extra-long tests is that the only way to align his lessons with the tests and yet avoid being accused of "teaching to the test" is to include so much content on the test that anyone who scores in the top cluster in the class will fully earn an "A."

The School and Its Leadership

Pine Grove Elementary School reminds most visitors of a turn-of-the-century school. Each of its six rooms accommodates a grade level. The principal, Ms. Janice Blackwood, teaches two periods each day. This keeps her abreast of teaching and its new developments and challenges, and it makes both the students and teachers at Pine Grove Elementary respect the fact that she understands the perspectives of both teachers and students. Her pragmatic philosophy seems to fit this locale.

The faculty members at Pine Grove are congenial. Mr. Tom Burns has offered to help Hans "learn the ropes" at this school, and Hans knew his offer was serious. When the first annual attendance report was due, Tom sat down and showed him how to complete the report, step by step. Although this was a routine report that the other teachers completed while sitting in the faculty lounge and drinking coffee, or even while their students worked on assignments, the system seemed exceedingly complex to a teacher who had never seen it before.

Hans appreciated just knowing that there was someone in the school to whom he could turn with any type of problem. He also felt that the other teachers would be just as helpful if he ever needed them. From his first meeting with the other teachers, he could see that they would be equally helpful. They made Hans feel like a full-fledged member of the faculty.

Perhaps the thing Hans appreciated most about these teachers was their laid-back, easy-going dispositions. When compared to many contemporary work environments, to be able to work with people who never seem to panic over deadlines or rush to do anything was a welcome contrast. Hans concluded that the only thing that might prompt these teachers to rush was preparing for a fishing trip or a weekend in the mountains!

Hans could not help but wonder how well prepared these colleagues were to meet the new challenges that confront the nation's schools. He had serious doubts about their knowledge of new teaching methodology and new testing and evaluation methods. He chuckled to think that most of these teachers had probably never heard such terms as *curriculum alignment, authentic testing, valued outcomes,* and *performance assessment.* Then he felt guilty for his condescending attitudes, especially since these were such nice people. Thank goodness, the school did have forward-thinking leadership in its administration.

The principal, Ms. Blackwood, endorses the concept of experiential education and encourages the other teachers to combine direct instruction with hands-on experiences. At Pine Grove the hands-on approach is also appreciated by the rugged, work-oriented parents. Ms. Blackwood has provided strong leadership for the school for the past 15 years. To the residents, who respect her understanding but no-nonsense approach, she symbolizes Pine Grove. The students and teachers consider her firm, but fair.

On one occasion which involved two students changing their grades in their teacher's gradebook, Ms. Blackwood arranged a meeting with the students and their parents. She firmly assured them that any recurrence of the problem would find the students giving a public apology in their classes, and that notes of their dishonest behavior would be placed in their cumulative files. Needless to say, there were no further instances of this behavior. The incident also led to the development of a policy statement on cheating.

The Teacher

Hans Anderson did his student teaching in a large urban school. There he found many aspects of urban life unbearable. The pace was always too rapid. At first it was a rush to get everything done on time. Then it got worse. It seemed that he had to rush just to get things done at all. The bell system at school didn't help. There was never enough time to eat lunch or to get from one part of the building to another.

Then there was all the paperwork. The school didn't seem to realize that he needed to spend his time making lesson plans and tests and scoring tests. Hans knew that part of his problem stemmed from his lack of experience. He noticed that the more experienced teachers seemed to fill out the attendance reports and other required reports much faster then he could do them.

Apart from the constant rushing, Hans also missed the natural environment. In the city everything was cement and concrete. Yet all of his life he had been "Mr. Outdoors." He wondered what had lured him to accept an inner-city job.

The worst part of all for Hans was the lack of trust that he found in this new environment. Here people referred to those who take advantage of others as "street smart." Hans thought such reference was undeservingly complimentary. What a contrast this idea was from his upbringing, for he had always been taught to help people who need help, particularly those who are less fortunate. And what about respecting others, self-respect, and trust?

Hans' student-teaching experience, though brief, had taught him several lessons. Urban living had forced him to develop several time-management strategies.

For the first time in his life he carried on his person, at all times, a pocket calendar on which he recorded all of his future meetings. Each evening he also made up a "things to do" list for the next day. During the day, from time to time he would pull this list out of his shirt pocket and check off completed tasks.

Hans found the calendar and the "things to do" lists to be absolute necessities. He wondered how many other strategies his urban colleagues had developed to streamline their time. One common strategy was his fellow teachers' use of weekly machine-scored multiple-choice tests. In the teacher's lounge, a scoring machine marked answer sheets for tests with rapid speed. However, Hans had worked hard to develop a qualitative testing program. He knew that such a program took more teacher time to administer, but he believed that tests should be used to promote learning, which, after all, was his first responsibility as a teacher. He perceived his role in grading as one of the "necessary evils" that befall all teachers, and he thought that it militated against his being a well-respected teacher.

Altogether, these liabilities were too much; and Hans felt compelled to move away from the city. When his student-teaching program was finished a year ago, he moved to Paris County because he wanted to live in the mountains. The serenity and the natural setting have been all he had hoped for. The residents seem to have an unwritten code of acceptance. His love for the outdoors provides excellent opportunities for Hans to get close to his sixth-grade students. Saturdays are often spent hunting or fishing with some of these students and their parents.

As part of a science unit on plants, Hans takes nature hikes with several students. His students enjoy competing with each other as they use a key that he provides them to classify trees. They enjoy similar experiences when studying a unit on rocks and minerals, using outdoor hikes to collect specimens of fossils and sedimentary, igneous, and metamorphic rocks. They frequently visit a gravel pit, which the county road commissioner had dug to provide rocks for road beds, but which Hans and his students use to collect crinoid stems. Some have even found some petrified flowers and round bulbs that anchored these marine plants.

Most of the students show their appreciation by applying their efforts on classroom and homework assignments. The first year at Pine Grove Elementary has proven that Hans has found a permanent home, a place where people share his love of nature, and a school where he can use his hands-on teaching methods. Appreciating this job and all of its advantages, Hans has worked hard to get along with his fellow teachers. He keeps them informed about his field trips and invites them to bring their students along and join these experiences. Hans enjoys sharing, and he also wants to secure his position at Pine Grove for a long time.

The Incident

For Hans's classes, Friday is known as test day. Today was no different. As Hans often kids, "Friday is our sharing day; it's the day that I give you the opportunity to share some of your knowledge with me." At the beginning of each test period, Hans introduces a little levity to lower the anxiety. It is clearly understood that once the test is underway, there is to be no foolishness. Unlike some teachers who use test periods to catch up on their paperwork or to stand in their doorway and chat with their neighboring teachers, Hans never leaves the room during a test; in fact, he seldom uses test time to grade papers, fill out the monthly report, or perform other chores. Instead, Hans is determined to give his full attention to monitoring the test.

This Friday was typical. When the test was distributed, a silence fell across the room. Immediately each student began frantically working on the test. About five minutes into the test, in complete frustration, one student put down his pencil and said, "I give up." Another student followed suit. Then another. Soon a half-dozen students were refusing to take the rest of the test. They demanded that the weekly tests be discontinued, and that future major exams be adjusted to a reasonable length.

Hans knew that there was a high level of tension in this class, but he had never thought that the students would refuse to finish a test. At the end of the period, he knew that he had to decide how he would respond to these demands. He wouldn't mind discontinuing these practices if he were sure that they were not educationally sound, but he simply did not know. As he pondered his dilemma, he weighed the following factors:

- Pine Grove Elementary School is located in a rural, conservative community.
- The principal, Ms. Blackwood, is a strong, respected leader.
- Ms. Blackwood supports Hans's experiential approach to education.
- Here in Paris County, Hans enjoys teaching, and he even gives up many of his weekends to go fishing, hunting, and hiking with his students.
- He carefully monitors students as they take his tests.
- He has established a routine of giving weekly tests. Could this make students more sensitive to the seriousness of test taking? Less sensitive?

The Challenge

How would you respond to the immediate crisis? What precautions would you take to prevent further upheavals?

ISSUES FOR FURTHER REFLECTION

1. What are some alternative behaviors that Hans could take?
2. How would you rank order the behaviors listed in response to the previous question?
3. For each alternative, what additional information is needed, if any?
4. In what ways, if any, do community values affect your decision?
5. Why do some teachers give tests at definite intervals? How does this routine approach affect the degree of seriousness that students feel toward tests?

6. Should tests be used to motivate students? What are some ways to motivate these students?

7. Suppose you choose to offer the students a compromise and give up just one of the practices; the power exams, the rank ordering of scores, or the unannounced tests. Which would you give up? Why?

8. How should the type of local administration (for example, Ms. Blackwood) affect a teacher's testing program?

9. Is there any danger in combining humor with testing? If so, what is the danger and how can it be avoided?

10. What, if any, effect should the previous cheating incident have on Hans's decision?

11. Most students work hard to please their teacher. Should this affect the testing program? If so, how?

SUGGESTED READINGS

Dagley, D. L., & Orso, J. K. (1991) Integrating summative and formative modes evaluation. *NASSP Bulletin, 75*(536), 75–82.

Dembo, M. (1994). *Applying educational psychology in the classroom* (5th ed.). New York: Longman (see chapters 12, 13).

Ellsworth, R. A., Donnell, P., & Duell, O. K. (1990). Multiple-choice test items: What are textbook authors telling teachers? *Journal of Educational Research, 83*(5), 290–293.

Fielding, G., & Shaughnessy, J. (1990). Improving student assessment: Overcoming the obstacles. *NASSP Bulletin, 74*(529), 90–98.

Good, T., & Brophy, J. (1990). *Educational psychology: A realistic approach* (4th ed.). New York: Longman (see chapters 26–29).

Griswold, P. A. (1990, Feb.). Assessing relevance and reliability to improve the quality of teacher-made tests. *NASSP Bulletin, 74*(523), 18–23.

Gronlund, N. E. (1991). *How to write and use international objectives* (4th ed.). New York: Macmillan.

Henson, K. T. (1993). *Methods and strategies for teaching in secondary and middle schools* (2nd ed.). White Plains, NY: Longman (chapters 14, 15).

Newstead, S. E. (1992). A study of two "quick and easy" methods of assessing individual differences in student learning. *British Journal of Educational Psychology, 62*(3), 299–312.

Parsons, J., & Jones, C. (1990). Not another test. *The Clearing House, 64*(1), 17–20.

Popham, W. J., & Hambleton, R. K. (1990). Can you pass the test on testing? *Principal, 69*(3), 38–39.

Walde, A. C., & Baker, K. (1990). How teachers view the parents' role in education. *Phi Delta Kappan, 72*(4), 319–322.

Wiggins, G. (1989). Teaching to the authentic test. *Educational Leadership, 46*(7), 41–47.

Wolfe, D. P. (1989). Portfolio assessment: Sampling student work. *Educational Leadership, 46*(7), 35–39.

Making the Grade?

PREPARING TO USE THE CASE

Background Information

Giving grades remains one of the most unpleasant tasks that teachers face. Grading too easily or too harshly creates problems of motivation for students. Constructing tests that appear unfair encites the anger of students. Giving grades that parents believe don't represent the ability of their children may elicit parental criticism. Not following school policy regarding grading invites criticism from other teachers and administrators.

It is never possible to avoid criticism entirely in assigning grades to student performance. A student, parent, other teacher, or administrator will, on occasion, challenge the grade assigned or the reasons for assigning it. Given this fact, it is critical that teachers use tests that are well designed and measure the outcomes taught. The content to be covered, the kinds of test items to be used, the weight of the items, how the test will be scored and the grade assigned, and when the test will be returned—as much information about the test and testing conditions as is possible—should be thoroughly explained. When tests are returned, an opportunity for students to ask questions should be provided.

Grades assigned to tests have an emotive value; that is, they affect students' self-concept and esteem. Accordingly, grades should be determined in ways so that they are used to describe student performance, not as a means to punish students. Finding activities that enable each student to be successful provides an additional challenge as grades are assigned.

In recent years, debate has surrounded the issue of "weighted grades." Some educators argue that gifted students who are enrolled in the most challenging courses should expect to receive no less than a grade of A or B. Otherwise, they argue, these students, concerned about their grade point average and its effect on college admissions and scholarships, will choose easier courses to take. This case focuses on this concern, as a beginning teacher hands back his first set of graded tests in a mathematics class. Whether or not to maintain the standard he has set for student performance is at issue.

Topics for Reflection
1. Developing a rationale for grading practices
2. Determining grades based on the results of student performance
3. The effects of grading on student behavior
4. The relationship between grades and self-esteem
5. The relationship between student ability and grading practices
6. The impact of political pressures on teacher decision making
7. The academic freedom of teachers

THE CASE

Binghamton City School District takes pride in its standards of educational excellence. The grades given should reflect the quality of work completed by the students. The following grading system is used:

A = superior

B = excellent

C = average

D = poor

F = failure

David Marks reread the grading policy published in *The Teachers Handbook: Binghamton City Schools.* He had also read through the 27 test papers from his second-period advanced mathematics class once. Before he marked the test papers, he wanted to be certain he was following procedures.

"Can't be too careful, especially with the gifted students," he thought to himself. "If I'm not precise, they'll challenge me. I want to be prepared."

There was no doubt in David's mind about the potential for challenge from his students. The 27 juniors and seniors in his class were admitted into the highly selective colloquium "Mind Problems" on the basis of their carrying an overall grade point average of 3.7 (on a 4.0 scale), an A grade in all high school math courses, and a 680 or better score on the mathematics section of the Scholastic Aptitude Test (SAT). In addition, the students had to have the written recommendation of two teachers attesting to their leadership potential.

For the remainder of the evening Mr. Marks graded the papers. For each paper, he reviewed the process used to solve the ten problems on the test along with the students' answers. He assigned a maximum of 5 points to the process and 5 points to the answer for a total of 100 possible points.

After he had marked all the papers, he made a list of the point totals. Beside the totals he noted how many students obtained each score. He put a line under 72, indicating 13 scores above and 14 scores below the line. He looked for "natural breaks" in the scores and put broken lines above 58, 64, 81, and 90. Next he put letter grades next to the scores within an area. Next to the score of 93 he put "A." For scores 84–90 he put "B"; for 66–81 he put "C"; for 62–64 he put "D"; and for 52–58 he put "F".

SCORES

93 II		A
90 I		
87 I	B	
86 I		
84 I		
81 III		
79 II		
75 I		
72 I		C
70 II		
68 I		
67 I		
66 II		
64 I		
63 II	D	
62 II		
58 I		
57 I	F	
52 I		

Mr. Marks entered a letter grade on each paper, using his grading scale. The next morning before the advanced mathematics class began he printed the number of As, Bs, Cs, Ds, and Fs on the chalkboard.

2	A
4	B
13	C
5	D
3	F

He was proud of the care with which he had graded his first test. He wanted to show his class that he had high expectations and was well organized.

After the students arrived and the bell rang, he distributed the test papers, saying: "I want to begin class by going over the tests. Each time I give a test I'll return your tests the next day and review them so that you can learn from your mistakes." He beamed with pride, as he thought of his professor who had taught test and measurements, who had noted the importance of immediate feedback.

He walked down each row and returned each student's paper. He had folded each paper in half, vertically, so that students could not easily see one another's score. Seating the students alphabetically made it efficient for returning papers. As he passed out the papers, he said, "I've put the number of students receiving A, B, C, D, and F grades on the chalkboard so that you can see how you did in comparison with the other students."

As he passed out the papers, students began grumbling.

"Quiet, please," Mr. Marks said. "We'll go over the test in a minute."

"I can't believe this," one student said aloud. "I've *never* received a B on a math test."

"Me neither," another student agreed.

Several students echoed displeasure about the grade marked on their papers.

As Mr. Marks went through the test, the students challenged him on every item. But he had prepared carefully and had an answer for each challenge. He was pleased with the quickness of his responses.

"I survived the challenge," he thought. He recalled his methods professor saying that you can loosen things up later, but you've got to show them you are in charge at the beginning.

During the remainder of the period, he lectured on a new math concept. When ten minutes were left, he assigned 25 problems from the mathematics text and told the students they could begin working on the problems. As they worked on the problems, he walked around the room, assisting students who requested help. Although he felt some tension in the room, he assumed that it was the result of his students' reaction to his having set such high expectations.

A couple of minutes before the bell rang, Mr. Marks approached Elaine Jamerson, who had raised her hand. As he neared her desk, he could tell she had been crying.

"What's wrong, Elaine?" Mr Marks asked.

"Do you know what you have done?" she questioned.

"What do you mean," he responded.

"Do you have any idea what grades mean to us?" she asked.

"I'm certain they are very important," he indicated. "But you have to realize this is just the first test. It's important that I show you how I will be assigning grades. It really doesn't mean that much yet."

"Doesn't mean much!" Elaine yelled. "You don't know!" She gathered her books, stood up, and shouted: "You don't care. About me. About anybody!" Sobbing, she walked hurriedly from the room.

Upset, Mr. Marks followed her, calling to her as she walked down the corridor: "Elaine. You're wrong. I *do* care. Let's talk. Come back."

The bell rang. The students filed past Mr. Marks, still standing outside the classroom door. As they passed by, the students were still grumbling about the grades.

Before he went to the cafeteria for lunch, Mr. Marks stopped by the main office to check his mail. He found two phone messages. One was from Mrs. Jamerson and another was from Mrs. Scrivens. "Jamerson and Scrivens must be the mothers of Elaine Jamerson and Marvin Scrivens—students in my second-period class," he thought.

He took the phone messages and left the other papers behind. He decided he would call after lunch. He made a habit of avoiding discussion of school activities and problems during the 40-minute lunch period. Typically, he ate with two coaches and an English teacher. They talked about sports, movies, and automobiles.

He finished lunch a few minutes early and went to the counseling center, where he could use the phone in the privacy of a counselor's office.

He called Mrs. Jamerson.

"Hello, the Jamerson residence," she answered.

"Mrs. Jamerson?" Mr. Marks asked.

"Yes?" she responded.

"This is Mr. Marks. You called," he said.

"Mr. Marks, Elaine called me after your class and asked me to come and get her. When I picked her up, she burst into tears. She cried so hard when she got home that she cried herself to sleep. She said she was humiliated in your class."

"I don't understand," Mr. Marks said.

"Probably not. Elaine works very hard to compete in the honors classes. Math is not her strongest subject. But she's never received an F. How do you explain giving her an F?" Mrs. Jamerson asked.

"She had one of the lowest scores in the class," Mr. Marks responded. "I believe it was next to the lowest."

"Compared to what?" Mrs. Jamerson asked.

"What do you mean, compared to what?" Mr. Marks responded.

"These young people are the brightest in the school. There are no average students in your class. So how could you fail anyone?" she asked.

"Mrs. Jamerson, I told Elaine that this was just the first test and that the grades don't mean that much. There will be plenty of opportunities for her to improve. I just wanted the students to know that I have very high expectations," he responded.

"I believe in high expectations, as much as anyone," Mrs. Jamerson retorted coldly. "I was *cum laude* at a private university, one of the finest liberal arts institutions in the country. So don't lecture me about high expectations!"

"I wasn't lecturing. I was just trying to explain," Mr. Marks said. "Please don't . . . ."

Mrs. Jamerson interrupted. "I won't have my daughter treated this way!" she snapped angrily, and hung up.

Mr. Marks was stunned. When he took the job at Binghamton, he had developed a set of personal policies. One was not to embarrass or humiliate a student. Another was to return parents' calls promptly. He was troubled by this incident. He was particularly puzzled by Mrs. Jamerson's behavior.

He sat down in a chair and stared at the ceiling. After a minute or two, he looked at the other note, which showed Mrs. Scrivens's phone number. After Mrs. Jamerson's reaction to his call, he wasn't certain he wanted to make this one. "Maybe I should wait until the students and their parents cool off," he thought.

"Oh, well," he whispered aloud to gain self-assurance, "I make a commitment to myself to return calls promptly. I must stand by my personal principles."

He dialed the other number. Mrs. Scrivens answered.

"Mrs. Scrivens, this is Mr. Marks," he blurted out before she could talk. "You called earlier. I suppose you wanted to talk about the second-period class."

"Yes," she responded. "Marvin has a 4.0 average. He has not had a low grade in anything since third grade. We plan for him to go to Harvard, Yale, or Stanford."

"I'm pleased that you have high hopes for Marvin, but what does this have to do with my class?" Mr. Marks asked.

"Well, the B that you gave Marvin on his paper today—do you really believe that the grade is indicative of his ability?" she asked.

"I'm not certain," Mr. Marks said. "This was just the first test. He did B work on *this* test."

"We can't risk jeopardizing Marvin's 4.0 average. We may have to have him removed from your class if you can't give some assurance that he will excel," Mrs. Scrivens remarked.

"I can't guarantee how he will finish the course. Like I said, this was just the first test," Mr. Marks stated.

"Well, we expect him to get all A's. *Every* test. I trust you'll do what you can to see that he does," Mrs. Scrivens stressed.

"The grade Marvin gets will depend on his performance," Mr. Marks said, "I can't guarantee anything. It's up to him."

"Do you know who I am, Mr. Marks?" Mrs. Scrivens asked rhetorically. "Well, my husband owns Scrivens Industries. For several years he served on the school board. He is a powerful man, who can take your job away from you, if he wants," she noted. "And don't you think he won't, if you don't do a better job of teaching."

"Mrs. Scrivens, I don't believe threatening me . . ."

Before he could finish the sentence, Mrs. Scrivens warned: "This is no threat, Mr. Marks. This is a fact. Get the point?"

She hung up.

Mr. Marks was upset. He had difficulty teaching the rest of the afternoon. After his last class, he went to see Martha Givens, head of the mathematics department.

"Can I talk with you for a couple of minutes?" he asked.

"About your second-period class?" Mrs. Givens responded.

"How did you know?" Mr. Marks asked in astonishment.

"I've had Elaine and Marvin in class. Mrs. Scrivens and Mrs. Jamerson both called me this morning during my planning period," she said. "I know all about it."

"I can't believe they called you," Mr. Marks said. "I didn't do anything wrong."

"It's a matter of judgment. Students in your advanced math class could take an easier class and be certain of getting an A to keep a high grade point average. But they didn't do that," Mrs. Givens said.

"I followed the school district policy in assigning grades. I was very careful in grading their papers," Mr. Marks added defensively. "Should I give everyone in the class A's and B's?"

"It's your class, Mr. Marks. You need to decide for yourself," Mrs. Givens concluded abruptly, as she walked away.

The Challenge

You are Mr. Marks. How will you approach the issue of grading?

ISSUES FOR FURTHER REFLECTION

1. Did you use good judgment in assigning grades? Defend your answer.
2. Should you continue grading tests the way you have begun or consider another approach? Explain your response.
3. What information in the case led you to your decision?
4. What additional information would you like to have in order to make a decision?
5. What influence on your decision should the district's published grading policy have?
6. To what extent should Mrs. Givens's view be considered?
7. What effect will the parents' remarks have on your decision?
8. Is there a difference between the evaluation of student performance and giving grades? Explain your answer.
9. How do you feel about "weighted" grades? Should academically gifted students be given higher grades by virtue of their ability?
10. What beliefs do you hold about giving grades? How important are they? What is their most appropriate use?

SUGGESTED READINGS

Canady, R., & Hotchkiss, P. (1989). It's a good score! Just a bad grade. *Phi Delta Kappan, 71*(1), 68–71.

Dembo, M. (1994). *Applying educational psychology in the classroom* (5th ed.). New York: Longman (see Part 5).

Driscoll, M. P. (1986). The relationship between grading standards and achievement: A new perspective. *Journal of Research and Development in Education, 19*(3), 13–17.

Good, T., & Brophy, J. (1990). *Educational psychology: A realistic approach* (4th ed.). New York: Longman (see Part 8).

Henson, K. (1993). *Methods and strategies for teaching in secondary and middle schools* (2nd ed.). New York: Longman (see chapters 7, 14, 15).

Hills, J. (1991). Apathy concerning grading and testing. *Phi Delta Kappan, 72*(7), 540–545.

Jongsma, K. (1991). Rethinking grading practices. *Reading Teacher, 45*(4), 318–320.

Lockhart, E. (Winter, 1990). Heavy grades? A study on weighted grades. *Journal of College Admissions, 126,* 9–16.

Montmarquette, C., & Mahseredjian, S. (1989). Could teacher grading practices account for unexplained variation in school achievements? *Economics of Education Review, 8*(4), 335–343.

Ornstein, A. (1989). The nature of grading. *Clearing House, 62*(8), 365–369.

Pasch, M., Sparks-Langer, G., Gardner, T., Starko, A., & Moody, C. (1991). *Teaching as decision making: Instructional practices for the successful teacher.* New York: Longman (see chapter 7, section 1).

Pestello, F. (1987). The social construction of grades. *Teaching Sociology, 15*(4), 414–417.

Pollo, H., & Humphreys, W. (Summer, 1988). Grading students. *New Directions for Teaching and Learning, (34),* 85–97.

Siegel, J., & Anderson, C. (1991). Considerations in calculating high school GPA and rank-in-class. *NASSP Bulletin, 75*(537), 96–109.

Stiggins, R. (1989). Inside high school grading practices. *Educational Measurement, 8*(2), 5–14.

Terwilliger, J. (1989). Classroom standard setting and grading practices. *Educational Measurement: Issues and Practice, 8*(2), 15–19.

Thomas, W. C. (1986). Grading—why are school policies necessary? What are the issues? *NASSP Bulletin, 70*(487), 23–26.

CASE 33

Organizing for Instruction

PREPARING TO USE THE CASE

Background Information

Each child who comes to school is different from the others. Some of the differences are obvious. The sex, race, approximate height and weight, body shape, hair and eye color, and tone of voice are most noticeable. Other differences are much more subtle.

While one may readily see that a child has the facial and body characteristics of an Asian, the cultural values the child possesses cannot as easily be identified. Similarly, other differences are less obvious, such as: preference for physical activity, noise level, eye contact, touching, or method of discipline.

Individual differences will affect how teachers respond to children. Each teacher holds some biases about children's appearance and behavior. Wearing a hat to class may create a disruption in one teacher's class, but not in another teacher's class. Slouching in a chair may cause the ire of one teacher, but not another. Some teachers expect higher achievement from some groups than others. For example, some teachers expect all Asian students to excel in mathematics and sciences. Some teachers expect all girls to have difficulty in mathematics. Some teachers treat students of color differentially, based on the darkness of their skin.

It is critical for teachers to consider individual and group differences in planning instruction. Knowing differences can assist in grouping students for collaborative lessons. Understanding individual preferences can help in assigning students to the most appropriate instructional strategy. Having as much knowledge about each child is vital for making informed, productive, instructional decisions.

In this case a recent graduate, on short notice, replaces a teacher who takes a medical leave. Faced with teaching a large, combined class of fifth- and sixth-graders, the replacement must quickly organize the students for instructional purposes. While she is familiar with the school, having completed early field experiences there during her undergraduate study, she has little information with which to make instructional decisions. Two pieces of information she has at her disposal pose a dilemma. One is a folder of written descriptions of each child, prepared by the regular teacher. The other is a list of standardized test scores. How to use these data and others is the challenge she faces in getting organized.

Topics for Reflection
1. Cognitive goals
2. Cultural bias
3. Individual differences
4. Individualized instruction
5. Instructional planning
6. Instructional strategies
7. Multicultural education

THE CASE

Shelly had not expected to get a full-time teaching position. She had married during the summer and planned to do part-time substituting. She and her husband, a computer engineer, had felt that part-time employment would provide flexibility for their adjustment to marriage and, at the same time, bring in additional income.

One week before the start of school they were surprised when the personnel director from City District called to see if Shelly would be interested in teaching a combined fifth and sixth grade at Woodrow Wilson Elementary. City District is an elementary district within a large urban school corporation. Over the past two decades, it has experienced an influx of minorities. What was once considered an elitist, white-collar community has become a melting pot. While the makeup of the population has changed dramatically, the reputation of City District as a center of educational excellence has not changed. The "white flight" that occurred in the community was not followed by a similar exodus among teachers. The aging faculty has held firm to high expectations for students, a major reason why the district has retained its reputation.

At the same time, civic support for facilities and activities has not waned. Community organizations continue to hold fund-raisers to generate additional funds for the district. During the last 12 years, two tax referenda passed, due largely to the active political support from these civic organizations. Large crowds at both sporting events and fine-arts performances illustrate the level of community support.

Woodrow Wilson, the oldest of six elementary schools in the district, opened to 470 students in 1917. Refurbished in 1937, 1954, and again in 1980, the school's traditional brick, factorylike face had been carefully maintained. Currently, the school serves 730 students. Additions have been added to accommodate the expanded student population without sacrificing the architectural character of the building.

Shelly and her husband discussed the opportunity and decided she should sign a contract. There were several reasons for the decision. Shelly had already been processed to be placed on the substitute list; hence she would not need to request transcripts, fill out forms, and be interviewed. She had completed early field experiences at Woodrow Wilson while she was a sophomore. The principal and several staff who knew her recommended Shelly for the job. Woodrow Wilson was a five-minute drive from their apartment and on the way to her husband's place of work. The thought of having more than twice the income they might have otherwise meant they would have money to buy some luxuries or to invest. The only negative thought was having to take over the job from Deanna Bailey on such short notice.

Shelly knew Deanna Bailey from her university days. She had observed the veteran teacher on several occasions. She remembered Mrs. Bailey as a demanding, highly organized, creative teacher. Shelly felt pressure, knowing that within three working days she would have to be prepared to teach 28 fifth- and sixth-graders from highly diverse backgrounds.

Shelly had met with Elicia Fernandez, the principal at Woodrow Wilson, and learned that Mrs. Bailey would probably not return. She had become seriously ill during the summer and the prognosis for a full recovery was not good. In typical fashion Mrs. Bailey had worked until the day before surgery. She had prepared a list of the names of the 28 students and had typed a brief description of what she knew about them. Shelly found these materials in a folder she was given. She read a few of the descriptions.

- Eduardo Ruiz, grade 5, has three brothers and two sisters—all older than he. His father is a factory worker and his mother cleans houses. None of his brothers or sisters has graduated from high school, although all of them range in age from 23 to 29. "Eddie," as his friends call him, is an outgoing, alert, verbal child. He is viewed as somewhat of a clown. He rarely misses school and seems to like everyone. His grandparents came to the United States from Uruguay as seasonal farm workers.

- Latana Juarez, grade 5, is an only child. She is supported by her mother, who works two jobs—during the day as a waitress in a restaurant and at night as a security guard. Latana sees her mother for a couple of hours each night and, otherwise, is left alone during the week. Sometimes on weekends her mother also must work. Latana is shy and introverted, has few friends, and has a spotty attendance record.

- Lucinda Brown, grade 5, is the child of a mixed marriage. "Candy," as her friends call her both because of her sweet disposition and her mother's occupation, has a Caucasian father and an African-American mother. Her father runs a barber shop in the community, while her mother sells homemade candy marketed from their house. Candy is a bubbly, fun-loving child. She enjoys reading mystery stories and writing poetry. She is viewed by others as creative.

- Henry Chin, grade 5, is one of two children who has been supported by his mother. His father was killed in the Vietnam War. His older brother is a computer salesman on the East Coast. He rarely sees or hears from his brother. His mother works as a seamstress for a clothing manufacturer. Henry skips school frequently. When he does, he tries to sneak into movie theaters in the neighborhood. He spends much of his time in front of a screen—either movie or television. He is an aggressive, loud child who gets angry when he does not get his way.

- Mallory Applegate, grade 5, is a frail, only child. She was born six weeks prematurely. Her father is a Methodist minister, her mother a stenographer for an insurance company. Mallory, because of continuing ill health, has few friends. Her peers have given her the nickname "Malaria." She daydreams often. She has a short attention span, is easily brought to tears, and is absent regularly because of illness.

- Ronnie Chang, grade 6, is an only child. He lives with his grandparents, both of whom are now retired and in their late sixties. His mother is deceased. Ronnie's father is an industrial plant supervisor in Taiwan. During the summer months, Ronnie returns to Taiwan to spend time with his father. He wishes that he lived with his father. Often he appears depressed. He does not mix easily with his peers. He argues often with his grandparents. He frequently misses school and hangs out with a junior high school gang called the "Kings." Ronnie enjoys rock music. He owns an electric guitar and is teaching himself to play.

- Carlota Ovando, grade 6, is one of three sisters. One sister—seven years older—is a senior in high school but may not graduate because she does not have the required number of credits. Another sister— three years older—is thinking about dropping out of school. She currently holds a part-time job washing dishes in a restaurant. Carlota's father is an upholsterer and her mother is a cook at a mission for the homeless. Carlota missed two years of school while the family traveled through the West and Midwest doing seasonal farm work. Carlota has been told she must begin thinking of ways she can help the family. Her parents want her to look for a job. Carlota enjoys reading and thinks she would like to be a newspaper reporter someday.

- Hoji Hikawa, grade 6, is the only son of a Japanese family that immigrated to the United States five years ago. When he came to America, he spoke little English but has made rapid progress. His father is an assembly-line foreman, and his mother works in the home and occasionally baby-sits. Hoji is a sports enthusiast. His favorite sport is judo. He takes judo lessons every Thursday night and every Saturday morning. He is outgoing and gets along well with other children. He enjoys all subjects in school.

- Jennifer Jensen, grade 6, is an adopted child who lives with a divorced mother, who had no other children. Her mother is a salesperson for a cosmetics manufacturer and on occasion must travel for several days at a time. During her absence, Jennifer stays with a next-door family of five. The neighbors have two children, both in college, and a grandmother living in the home. Jennifer enjoys the opportunity to stay with the family. Jennifer is athletic and enjoys swimming and running. She also enjoys history.

- Lisa Puerta, grade 6, is the older of two children. She has a sister who is two months old. Her father owns and operates a large machinery-repair business. Her mother is a bookkeeper in the business. Lisa and her sister spend most evenings after school in the office area of the business, where their parents work until after ten most nights. Her mother has taught Lisa many of the bookkeeping tasks and has permitted her to do some of the math work required for keeping financial records. Lisa enjoys spending time at the business because she gets to meet so many different people. Lisa is an outgoing, highly verbal girl who makes friends easily. She enjoys reading fiction.

"These are interesting descriptions," Shelly thought to herself. "I wonder if I can get any other information." As she leafed through the folder, she discovered a summary of test scores from the Iowa Tests of Basic Skills. (See Figure 1)

The Challenge

What information should Shelly use in order to organize the children for instruction? How should she organize the children for instruction?

ISSUES FOR FURTHER REFLECTION

1. Was it wise for Mrs. Bailey to leave the descriptions of the students along with a summary of test scores? Explain your answer.
2. To what extent will these descriptions influence the way in which the students are organized for instruction? For example:
   a. What would you do to encourage Eduardo Ruiz to take his studies seriously?
   b. Given the fact that Latana Luarez has little contact with either adults or peers, what would you do to enhance her chances of developing adult and childhood friends? How might you organize instruction to improve her attendance record?
   c. As a child from a racially mixed marriage, Lucinda Brown may face ridicule or embarrassment from her classmates. What could you do to prevent such ridicule from occurring? Or, if it did occur, how would you respond to it?
   d. Henry Chin has a strong interest in movies and television. In what ways could you use the media to get Henry more interested in schoolwork?
   e. Mallory Applegate has already been stigmatized by her peers' behavior toward her. Given her condition and the way she has been treated in the past, how would you improve both her social and her educational standing in your classroom?

Students' Names	Age	C	V	R	La	Lb	Lc	Ld	L	Wa	Wb	W	Ma	Mb	Mc	M
GRADE 5																
M/H Eduardo Ruiz	12	4.2	4.2	3.8	4.0	4.3	4.2	4.1	4.2	3.8	4.2	4.0	4.1	4.3	4.0	4.1
F/H Latana Juarez	10	4.1	4.3	4.2	3.4	5.0	4.4	3.3	4.0	2.2	5.9	4.0	4.1	4.3	3.1	3.8
M/AF James Hightower	10	4.6	6.0	6.9	5.0	4.8	5.6	6.3	5.4	5.7	5.3	5.5	4.2	4.7	4.4	4.4
M/C Edward Fisherly	10	4.2	4.2	4.6	4.5	3.9	4.4	5.5	4.6	4.0	3.8	3.9	3.7	3.2	3.6	3.5
F/AF Lucinda Brown	10	6.1	6.1	7.5	6.4	5.0	6.2	8.5	6.5	7.7	6.9	7.3	5.2	5.5	5.1	5.3
M/AF Eddie Smith	10	5.5	5.5	4.5	6.4	5.0	5.6	6.5	5.9	5.9	6.4	6.2	5.2	5.8	5.4	5.5
M/C Henry Newer	11	6.8	7.2	6.7	5.4	6.4	4.2	6.5	5.6	6.3	5.3	5.8	6.2	7.2	5.2	6.2
M/AR Abdullah Al-Beran	10	6.4	6.6	7.1	5.6	5.5	7.5	7.1	6.4	5.4	6.6	6.0	6.2	7.2	5.5	6.3
M/AS Henry Chin	10	3.9	4.4	4.7	3.7	3.3	3.2	4.8	3.8	2.8	3.4	3.1	3.4	3.6	3.3	3.4
M/AS Rudy Talupu	10	6.0	6.0	6.9	6.4	5.0	5.3	6.8	5.9	5.8	6.4	6.0	6.5	6.3	4.3	5.8
F/C Mallory Applegate	10	5.1	5.1	5.3	5.9	4.8	4.4	5.8	5.2	5.4	2.2	3.3	4.1	3.6	4.3	4.0
F/H Maria Notchez	10	5.1	6.6	5.2	5.8	4.1	6.5	5.8	5.6	5.1	6.0	5.6	5.8	4.3	4.8	4.9
M/H Roberto Reliz	10	6.2	6.3	7.3	5.0	6.0	5.6	5.3	5.5	6.3	6.6	6.0	5.9	5.8	5.5	5.7
F/AF Yolanda Smith	9	6.1	6.3	6.7	5.8	5.5	6.8	6.3	6.6	5.0	7.2	6.1	5.9	5.2	4.8	5.3
GRADE 6																
M/AS Ronnie Chang	11	5.0	5.2	4.9	3.7	4.4	4.8	4.5	4.4	6.1	5.1	5.6	5.8	4.3	4.9	5.0
F/H Carlota Ovando	13	6.4	6.7	7.7	6.4	6.0	6.5	6.1	6.3	6.7	5.6	6.3	4.2	5.8	4.8	4.9
F/AF Cindy LaVerne	11	5.0	5.0	5.6	5.0	4.8	5.5	5.1	5.1	3.3	6.1	4.7	3.8	4.9	5.6	4.8
F/AS Alvina Ming	11	7.1	6.7	7.7	8.1	7.3	7.2	5.6	7.1	6.9	5.6	6.8	9.0	6.8	5.6	7.3
M/AS Hoji Hikawa	11	8.0	7.8	8.9	8.1	5.8	8.2	7.8	7.5	8.5	7.8	8.2	7.9	7.6	6.9	7.5
F/C Jennifer Jensen	11	7.6	6.9	7.7	8.6	8.1	7.2	9.7	8.4	9.0	7.6	8.3	7.5	7.3	5.8	6.9
M/AF Luther Bradford	12	7.6	7.5	7.9	6.1	6.7	6.2	6.7	6.4	9.0	8.3	8.7	7.7	8.0	6.9	7.5
M/C John Jones	11	7.2	8.1	6.4	6.8	6.7	7.2	7.5	7.1	7.4	6.9	7.2	8.1	7.6	6.6	7.2

Student																
M/H Edwardo Flavo	11	7.4	7.8	7.7	7.2	8.5	7.9	8.6	8.1	7.9	5.6	6.8	7.3	7.3	5.9	6.8
F/H Lisa Puerta	12	8.0	8.4	8.4	7.8	6.0	7.2	9.1	7.5	9.2	8.3	8.8	7.2	7.0	6.9	7.0
M/AF Lew Bensen	11	7.4	6.9	7.5	7.4	6.3	8.2	7.8	7.4	7.8	8.3	8.1	7.5	7.6	6.5	7.2
M/H Juan Salizer	11	7.5	6.7	8.1	8.9	8.8	9.1	6.4	8.3	6.5	6.0	6.3	7.9	8.0	8.0	8.0
F/AF Carrie Evans	11	5.5	5.5	4.4	5.9	5.0	5.9	5.6	5.6	5.8	5.5	5.7	6.1	6.4	5.7	6.1
M/C Tom Rose	11	7.9	8.1	7.9	9.2	8.5	9.1	7.5	8.6	7.4	7.3	7.4	6.6	9.4	5.8	6.1

GRADE EQUIVALENTS

The scale for grade equivalents ranges from 0.0 through 12.9 representing the 13 years of school (K–12) and the 10 months in the traditional school year. September is viewed as the start of the year (.0), October is identified as .1, November as .2, and so forth to June (.9). A grade equivalent represents the grade and month in school of students in the norm group whose test performance is theoretically equivalent to the test performance of a given student.

C = Composite
V = Vocabulary
R = Reading
La = Spelling
Lb = Capitalization
Lc = Punctuation
L = Language (total)

Wa = Visual
Wb = References
Wc = Work/study (total)
Ma = Math concepts
Mb = Math problems
Mc = Math computation
M = Math (total)

STUDENT CODE

M/AF = Male/Afro-American
F/AF = Female/Afro-American
M/AR = Male/Arab
F/AR = Female/Arab
M/AS = Male/Asian
F/AS = Female/Asian
M/C = Male/Caucasian
F/C = Female/Caucasian
M/H = Male/Hispanic
F/H = Female/Hispanic

FIGURE 1 Fifth- and sixth-grade class grade equivalents—Iowa tests of basic skills

    f. Ronnie Chang has substituted gang association for the absence of his father. What can you do to challenge his gang association and get him excited about classroom instruction?

    g. Carlota Ovando's parents hold unrealistic expectations for her. They want her to get a job. She has no successful role models in terms of educational attainment. How could you organize instruction to build on her interests and to also confront the obstacles to long-term educational success imposed by her family situation?

    h. Some students appear to be highly motivated. Hoji Hikawa seems to be one of them. What would you do to maintain his high level of motivation?

    i. Jennifer Jensen appears to be successful. In time, however, how might her mother's continual, lengthy absences affect Jennifer's classroom behavior? How would you respond?

    j. Lisa Puerta has experienced success by virtue of her help in the family business. How can these experiences at home be used in the classroom to enhance her educational success?

3. How can the statistical data provided be used for organizing students for instruction? Explain why these data are useful. What other data might be helpful?

4. Should information be sought from other teachers who may know these students? Defend your answer.

5. Should parents be used as a data source for organizing students for instruction? Explain your answer.

6. In what ways might information from the students themselves be helpful? How would you collect the data?

7. How much data about the students should be collected in order to make an adequate decision for grouping students for instruction?

8. From each description of the ten children, identify what information is relevant for planning instruction. Using the relevant information, explain an instructional strategy that you believe would be most effective for teaching each child. Provide a rationale for each choice.

SUGGESTED READINGS

Beane, J. (1981). Sorting out the self-esteem controversy. *Educational Leadership, 49*(1), 25–30.

Belle, D., & Burr, R. (1991). Why children do not confide: An exploratory analysis. *Child Study Journal, 21*(4), 217–234.

Canfield, J. (1990). Improving students' self-esteem. *Educational Leadership, 48*(1), 48–50.

Dembo, M. (1994). *Applying educational psychology in the classroom* (5th ed.). New York: Longman (see chapters 8, 9, 10, 11, 12, 13).

Dewhurst, D. (1991). Should teachers enhance their pupils' self-esteem. *Journal of Moral Education, 20*(1), 3–11.

Elliott, R. (1988). Tests, abilities, race, and conflict. *Intelligence, 12*(4), 333–350.

Good, T., & Brophy, J. (1990). *Educational psychology: A realistic approach* (4th ed.). New York: Longman (see chapters 23, 24, 25, 26).

Henson, K. (1993). *Methods and strategies for teaching in secondary and middle schools* (2nd ed.). New York: Longman (see chapters 7, 9).

McCombs, R., & Gray, J. (1988). Effects of race, class, and IQ information on judgments of parochial grade school teachers. *Journal of Social Psychology, 128*(5), 647–652.

Miller-Jones, D. (1988). Culture and testing. *American Psychologist, 44*(2), 360–366.

Oakes, J. (1986). Keeping track, part 2: Curriculum inequality and school reform. *Phi Delta Kappan, 68*(2), 148–154.

Partenio, L., & Taylor, R. (1985). The relationship of teacher ratings and IQ: A question of bias? *School Psychology Review, 14*(1), 79–83.

Pasch, M., Sparks-Langer, G., Gardner, T., Starko, A., & Moody, C. (1991). *Teaching as decision making: Instructional practices for the successful teacher.* New York: Longman (see chapters 8, 9).

Powers, S., Escamilla, K., Haussler, M., et. al. (1986). The California achievement test as a predictor of reading ability across race and sex. *Educational and Psychological Measurement, 46*(4), 1067–1070.

Sharma, S. (1986). Assessment strategies for minority groups. *Journal of Black Studies, 17*(1), 111–124.

Slavin, R. (1987). Ability grouping and student achievement in elementary schools: A best-evidence synthesis. *Review of Educational Research, 57*(3), 293–336.

CASE 34

A Teacher Is Dedicated to Promoting Creativity in All Students

PREPARING TO USE THE CASE

Background Information

Storyteller Garrison Keillor says that at Lake Wobegon all the men are good looking, all the women are strong, and all the children are above average. Today the majority of parents think that their children are above average. Theories of multiple intelligence reinforce the idea that each child is superior in some area(s).

As a teacher, you will learn that many parents will insist that you teach their children how to develop their creative abilities.

In recent years, the once-popular belief that intelligence is an innate, rigid characteristic has been questioned. This change in the way people view learners is reflected in many of the education reform movements. For example, in one state's reform program, a basic underlying premise (which is stated in writing) is that all students can learn. This perspective leaves no room for excuses and makes every teacher accountable for the academic success of all students in their classrooms.

The continuing migration of other cultures to America is another factor that exacerbates the need for teachers to be committed to individualized learning. Each culture has unique qualities. Teachers who fail to acknowledge and appreciate these qualities can never reach academic effectiveness with their students.

The following case presents a young teacher whose philosophy regarding lessons and how they should be taught varies significantly with the principal's philosophy. It is unfortunate that some principals, such as Mr. Marshall, do not encourage teachers to try to meet the needs of individual students. One thing is certain, you will meet administrators like Mr. Marshall who will try to encourage you and all other teachers on their faculty to use only direct instruction, because much of the recent effective teaching research emphasizes the use of direct instruction.

The continuing breakdown of the family by divorce, the hurried pace of current lifestyles, and the increasing role of television have all worked against achievement and social development of students by making life impersonal. Today's youths are often isolated from quality social contact at home. When they come to school, they do not always purposefully choose to be antisocial; often they do not know how to socialize. Because they have no real friends, many children do not learn to trust, share, and appreciate others. The result is they also do not trust and appreciate themselves. Unfortunately, this leads them to dislike themselves. Negative self-concepts are associated with low achievement and misbehavior. As you proceed, realize that a major responsibility of all teachers is to help students develop positive self-concepts.

The following case contains examples of how teachers can reach out and help individual students.

Topics for Reflection
1. Meeting the needs of individual students
2. Recognizing differences among students
3. Demanding success of all students
4. Helping students help themselves
5. Altering the environment to promote individual strengths
6. Promoting creativity

THE CASE

Hudson Heights is an urban residential and business area within the metropolitan New York City area. On a clear day, from some locations in Hudson Heights, residents can see the Statue of Liberty. To visitors, it is clear that most residents of the community are not enjoying the wealth that they see everyday. Row after row of run-down government housing with little or no lawn space forces children to play in the streets. Attempts to reestablish a park have proven financially impossible. Most streets are littered with fast-food wrappers, bottles, and cans. In the business district, there seems to be a liquor store on almost every corner. Signs remind vandals that they are under constant crime-watch surveillance, but many of the signs have been defaced with spray paint. One drive through the community tells the visitor that this is what Plato predicted over 2,000 years ago when, in his book *The Republic,* he warned readers about the decay that would occur when urban communities became too congested.

The people who pass down the sidewalks in this community represent a myriad of cultures. The dress lengths and designs announce the profession of many of the young women. Drugs play a central role in the lifestyle and culture of this community. To be sure, Hudson Heights also has law-abiding citizens, but one has to marvel at their ability to live in a community where crime is the norm.

The School

Hudson Elementary appears as old as the city itself. The aged building has suffered 50 very long years of vandalism. It stands like an old general scarred from its attacks, yet stubbornly refusing defeat. The inscription above the front door reads IN SEARCH OF TRVTH. Mr. Marshall, the new principal, is a strong disciplinarian who equates good teaching with learning those facts that will lead to a good job. He used the first faculty meeting to advise the teachers that he will be visiting all classes and to remind them that he believes in traditional teaching methods.

The hallways at Hudson Elementary are dark and narrow; like the classrooms, they have high ceilings. The old varnish and wood stain on the walls and floors have blackened over the years. All things considered, the general physical appearance of the building can accurately be described as depressing.

The Teacher

The preceding observation describes how Hudson Elementary School appears to an outsider. Sandy Mears, a fifth-grade teacher at Hudson has an entirely different perception of the school. To Sandy, Hudson Elementary is a beautiful place. She would agree that the varnish on the walls and floor is dark and unattractive, like the rest of the building, but to Sandy the physical appearance of the school is only a minor, insignificant part. To understand Sandy's perspective, one would need to visit one of her classes. We will do that, but first let's meet the school's administrators.

Last July, Mr. Sam Everett retired after serving as vice-principal at Hudson Elementary for 26 years. Judy Calloway has been serving and will continue to serve as interim vice-principal until the board finds the "right" person for the job. Judy, who served as an administrative intern while working on her specialist degree, has done a remarkable job and is well liked by the faculty and students. Because of her upbeat disposition, students and teachers alike usually seek out Ms. Calloway to answer their requests.

Sandy considers the administration at Hudson Elementary to be excellent. She has frequently requested special privileges for her classes, and they have always been granted. She interprets this strong support as approval of her efforts— at least as an indication that Judy Calloway approves.

The other teachers seem to spend most of their planning periods in the teachers' lounge, where their topics for discussion cover almost everything except their lessons. Most of these teachers insist that they need this period to rest and recharge for the other classes that require more energy than they have available.

From her very first visit to the school, Sandy noticed that the teachers here are well adjusted to the school climate. They do what must be done. That is neither a criticism nor a compliment, just an observation. In a literal sense, they do their jobs, but Sandy wants more for her classes, and she is willing to use her planning periods and her evenings and weekends to see that they get it.

Once inside Sandy's classroom, it is obvious why, for her, the unattractive appearance of the building fades in importance. Her room promotes enthusiasm.

In it, busy students are having fun while they study science. Although most of them come from low socioeconomic backgrounds, these students feel good about themselves. They know that they are capable, not because they have unusually high innate abilities, for they are average students, but because Sandy knows how to help students discover their potentialities.

The Incident

In her teacher education program, Sandy became interested in creativity as a field of study. This began when a visiting professor conducted a workshop for her language-arts methods course. As a participant in the workshop, Sandy learned about several student activities that teachers can use to help students develop their creative abilities. As required projects for her other methods courses, Sandy chose to develop similar activities to enable her future students to become more creative.

Sandy's sixth-grade science class is a good example. The current unit of study focuses on rivers, a topic that the group is also currently studying in their social studies class. At the front of the room is a table surrounded by several students. On the table is a box of large drinking straws, a few pounds of modeling clay, a set of scales, and a stack of books. Several pairs of students are working independently. Each two-person team is designing a bridge. The object of their challenge is to see which team can design the strongest bridge, using only six ounces of clay and twelve straws. A few teams have already completed their bridges and are now testing them to see how many books they will support.

Another table holds several trays of water, some modeling clay, and a jar of marbles. These students are also working in pairs. Their challenge is to use only three ounces of modeling clay to build a boat that has greater buoyancy than those built by their classmates. When each pair of students completes the design and construction of their boat, they will test it to see whether it floats, and if so, how many marbles the boat will support before it sinks.

Throughout the room, groups of students are conducting similar activities. At each table, students are carefully recording the results of all teams. At the end of the hour students will rotate to a different table until all students have participated in all of the projects. The winners of each project will explain why they designed their project as they did. Sandy will ask specific questions to get students to think further about the tasks. Some of her favorite questions are: What were the results? Why did this occur? How could you improve your project? If you could have one additional material to use in designing or constructing the project, what material would you choose? Why? Sandy also insists that it is essential for the students to ask questions. She believes that learning how to ask the right question is as important as knowing how to find the right answer.

Sandy tries never to miss a chance to recognize her students' accomplishments, but she never gives false praise. She recognizes student success orally and visually. All winning projects are displayed for others to see. Her goal is to have something belonging to every student on display all the time. Sandy groups students so that all will have an equal chance to develop a winning project. She proudly points out that some of her students whose test scores are consistently low succeed in building winning projects.

After Mr. Marshall's visit to her class, Sandy's concern over his comments during the recent faculty meeting is understandable. During the meeting, Mr. Marshall clearly communicated that he would not tolerate unorthodox teaching methods, for according to Mr. Marshall, "Recent studies have shown that direct instruction and time on task are producing the most achievement in classrooms across the country." Sandy has begun worrying about Mr. Marshall's forthcoming visit to her classroom. She wonders how she can plan for the anticipated conflict that may arise.

The pace is moderate. Sandy knows that a brisk pace can be motivational, yet she is careful not to proceed so quickly that some of the more easily stressed students will become frustrated and anxious. Sandy also knows that just as some children are more anxious than others, some can grasp the general science concepts and principles more quickly than others. But Sandy is determined that all students will learn these major concepts and principles. She uses peer tutors to break these generalizations down into small steps so that the low achievers can more readily understand them.

The room is furnished to look more like a family room than a classroom. Sandy has collected pictures, pillows, hanging plants, and wall tapestries which she gladly keeps in her room for the students to enjoy. She also has a small bookcase with several books whose difficulty levels range from elementary through junior high.

In each work group, the roles are varied. Some students are given (actually they usually choose) the jobs of weighing, measuring, and recording the results. Other students will have an opportunity to tell their classmates what they have learned. These students summarize the steps of each activity in their group. Then they clarify each step, asking questions of their audience (the entire class), and encouraging the audience to ask questions. To further promote creativity, these students ask their peers to hypothesize what would happen if certain parts of the activities were changed. For example, what do you think would happen if the rectangular-shaped clay boats were changed into circular boats? Would this increase or decrease their buoyancy?

When the presentations are complete, students are taught to compliment each other. Sandy spends more time urging the boys to compliment the girls than vice versa.

Often Sandy will bring a student who has particular knowledge relevant to a group's task over to share that expertise. Sometimes the custodial staff and lunchroom workers are invited to speak to the class.

In addition to the step-by-step structural activities, other activities are used which are far less structured. For example, while some students carefully weigh and measure, others are encouraged to provide estimates or guesses.

Each day, Sandy circulates among the students, stopping at each work station long enough to ask a few quick questions just to make sure that the group is making progress. This also provides her with an opportunity to compliment students on their progress.

Sandy knows that her commitment to student activities and inquiry is so strong that it cannot be compromised. But she also knows that Mr. Marshall's aversion to experimentation and to student-centered curricula is equally nonnegotiable.

During her student teaching, Sandy helped her cooperating teacher prepare for and conduct a local science fair. In fact, she also served as one of the judges. Sandy saw that some of the quieter students were willing to discuss their projects with the judges and with visitors who came to the science fair. She concluded that this one spin-off from the fair—getting the quiet students to participate and discuss their projects—was enough reason to hold a fair.

Ever since her arrival at Hudson, she has been trying to muster up enough courage to ask Mr. Marshall to let her, the other teachers, and the students put on a science fair. Perhaps when Mr. Marshall revisits her class and sees how enthusiastic the students are and how hard they work, then he will agree to a science fair.

The Challenge

Put yourself in Sandy's place. Would you ask Mr. Marshall for permission to hold a science fair? Would you discontinue your individualized teaching program and plan more direct-instruction lessons?

ISSUES FOR FURTHER REFLECTION

1. How can teachers group students to stimulate creativity?
2. For each of your disciplines, describe an activity that would stimulate creativity.
3. Choose one creative activity (which may or may not be one that Sandy used), and make a list of questions to promote further thinking.
4. How can teachers motivate students to share the teacher's enthusiasm?
5. List some ways that teachers can show their enthusiasm for their subject.
6. Why is it important that students ask questions?
7. What advantages are there in assigning some structural tasks and some nonstructural tasks?
8. How can Sandy convince her principal that promoting creativity is a worthy goal?
9. How important is each of the following?
    a. The depressing physical appearance of this school.
    b. The fact that these students come from low socioeconomic families.
    c. Sandy's use of an interdisciplinary approach.
    d. Motivation of Sandy's students.
    e. Sandy's use of reinforcement and recognition.
    f. The sense that in Sandy's class, every student is a winner.
    g. Enthusiasm of both Sandy and her students.
    h. The average ability of the students in Sandy's room.
    i. Occasional overachievement by most students in the room.
    j. Sandy's high expectations of all students.

k. Encouraging students to ask questions.

l. Constant monitoring by the student.

m. The moderate workplace.

SUGGESTED READINGS

Blumenthal, C., Holmes, G. V., & Pound, L. (1991). Academic success for students at-risk. In R. C. Morris (Ed.), *Youth at-Risk,* Scranton, PA: Technomic.

Brophy, J. (1991). Effective schooling for disadvantaged students. In M. S. Knapp and P. M. Shields (Eds.), *Better schooling for the children of poverty: Alternatives to conventional wisdom* (pp. 211–234). Berkeley, CA: McCutchan.

Caissy, G. A. (1992). Developing information processing skills in the middle school. *The Clearing House, 65*(3), 149–151.

Crosby, E. A. (1993). The at-risk decade. *Phi Delta Kappan, 74*(8), 598–604.

Dembo, M. (1994). *Applying educational psychology in the classroom* (5th ed.). New York: Longman (see chapters 7, 8, 9, 10, 11).

Doyle, W. (1991). Classroom tasks: The core of learning from teaching. In M. S. Knapp and P. M. Shields (Eds.), *Better schooling for the children of poverty: Alternatives to conventional wisdom.* Berkeley, CA: McCutchan.

Geisert, G. & Dunn, R. (1991). Effective use of computers: Assignments based on individual learning style. *The Clearing House, 64*(4), 219–223.

Good, T., & Brophy, J. (1990). *Educational psychology: A realistic approach* (4th ed.). New York: Longman (Part 6).

Henson, K. T. (1993). *Methods and strategies for teaching in secondary and middle schools* (2nd ed.). White Plains, NY: Longman (chapter 13: From discipline to self-discipline).

Martin, J. E. (1992). Gifted behaviors—Excellence for all. *The Clearing House, 66*(1), 37–40.

Means, B., & Kapp, M. S. (1991). Introduction: Rethinking teaching for disadvantaged students. In B. Means, C. Chelemer, and M.S. Knapp (Eds.), *Teaching advanced skills to at-risk students* (pp. 1–26). San Francisco: Jossey Bass.

Morris, R. C. (1991), (Ed.). *Youth at Risk.* Lancaster, PA: Technomic.

Neely, R. O. & Alm, D. (1992). Meeting individual needs: A learning styles success story. *The Clearing House, 66*(2), 109–113.

Newstead, S. E. (1992). A study of two "quick and easy" methods of assessing individual differences in student learning. *British Journal of Educational Psychology, 62,* 299–312.

Prawat, R. S. (1992). From individual differences to learning communities—our changing focus. *Educational Leadership, 49*(7), 9–13.

Theilheimer, R. (1991). Involving children in their own learning. *The Clearing House, 65*(2), 123–125.

Thomas, J. (1992). Individualized teaching. *Oxford Review of Education, 18*(1), 59–74.

Torrance, E. P. (1992). Creatively gifted, learning disabled individuals. *Educational Forum, 56*(4), 399–404.

CASE 35

Grouping and Student Diversity

PREPARING TO USE THE CASE

Background Information

The practice of individualized instruction is predicated on an awareness that students have unique needs. They differ in such respects as personality, interests, life experiences, self-esteem, physical characteristics, self-confidence, intellectual ability, and achievement. Students even differ in the ways that they learn. In a growing number of schools, diversity is also related to cultural, racial, and ethnic characteristics.

Historically, public schools have used three processes in an effort to address differing student needs: (1) special placements, (2) in-class ability grouping, and (3) tracking. Special placements have been used to take care of students with the most diverse needs (e.g., special education). Problems associated with this process resulted in legal requirements for "mainstreaming" in the early 1970s; more recently, there are efforts to require total assimilation of special-need pupils into regular classrooms. Tracking has been used primarily in secondary schools as a means of separating students on the basis of ability and/or achievement (e.g., creating three levels of eighth-grade mathematics). In-class ability grouping has been most commonly used in elementary classrooms. All three of these techniques have been predicated largely on student ability.

Ideally, the process of in-class ability grouping is intended to divide a class into smaller groups so that instruction can be targeted more directly to specific student needs. At first glance, this appears to be a rational solution to individualizing instruction. After all, one cannot expect an elementary teacher to devise separate instructional plans every day for 25 or 30 students. But in reality, ability grouping spawns a number of undesirable outcomes. For example, some children may be placed in the wrong group (measures of intelligence are subject to error); once placed in groups, students may be labeled for life (a condition that ignores the fact that intelligence is not a fixed attribute); and many students placed in low-ability groups become demoralized (when in fact they need to be more highly motivated). Accordingly, ability grouping has been heavily criticized as an instructional technique.

The undesirable by-products of in-class ability grouping are becoming better known at a time when many classrooms in America are becoming more diverse. For a good number of teachers, this presents a major challenge. On the one hand, they do not want to use an instructional practice that can potentially damage some of the children, but on the other hand, they must find ways to achieve higher levels of individualization because of a growing diversity in student needs. It is within this context that many are looking toward technology as a promising resource that may allow teachers to alter their traditional roles so that classroom experiences can be targeted more directly to individual students.

In this case, a beginning teacher in a suburban elementary school is overwhelmed by the individual differences of her students. She realizes that some of the teachers in her school employ ability grouping; and this is one of the alternatives that she considers. She rejects the idea, however, and opts to create student groups on the basis of multiple criteria.

Topics for Reflection
1. Individual student differences
2. Grouping for instruction
3. Multicultural education
4. Cooperative learning
5. Learning styles

THE CASE

The Community

Mayburn was one of the first affluent suburbs to develop on the outskirts of a major eastern city after World War II. For nearly 30 years, it was the location of choice for upper-middle-class families in the area. Toward the end of the 1970s, the community started to encounter change. Many of the homes were now reaching a point where they required major repairs, and newer and more modern suburbs had been developed further from the city. Mayburn became a buffer zone between the city and the newest suburbs.

Many affluent minority families have moved to Mayburn in the past decade. Approximately one-fourth of all homeowners in the town are African Americans. The cost of houses remains relatively high, so although the racial balance of the community has changed, it remains middle to upper-middle class with regard to socioeconomic status.

The School

When Mayburn was developed, four elementary schools were placed in strategic locations so that most children could walk to school. Nathan Hale Elementary School is located on the west side of town, and the exterior of this 1951 building looks more like a facility at a liberal arts college than a typical elementary school. Unlike many other schools, it does not have a cold, institutional character. The library, for example, has a large fireplace.

In 1979, court-ordered desegregation resulted in a one-way busing plan that brought approximately 70 inner-city children to Nathan Hale. That figure and the school's total enrollment (approximately 300) have remained constant over the years; however, the racial balance in the school has changed. When the busing plan was initiated at the start of the 1979–1980 school year, the minority population in the school was about 25%. Now it is approximately 60%. The change in racial balance reflects the growing minority population in Mayburn itself.

Basically, there are two classes at each grade level, from kindergarten through grade 5. Of the 14 teachers who work at the school (including special teachers in art, music, and physical education), 5 are African Americans. Eleven have worked at the school for more than 10 years.

The Teacher

Tina Almatti grew up in a metropolitan area in Rhode Island. Her father operated his own plumbing business, and her mother, a housewife, raised seven children. Tina is the youngest member of her family, and she attended a relatively large, private university in her home state. She received a scholarship from the institution after having graduated third in her high school class of 308 students.

Tina majored in elementary education and completed a minor in sociology. Despite becoming highly involved in student activities as a college student, she graduated magna cum laude. In her placement file is a letter from one of her professors who wrote: "Tina is the most creative, energetic student I have known in 15 years of college teaching. She is a 'can't miss' prospect."

After interviewing with a number of school districts during the spring semester of her senior year, Tina received three job offers. She selected Mayburn because she was so impressed with the administration and teaching staff at the school. While she encountered primarily personnel directors in her other interviews, she had an opportunity to meet most of the teachers and the principal when she visited Mayburn.

The Problem

Tina had learned some things about Mayburn prior to moving there, so she was aware that the student population was somewhat diverse. But when she encountered her fourth-grade class in the fall, she realized that she had really underestimated the differences in their needs. There were 26 students in her class; 14 of the students were African Americans, 7 of whom were bused to Nathan Hale in conjunction with the desegregation program.

During the first few weeks of school, Tina spent a great deal of time trying to find out as much as she could about the children. Nathan Hale was fortunate to have a full-time counselor, and the permanent files of the students were well maintained. For instance, ability-test scores from the first and third grades were available; there was extensive information on past academic performance; and the counselor had done an excellent job of accumulating family-related information on all of the children. As she read the files carefully, Tina became even more amazed by the differences in the students with whom she had to work.

Her day-to-day observations in the classroom also served to convince her that she needed to find a way to provide instruction that would be more directly targeted to individual student needs. She noted, for example, that some students enjoyed competitive activities, while others liked group work. Some did better with skill-related tasks; others were most successful when working with abstract problems. Thus the children were not only different in ability, race, socioeconomic status, and achievement, they also showed tremendous variance in learning styles.

As a first step in the effort to create higher levels of individualized instruction, Tina developed profiles for each of the 26 students. Extracting information from student files, she made note cards that she could use for reference purposes; even in the classroom. When she completed the cards, her perspective of the range of diversity among her students was enhanced. She could see more clearly how the children bused from the inner city differed from the those who lived in Mayburn. She could see how diverse the group was with regard to past achievement.

The following four student profiles show the level of diversity in her class.

Name: Elaine B.   **Race:** African American
Age: 9   **Height:** 4'9"   **Weight:** 82   **IQ:** 120–123
Past Academic Performance: Very good. Creative and works hard.
Family: Parents married; father an engineer, mother an account executive for advertising firm; one older brother (age 13).
Primary Interests: Science, social studies.
Strengths: Self-starter; bright; high need to achieve.
Primary Needs: To learn to work with others; to improve social skills; to reduce self-induced stress.

Name: Joseph K.   **Race:** African American
Age: 10   **Height:** 5'1"   **Weight:** 102   **IQ:** 95–98
Past Academic Performance: Performance varies depending on subject areas; good in math; does not like art, language arts, social studies.
Family: Parents divorced; mother remarried; stepfather is custodian, mother unemployed; two siblings, brother (age 6) and sister (age 5).
Primary Interests: Basketball, collecting baseball cards.
Strengths: Has good math skills; works very well with others; very popular with other students; excels in physical tasks.
Primary Needs: To improve attention span; to develop a more balanced interest in academic work; to develop self-discipline, especially as related to completing individual tasks.

Name: Ann T.   **Race:** Caucasian
Age: 10   **Height:** 4′10″   **Weight:** 92   **IQ:** 109–112
Past Academic Performance: Inconsistent. Exhibits periods of high interest, but grades have been uneven.
Family: Adopted; stepfather is bank executive, stepmother is nurse; no siblings.
Primary Interests: Music, drama.
Academic Strengths: Very creative; cooperative when working with others; appears to have good reasoning skills; does reasonably well with abstract problem solving.
Primary Needs: To be more task oriented (is easily distracted); to improve basic skills in math and writing; to learn to assume responsibility; to show more maturity.

Name: Darrell J.   **Race:** Caucasian
Age: 11   **Height:** 5′2″   **Weight:** 180   **IQ:** 85–89
Past Academic Performance: Poor, retained in first grade.
Family: Parents divorced; mother employed with real estate company; no siblings.
Primary Interests: Science-fiction stories.
Strengths: Does reasonably well in art; does not misbehave.
Primary Needs: Low self-esteem; does not relate well to other children, especially African-American students; shows little interest in schoolwork, and as a result, requires constant encouragement; needs to become more independent.

As the first month of school was ending, Tina realized that she was not able to address individual needs as long as she tried to teach the same subject matter and skills to the entire class using the uniform instructional practices. Her first thought was to group the students according to IQ scores and past achievement. She was aware that several teachers in the school were still using ability grouping, especially in the early grades for reading and mathematics. But based largely on professional material she had read as a student in college, Tina was opposed to forming groups utilizing this single criterion. There were too many other issues that she thought were important. These included concerns for learning styles, social development, multiculturism, student interest, and student compatibility.

Tina remembered visiting a school during her junior year in college that was using cooperative learning. Her professors had talked about this teaching paradigm being used to mix students of varied academic abilities, but she was surprised to learn that the school she visited was using the technique largely to mix children of different races so that they would become comfortable working with each other. Given the diversity of students in her class, she decided that some form of cooperative learning would help her achieve her goal of more individualized instruction.

The decision was made to form five groups. This seemed to be a manageable number. Some broad guidelines for placing students in the groups were established:

1. No group could contain more than 65% of students of the same race. If groups were to be formed, they might as well be used to deal with culture-related goals in a diverse-population school.
2. The groups would be as heterogeneous as possible with regard to ability. This would allow the more able students to assist students with lesser ability.
3. Effort would be made to balance interests in the groups. For example, a student with a high interest in art or music would be put in a group with a student who had a high interest in math or science.
4. Effort would be made to balance personalities. An extroverted student, for instance, would not be placed in a group that consisted entirely of the same personality types.
5. Children who were bused to Nathan Hale from the inner-city schools would be dispersed across the groups. No more than two of these students would be assigned to any given group.
6. Since some of the students were physically and emotionally more developed than others, an effort would be made to mix the students with different levels of maturity.
7. An attempt would be made to group students with similar learning styles.

Tina mapped out her plan as best she could. She developed goals in three broad categories that she labeled, "Academic," "Social," and "Multicultural." The goals required her to make periodic assessments to determine whether the grouping procedure was effective. When she completed her plan, she made an appointment to see Paul Bowers, the principal, to discuss her intentions and to see if he would provide her with two additional computers. Each classroom in the school had three, but Tina wanted one for each group.

Mr. Bowers listened intently as Tina related her plan to create instructional groups. He was particularly fascinated by her intention to group students who exhibited diverse characteristics but shared similarities with regard to learning styles. When she was finished, he praised her efforts but cautioned her about being too ambitious during her first year of teaching. He said he would find resources to get the extra two computers; but he would only do so if Tina shared her plan with Dr. Barbara Sake, the district's director of curriculum. The principal wanted to make sure there would be no objections from the central office of the school district. Further, he indicated that if the plan was put into effect, he was willing to get personally involved. He found it to be a refreshing and promising idea.

The Challenge

Assess Tina's plan for dealing with diversity in the fourth-grade classroom. Do you see any potential problems?

ISSUES FOR FURTHER REFLECTION

1. Why do you think some teachers still use in-class ability grouping to deal with student diversity?

2. What are the shortcomings of in-class ability grouping?

3. How will students react to Tina's plan? How will parents react?

4. From what you read in this case, is the level of diversity in Tina's classroom typical for public schools in America today? Why or why not?

5. Can you think of other instructional techniques that Tina could use to try to address individual student needs in her class?

6. Is it fair to ask more able students to assist with the instruction of less able students?

7. Some critics argue that one value of cooperative learning is that it reduces the negative effects of student competition. Do you agree that competition is a bad experience for students?

8. Is it a good idea to mix children of different personality types? Why or why not?

9. Should a beginning teacher be assuming such a difficult project?

10. To what degree do you believe that principals should encourage teachers to experiment? What potential problems may evolve from experimentation?

11. Many teachers continue to teach to an imaginary norm by providing the same instruction for the entire class. Who is likely to be most negatively affected by such an instructional approach?

12. Do you agree that children become more alike as they mature? What is the basis of your answer?

13. Some critics of education argue that schools should teach the basics and leave social and emotional development to the family. As an educator, how do you react to this sentiment?

14. Would you feel comfortable creating instructional groups based on multiple criteria in your first year of teaching? Why or why not?

15. In what way could heterogeneous groups improve the adjustment of students who are bused to another community?

SUGGESTED READINGS

Anderson, J. (1992). Acknowledging the learning styles of diverse student populations: Implications for instructional design. *New Directions for Teaching and Learning, 49,* 19–33.

Andrews, R. (1990). The development of a learning styles program in a low socioeconomic, underachieving North Carolina elementary school. *Journal of Reading, Writing, and Learning Disabilities International, 6*(3), 307–313.

Brandt, R. (1990). On learning styles: A conversation with Pat Guild. *Educational Leadership, 48*(2), 10–13.

Davis, B. (1985). Effects of cooperative learning on race/human relations: Study of a district program. *Spectrum, 3*(1), 37–43.

Dembo, M. (1994). *Applying educational psychology in the classroom* (5th ed.). New York: Longman (see chapters 9, 10).

Dunn, R., & Griggs, S. (1990). Research on the learning style characteristics of selected racial and ethnic groups. *Journal of Reading, Writing, and Learning Disabilities International, 6*(3), 261–280.

Epstein, J. (1985). After the bus arrives: Resegregation in desegregated schools. *Journal of Social Issues, 41*(3), 23–43.

Feeney, J. (1992). Oh, to fly with bluebirds...Looking back on tracking. *Schools in the Middle, 2*(1), 38–39.

Good, T., & Brophy, J. (1990). *Educational psychology: A realistic approach* (4th ed.). New York: Longman (see chapters 23, 24, 25).

Henson, K. (1993). *Methods and strategies for teaching in secondary and middle schools* (2nd ed.). New York: Longman (see chapters 7, 8, 9).

Larke, P. (1992). Effective multicultural teachers: Meeting the challenges of diverse classrooms. *Equity and Excellence, 25,*(2–4), 133–138.

Mills, C., & Tangherlini, C. (1992). Finding the optimal match: Another look at ability grouping and cooperative learning. *Equity and Excellence, 25*(2–4), 205–208.

Reis, S. (1992). Advocacy: The grouping issue. *Roeper Review, 14*(4), 225–227.

Riechmann-Hruska, S. (1989). Learning styles and individual differences in learning. *Equity and Excellence, 24*(3), 25–27.

Shedlin, A. (1986). New lenses for viewing elementary schools. *Phi Delta Kappan, 68*(2), 139–142.

Slavin, R. (1981). Cooperative learning and desegregation. *Journal of Educational Equity and Leadership, 1*(3), 145–161.

Slavin, R., & Oickle, E. (1981). Effects of cooperative learning teams on student achievement and race relations: Treatment by race interactions. *Sociology of Education, 54*(3), 174–180.

Valle, J. (1990). The development of learning styles program in an affluent, suburban New York elementary school. *Journal of Reading, Writing, and Learning Disabilities International, 6*(3), 315–322.

Wheelock, A., & Hawley, W. (1992). *What next? Promoting alternatives to ability grouping.* (ERIC Document Reproduction Service No. ED 353 220)

Yanok, J. (1988). Individualized instruction: A GOOD approach. *Academic Therapy, 24*(2), 163–167.